Platy Remodulatable Aerial for Open-airfield EM Coupling

Nea Vasilissa

Platy Remodulatable Aerial for Open-airfield EM Coupling

First Edition November 2025

Written by Nea Vasilissa

TABLE OF CONTENTS

Page No.

CHAPTER 1
INTRODUCTION

1.1 Overview

In today's world, wireless communication technologies demand high-performance antennas that can operate reliably even in remote environments. To achieve the required performance, these devices need to be compact and efficient. Antennas play a central role in any wireless system because they handle the transmission and reception of electromagnetic signals. For this reason, researchers are increasingly focused on designing miniaturized antennas that can be integrated easily into a wide range of communication devices [1]. The growing need for mobility, multifunctionality, and compactness has pushed antenna research to new heights. Technology also evolves rapidly, devices released today often become outdated within a short period. Traditional single-antenna structures, which operate over a fixed bandwidth, are no longer sufficient for modern applications that demand flexibility and adaptability. As a result, their performance suffers under dynamic conditions. To overcome these limitations, the concept of antenna reconfigurability has emerged. Reconfigurable antennas can adjust their operating characteristics according to changing environmental conditions or application needs [2]. This not only adds extra functionality but also reduces the overall size and cost of wireless systems. Consequently, reconfigurable antennas have significantly enhanced modern communication systems and continue to meet the diverse needs of users across various scenarios.

1.2 Reconfigurable Antenna

Antennas are essential components of communication systems because they are responsible for transmitting and receiving electromagnetic waves. The term "configuration" refers to arranging or adjusting various elements of a system to achieve a specific purpose. In the context of antennas, configuration involves selecting parameters such as the patch shape, substrate characteristics, element position, and feed type so that the antenna operates at the required frequency and polarization [2]. When any of these key characteristics are altered, the entire system must be adjusted or reconfigured to meet the new performance requirements.

Therefore, the reconfigurability approach has to be introduced into the antenna design. Reconfigurable antennas have been considered one of the fascinating topics among numerous antenna designers. The performance parameters of the reconfigurable antenna are altered by changing the current distribution on the antenna surface by employing mechanically movable parts, attenuators, tunable and/or active materials as well as phase shifters [3]. These distinct types of antennas can be arranged either in the form of a single antenna or in a group of antennas. These devices can dynamically alter the important characteristics of an antenna such as frequency, radiation pattern, and polarization in the desired manner. In other words, a reconfigurable antenna can switch the pattern from unidirectional to bidirectional, polarization from left-hand circular to right-hand circular, resonant frequency from one value to another, or vice-versa [4]. Therefore, reconfigurable antennas behave as indispensable parts of modern wireless systems due to their capability to change the radiation characteristics dynamically.

Various factors are responsible for influencing the design of reconfigurable antennas. Still, there are some points that one must consider while designing such type of antennas [5]:

- Which reconfiguration characteristic – frequency, pattern, polarization, or compound has to be attained for achieving the desired performance?
- How the varying radiation mechanisms are configured for achieving the desired characteristic?
- Which reconfiguration method works well for minimizing the negative effects on the antenna radiation?

1.2.1 NECESSITY OF RECONFIGURABLE ANTENNAS

Reconfigurable antennas can be arranged in the form of a single element or an array. In the case of single-element scenarios, a single antenna element is used. It can either be a monopole or microstrip antenna. But for diversity reception, a large number of single element antennas are used in small packages for the correct reception of usable signals. Generally, a single antenna is required at the transmission end. However, due to the unpredictable electromagnetic conditions imposed by the portability, the signal transmission from the portable device to the main station becomes difficult over the communication link. Hence, the performance of the antenna gets degrades gradually. Nowadays, the reconfigurability approach is included in the antenna structures that provide a lot of inherent benefits such as multifunctional capabilities, size reduction, improvement in the quality and capacity of the communication link, etc. For tuning the operational frequency of the communication device, it is possible to alter the operating bands, eliminate the interfering signals, and tune the antenna according to the changing environmental scenarios. If there is any modification in the radiation pattern of an antenna, then it might be steered towards the access point with less transmission power, resulting in a battery consumption saving. The employment of reconfigurability in the antenna arrays can offer large degrees of freedom, which further results in sufficient large frequency bandwidths. Moreover, it offers larger scan volumes.

1.2.2 ADVANTAGES OF RECONFIGURABLE ANTENNAS

In comparison to the conventional antenna, the reconfigurable antenna offers several benefits [2-5]:

- Improves the quality and capacity of the communication link
- Offers multi-band functional capabilities
- Improves the performance of the radio system
- Reduces the size and simplifies the complexity of the system
- Provides myriad of services in a compact structure
- Easy to install and expand
- Promising candidate for future-generation communication systems

1.3 Reconfigurable Antenna Types

For designing a reconfigurable antenna, it is necessary to determine the required reconfiguration property and the reconfiguration technique [4]. The reconfigurable antennas can be categorized on the following basis:

- On the basis of reconfigured parameter
- On the basis of reconfiguration mechanism

1.3.1 ON THE BASIS OF RECONFIGURED PARAMETER

The reconfigurable antennas are classified into four types on the basis of the parameter to be reconfigured. These antennas are named as frequency, radiation pattern, polarization, and compound reconfigurable antennas. A brief description of these antennas is given below [5]:

1.3.1.1 Frequency Reconfigurable Antenna

Frequency Reconfigurable Antennas (FRAs) or tunable antennas are those that can dynamically alter their frequency of operation while keeping the radiation pattern and polarization intact [6]. For example: cognitive radio. These antennas are typically deployed in those situations where several antennas converge at a point. As a result, the requirement of multiple antennas is replaced by a single reconfigurable antenna. The reconfigurability can be achieved either electrically or mechanically by modifying the dimensions of the antenna using Positive Intrinsic Negative (PIN) diodes, varactor diodes, and tunable materials. They are generally classified under two categories: continuous and switched. Continuous tuning allows smooth transitions to occur within the operating bands, whereas the switched tuning is applicable at different frequency bands [6].

1.3.1.2 Radiation Pattern Reconfigurable Antenna

Radiation pattern reconfigurable antennas are those that can change the antenna pattern or beam from one form to another, for instance: unidirectional to bidirectional, multidirectional, and omnidirectional, or vice versa. They are employed in mobile phones. The radiation characteristics are changed by varying the surface current distribution on an antenna. The current arrangement further creates the spatial distribution of the antenna's radiation [7]. Thus, the antenna designers must determine the magnitude and phase values of surface current so as to design a pattern reconfigurable antenna.

1.3.1.3 Polarization Reconfigurable Antenna

Polarization is one of the important parameters of a reconfigurable antenna. Polarization reconfigurable antennas are those that can switch between various polarization modes that include horizontal polarization, vertical polarization, linear polarization, left-hand circular polarization or right-hand circular polarization. For example: Multi-In Multi-Out (MIMO) antenna. By varying the current distribution, the wave polarization of an antenna in the far field can be achieved [8]. Due to this, the polarization mismatch loss in portable devices reduces that frequently occurs in versatile specialized devices.

1.3.1.4 Compound Reconfigurable Antenna or Hybrid Antenna

Compound reconfiguration is a synchronous reconfiguration of two or more single parameters simultaneously. It is also called as multi-parameter reconfiguration. In such type of reconfiguration, two approaches are involved. The first approach covers only two parameters such as frequency-polarization, frequency-pattern, and pattern-polarization, whereas in the second approach, all three parameters such as frequency, pattern, and polarization are combined simultaneously [4].

1.3.2 ON THE BASIS OF THE RECONFIGURATION MECHANISM

To attain the desired functionality, various reconfiguration mechanisms such as electrical, mechanical, optical, physical, and material change-based are employed for configuring the characteristics of an antenna and redistribution of the current. The antenna designer must select appropriate techniques to eliminate the imposed constraints and to efficiently complete the antenna tasks [9].

1.3.2.1 Electrically Reconfigurable Antenna

Electrically reconfigurable antenna relies on band switching and continuous switching techniques to connect/ disconnect the various antenna parts [6]. The band switching is based on PIN diodes and on Radio-Frequency Micro-Electromechanical Switches (RF-MEMS). For realizing continuous and fast tuning, varactor diodes are employed [10]. In such devices, the capacitance changes as a result of the biasing voltage variation. Both cases require Direct Current (DC) for their operation. However, they exhibit some limitations such as negative biasing effects, nonlinearity, power consumption, reliability of components, as well as slow tuning [6].

1.3.2.2 Mechanically Reconfigurable Antenna

The structure of this type of antenna consists of mechanically movable parts such as a pulley, weight, and motor. The main limitation of this type of reconfigurable device is that its size varies in accordance with the tuning frequency. Further, for mechanical movements, actuators are employed. Hence, they make the overall structure complex, bulky, as well as costly [2].

1.3.2.3 Optically Reconfigurable Antenna

In this technique, laser diodes are employed for enlightening the switch with a light of suitable wavelength on a semiconductor material. This creates a photoconductive connection that occurs when electrons flow from the valence band to the conduction band. Thus, switching from an OFF to an ON state takes place [11]. The main advantages of this technique are faster switching, activation, linear behavior, no harmonics, and intermodulation distortion. In addition, biasing lines are not required in this method. This technique requires a laser light and a separate mechanism to operate the optical switches which results in an increased cost and complexity of the system [12].

1.3.2.4 Physically Reconfigurable Antenna

Such antennas are based on the physical modification in the radiating structure of the antenna or some structural changes in its important parts. The main advantage possessed by this technique is that it does not require any kind of biasing, switching, or optical integration. But, it suffers from the physical reconfiguration effect of individual devices, increased size, cost, and power requirements [13].

1.3.2.5 Material Change based Reconfigurable Antenna

The antennas that are made reconfigurable by employing materials like liquid crystals, ferrites, and metasurface are called material change based reconfigurable antennas. This property is achieved by changing its relative permittivity and permeability. A liquid crystal is a form of nonlinear material in which liquid flows but is arranged in the same way as molecules are [14]. By changing the orientation of the molecules, it is possible to change the dielectric constant under distinct voltage levels. In the case of ferrites, a static electromagnetic field is applied that can change the relative permittivity and permeability. The metasurfaces are the Two-Dimensional (2D) equivalents of the Three-Dimensional (3D) metamaterials that can change their relative permittivity and permeability. Moreover, they not only minimize the size and cost of design but also provide high gain and efficiency [15].

1.4 Metamaterials

Metamaterials have gained significant attraction because of their emerging properties since their inception. Present-day technological advancements have promoted the utilization of novel materials and their composites in many interdisciplinary fields that ranges from electronics to mechanics, agriculture, medicine, and so on [16]. These materials provide excellent flexibility in material design and introduce a new perspective on material understanding due to their ability to customize dielectric properties and tunable responses. The unique design ability of these materials makes them different from conventional ones [17]. Thus, a new era has been opened out for researchers in the field of material science [18]. The word 'metamaterial' is named after the Greek word 'meta' which means a combination of two words: meta and material. Meta is a prefix that is something beyond normal, altered, or unattainable by natural materials. Metamaterials, also called Double Negative (DNG) materials are a class of artificially engineered composite materials designed to exhibit exceptional properties that are difficult to seek out in natural materials [19]. Rodger M.

Walser defined metamaterials as, "Macroscopic composites possessing a synthetic, 3D as well as cellular structure in a periodic manner, which is designed to generate two or more outputs in an optimized combination that is not easily found in nature" [20]. Metamaterials are periodically arranged arrays possessing uncommon electromagnetic properties that generally emerge from the design and structure of a cell instead of the material they are composed of. In other words, they offer distinct properties from their constituent materials. They too follow classical electrodynamics principles. In a strict sense, metamaterials are considered to be composed of periodic cells whose largest dimension is smaller than the wavelength λ under consideration. As a result, they can be viewed as 'molecules' whose properties can be modeled using global parameters such as permeability, permittivity, and refractive index just like natural molecules [21].

In microwave devices, metamaterials are commonly employed to enhance their performance. Moreover, they have significant applications in amplifiers, filters, and power dividers. Further, they are used to improve the separation between tightly packed MIMO antenna systems because they are capable to provide band gaps in the structures [22]. This concept is generally introduced for miniaturizing the size of the patch antenna structure and enhancing its characteristics [23]. The two most exploited topologies of metamaterials are Split-Ring Resonator (SRR) and Complementary Split-Ring Resonator (CSRR) [24]. Basically, they act as the building blocks of metamaterials and have been utilized widely for the synthesis of various structures and components such as sensors, filters, absorbers, and RF antennas [25].

1.4.1 EVOLUTION OF METAMATERIALS

The metamaterials evolute when the first microwave experiment was conducted on twisted chiral structures by J. C. Bose in 1898 [26]. This is one of the foremost efforts that confirm the existence of artificial materials. During 1904-1905, the two important characteristics observed during investigations by Lamb and Pocklington in an artificial substance are anti-parallel directions of phase and group velocity, as well as negative refractive index. Such properties are different from typical materials [27] and [28]. Later, in 1914, K. F. Lindman studied the effect of chiral media on electromagnetic waves by randomly embedding wire helices [29]. Further, W. E. Kock in 1948 demonstrated a metal lens antenna that has the capability of focusing electromagnetic waves with the help of conducting plates [30]. Thus, this pioneering work has inspired several researchers and engineers working in the domain of such type of materials [31]. Afterwards, similar characteristics were explored by

Mandelstam in 1945 by considering one-dimensional analogue index system [32]. Following this concept, negative refractive index materials attracted substantial research attention in the 1950s. The simultaneous existence of negative permittivity and permeability was first explained by Veselago in 1968. He explained that the plane waves propagating in such type of media result in a left-handed triplet including the combination of electric field intensity vector (E), magnetic field intensity vector (H), and wave vector (k). He also investigated negative refractive index and reversed laws such as Snell's law, Doppler Effect, and Cerenkov Effect in similar types of media. This theory sets a major theoretical breakthrough for other researchers belonging to the antenna field [33]. However, after three decades, the prototype of metamaterial was implemented. In 1996, Pendry and his co-workers firstly introduced artificially electric plasmas using a thin wire structure [34]. Later in 1999, the first artificially magnetic plasma using SRRs was introduced by the same team [35]. Based on this, Smith successfully projected a DNG material by uniting SRRs and thin wire structures for simultaneously synthesizing the negative values of permeability and permittivity [36]. After nearly three decades of being dormant as an impractical concept, Shelby et al. experimentally demonstrated a medium that possesses negative refractive index [37]. In 2010, Sabah designed a triangular-shaped SRR and wire strip-based metamaterial structure that showed its functionality for S- and C-microwave bands [38]. Thereafter, numerous novel structures have been designed and implemented based on the resonators and wire combinations.

1.4.2 CONSTITUTIVE PARAMETERS

A well-accepted fact illustrates that when an electromagnetic wave travels through a composite medium, electric and magnetic dipole moments are induced in the metallic inclusions. The effective permittivity and permeability of the composite medium are closely associated with these dipole moments. It is possible to synthesize materials with a particular electromagnetic response, as the manufacturer is capable to control the scale, density, shape, and orientation of the inclusions. Thus, these artificially engineered materials called metamaterials may have negative values for both constitutive parameters when the individual elements are resonant. These resonant individual elements are responsible for the negative values of the refractive index. The refractive index signifies the amount of refraction and reflection. Due to this feature, as the frequency changes, the phase response reverses. These materials are also called DNG, Left-Handed Media (LHM), and Backward-Wave Media (BWM) [39]. The main parameters responsible for determining electromagnetic behavior are permittivity (ε) and permeability (μ). These two parameters also act as the basis for determining other material properties such as refractive index, wave impedance, loss tangent, etc. [40]. These parameters are defined as follows:

In case, when a dielectric or magnetic material is absent, the following equations describe the relation:

$$D_i = \varepsilon_0 . E \tag{1.1}$$

$$B_i = \mu_0 . H \tag{1.2}$$

where, D_i represents the electric induction and B_i represents the magnetic induction. The parameters E and H specify the corresponding electric field and magnetic field. The variables ε_0 and μ_0 indicate the respective permittivity and permeability associated with the free space. For calculations, the value of parameter $\varepsilon_0 = 8.854 \times 10^{-12}$ F/m and parameter $\mu_0 = 4\pi \times 10^{-7}$ Vs/Am. The following way relates the dielectric permittivity and magnetic permeability of free space:

$$c^2 = \frac{1}{\varepsilon_0 . \mu_0} \tag{1.3}$$

here, c specifies the speed of light whose value is 3×10^8 m/s. When an electromagnetic field interacts with the material medium, Equations (1.1) and (1.2) becomes

$$D = \varepsilon_0 . \varepsilon_r . E \tag{1.4}$$

$$B = \mu_0 . \mu_r . H \tag{1.5}$$

where ε_r and μ_r represent the associated value of relative permittivity and permeability. The following equations describe the real and imaginary parts:

$$\varepsilon = \varepsilon' - j . \varepsilon'' \tag{1.6}$$

$$\mu = \mu' - j . \mu'' \tag{1.7}$$

where j represents the imaginary part and the value of $j^2 = -1$. The real part indicates the stored energy, whereas the energy losses are represented by the imaginary part. Thus, permittivity is a term that connects the material's ability to transfer electrical energy. Permeability is a parameter that illustrates the amount of magnetization corresponding to an applied magnetic field that the material obtains. Permittivity measures the total electric dipole moment/unit volume generated by a material medium, whereas permeability determines the magnetic dipole moment generated with respect to the unit volume. These parameters help in determining other factors such as refractive index, phase velocity, loss, and impedance [41]. Based on these two parameters, metamaterials are classified into four different groups.

1.4.3 CLASSIFICATION OF METAMATERIALS

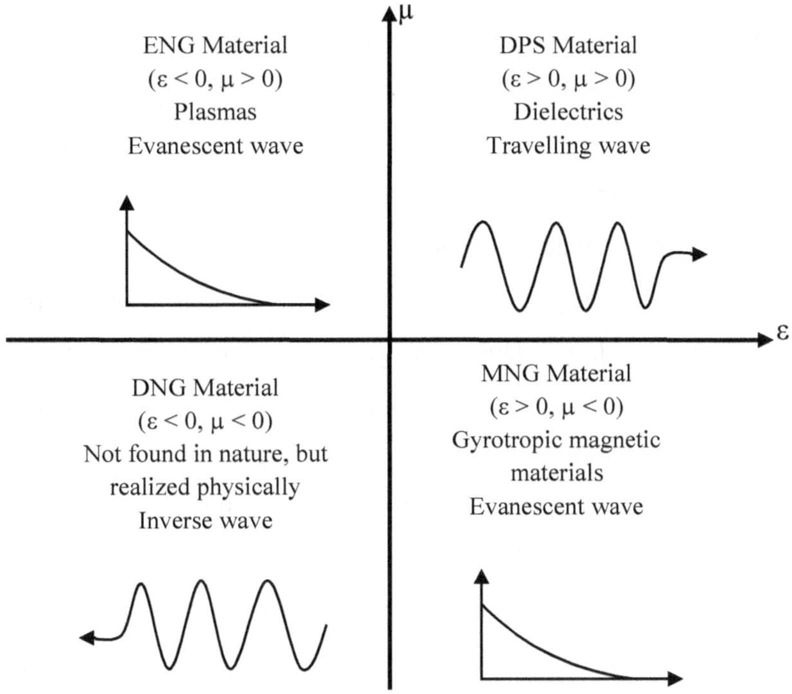

Figure 1.1 Classification of metamaterials [44]

The materials that exhibit positive permittivity and permeability are called as Double Positive (DPS) materials. In other words, such materials follow special conditions i.e. $\varepsilon > 0$ and $\mu > 0$. Dielectrics, the most naturally occurring media, fall under this category. If the materials exhibit negative permittivity and positive permeability i.e. $\varepsilon < 0$ and $\mu > 0$, then such materials are termed as Epsilon Negative (ENG) materials. In some frequency regions, plasmas exhibit this feature. In the case of DNG material, the permittivity and permeability values are negative i.e. $\varepsilon < 0$, $\mu < 0$. Antiparallel phase and group velocities mainly characterize these materials. Further, if the materials exhibit positive permittivity and negative permeability i.e. $\varepsilon > 0$, $\mu < 0$, then those materials are termed as Mu-Negative (MNG) materials. Gyrotropic magnetic materials fall under this category [42] and [43]. Figure 1.1 depicts the classification of metamaterials [44].

1.5 Metasurfaces

In recent years, it has been examined that a large number of scientists showed huge interest in 2D planar metamaterials, namely metasurfaces. Metasurface exhibits similar phenomena as that of metamaterials and have very smaller thickness i.e. only a fraction of wavelength. Moreover, they are easier to fabricate and have negligible associated losses. A large range of optical devices have been implemented by employing metasurfaces, whereas the majority of them are based on abrupt phase changes for the manipulation of wavefront of light. Metasurfaces are basically planar metamaterials. Just like the metamaterials, the electric and magnetic polarizabilities are responsible for characterizing the response. These 2D equivalents are also called metafilms. Because of the customized values of permittivity and permeability, metamaterials can regulate the light propagation. This effect is still used in these materials to manipulate the electromagnetic waves. This, in turn, makes the overall structure bulkier, whereas the metasurfaces can manipulate these waves over a single and extremely thin layer. The 2D nature of metasurfaces offers a promising alternative, thereby making the structure less bulky, and providing the possibility of lower structural losses, easy fabrication, and integration [39]. They provide a variety of applications in the electromagnetic domain that range from low microwave to optical frequencies including controllable smart surfaces, terahertz switches, miniaturized cavity resonators, angular independent surfaces, biomedical devices, and so on [15]. Due to their versatile nature, multifunctionality, ease of integration, and ultrathin features, these lately invented materials have recently attracted conspectus attention in comparison to their traditional counterparts [45].

Metasurfaces, the 2D version of metamaterials, are artificially engineered infinitely arranged ultrathin layer materials. They are made up of subwavelength meta-atoms called unit cells that are organized on a planar surface. The building blocks of metasurfaces consist of various material compositions that are arranged in various geometrical shapes to send the desired response to electromagnetic waves. Owing to their subwavelength periodicity, these materials can be characterized by effective, uniform surface material parameters that include electric and magnetic sheet conductivities. They can also have various interesting properties and unique capabilities to control electromagnetic waves, according to the resonance properties and shape of meta-atoms [46] and [47].

1.6 Artificial Neural Network

Artificial Neural Networks (ANNs) have garnered the attention of several scientists and engineers from a variety of disciplines because of their potential to simulate complex systems. The ANN concept is based on the human brain's ability to execute complex and intelligent computations very quickly. It can be defined as "a system consisting of many simple processing units working in parallel, the function of which depends on the network structure, the strength of the connections, and the processing performed in the computation element or node" [48]. The ANN systems are capable of learning very rapidly and this process is carried out by providing the ANN with sufficient number of patterns. Further, the synaptic weights associated with the connections between neurons are modified. As a result, the training patterns are stored in the ANN as weights. The network can then be used to predict output parameters. It also reduces the computational time during the designing process [48].

1.7 Numerical Methods used for Electromagnetic Modeling

There are several difficult problems in the field of antenna design and analysis that can only be solved by numerical methods. Below are the important methods utilized for the prediction of electromagnetic fields in the antennas:

1.7.1 FINITE DIFFERENCE TIME DOMAIN

The Finite Difference Time Domain (FDTD) method was firstly proposed in 1966 by K.S Yee for a basic cartesian coordinate system. Generally, it is considered as one of the most accepted time-domain methods for solving electromagnetic problems. It covers a wide frequency range, and can find out the properties of LHM. Moreover, this method is simple and even applied to 3D codes. This approach is not suitable for electrically massive systems, but it is well-suitable for systems incorporating pulses [49].

1.7.2 FINITE INTEGRAL TIME DOMAIN

In 1977, Thomas Weiland proposed the Finite Integral Time Domain (FITD) method for solving electromagnetic field-related problems. This method is based on the integral form of Maxwell's equations to numerically solve the problems. Computer Simulation Technology (CST) Microwave Studio is the most prominent package of FITD. The FITD method allows simpler derivation of schemes for irregular space discretizations and can generate results both in time and spectral domains. However, there is no particular difference between standard FITD and FDTD codes [50].

1.7.3 TRANSMISSION LINE MATRIX

The Transmission Line Matrix (TLM) method is based on the space and time discretization technique for the computation of electromagnetic field that replaces field domains by the networks of transmission lines. Along with the FDTD method, this method is also an important one and is used when microwave circuits with lumped elements are to be simulated. Using the code MEFiSTo-3D, one can design and implement some special transmission lines for metamaterials. This code uses a different approach for modeling NIMs [51].

1.7.4 METHODS OF MOMENTS

Method of Moments (MoM) is a technique used in the frequency domain to solve electromagnetic problems or volume integral equations. This method can solve problems in a variety of sectors associated with engineering and research, including electromagnetics. Roger F. Harrington first employed MoM to solve electromagnetic difficulties in 1960s [52]. It is a method of estimation of population parameters. It discretizes only the domains that contain field sources, which in turn removes problems caused by the discretization or truncation of infinite space. Therefore, the MoMs do not require absorbing boundary conditions. The preciseness in the results is a main benefit of this method as it follows fundamentally precise equations and provides a straightforward mathematical explanation for these equations [52] and [53].

1.7.5 FINITE ELEMENT METHOD

The Finite Element Method (FEM) was originally used by P. Silvester for electromagnetic field-related problems [49]. It is a finite difference approximation method and is used to determine estimated results of Partial Differential Equations (PDE) and integral equations. The differential equation is entirely simplified to obtain the solution. It is then numerically integrated using Euler's method, which is a very common approach. The attraction of FEM method is its adaptability in modeling in-homogeneities and complex geometries [49]. Softwares based on FEM are High Frequency Structure Simulator, Maxwell3D, and FEMLAB (COMSOL MULTIPHYSICS).

1.8 Simulation Tools Employed for Designing the Proposed Reconfigurable Antennas

High Frequency Structure Simulator and MATrix LABoratory are the tools that are employed while designing the proposed reconfigurable antennas. The high frequency simulation tool is an interactive and efficient software package for determining the electromagnetic behavior of the antennas [54]. This valuable tool allows the designers to create the models virtually, and then calculate vital performance parameters and 3D electromagnetic fields. MATrix LABoratory software is a numerical computing platform that has been employed for extracting the material properties of the object's output fields [56].

1.8.1 HIGH FREQUENCY STRUCTURE SIMULATOR

The Ansys High Frequency Structure Simulator (HFSS) is a 3D full-wave commercially available simulation tool utilized for the designing of high-frequency products such as antennas, waveguide components, integrated circuit packages, printed circuit boards. It can also be used in various RF and microwave applications. It utilizes brilliant graphics, adaptive meshing, and FEM for visualizing the radiation and transmission behavior of 3D electromagnetic fields [54]. It uses automatically generated meshes for faster, efficient, and more reliable simulations. The designing of an antenna requires geometry creation, specification of material properties, and solution frequency along with suitable boundary conditions, and excitations. Using this tool, one can calculate S parameters, resonant frequencies, and their fields. It is also a powerful field-solving engine that offers flexible capabilities to simplify the design entries and optimal solutions through parametric investigations. This valuable tool provides a good option for high frequency productive research, development, and virtual prototyping [55].

1.8.2 MATrix LABORATORY

MATrix LABoratory (MATLAB) is a high-performance multi-paradigm numerical computing platform developed by Cleve Moler. It is a high performance technical computing language that can perform various tasks in its interactive environment. It acts as an excellent tool for performing various functions such as matrix manipulations, data analysis, implementation of algorithms, and various other scientific computations using its vast library of built-in functions and graphics [56]. It is an efficient computational tool for the analysis of data in several domains belonging to science, mathematics, and engineering. The code generated in MATLAB can easily integrate with other languages, thus enabling one to deploy algorithms and applications within their production systems. MATrix LABoratory has a facility of Live Editor for generating the script files. It has a modern programming language environment with sophisticated data structures and debugging tools for supporting object oriented programming [57]. Additionally, it has several types of toolboxes. This tool is versatile, reliable, provides an easy learning environment, and is widely employed by various professionals and engineers.

1.9 Motivation

The introduction of wireless devices and mobile phones has completely transformed our lifestyles. During the evolutionary phase of development, numerous antennas have been designed and developed for wireless applications. With time, the demand for designing innovative, compact, and multiband antennas has become more challenging. To tackle such challenges, continuous and in-depth research is required for designing novel antennas that are capable of operating at different frequency bands. In this domain, previous research work illustrates that there is more emphasis on the designing of reconfigurable antennas with general reconfiguration mechanisms. However, less work has been done for designing the reconfigurable antennas based on smart materials. The notion to design FRAs using smart materials was the outcome of the extensive literature review. The emergence of metasurfaces satisfies the need of antenna designers by minimizing the antenna size and improving its radiation characteristics.

Nowadays, antenna applications have sparked a lot of interest in metasurface designing. Metasurface based antennas have a higher potential to overcome the limiting efficiency and bandwidth limitations suffered by conventionally constructed electrically small antennas. They can be designed to span a greater frequency range, and allow better utilization of limited space on compact platforms. They meet the desired requirement by allowing antennas to be as small as one-tenth the wavelength of the signal. In comparison to traditional patch antennas, they result in a five-fold reduction in size. Thus, these antennas have shown to exhibit unparalleled performance, and researchers are continually working to open up new doors to all sorts of possibilities that seemed impossible even a few years ago. Their 2D nature offers easy fabrication and integration. In this research work, different forms of metasurface based novel FRAs have been designed and developed for wireless applications. These antennas are capable to enhance the overall performance and system capability. These novel planar antennas are compact, provide wide bandwidth, and have large fractional tuning range.

1.10 Research Gaps

The reconfiguration mechanism employed in implementing most of the reconfigurable antennas so far was achieved through electrical, optical, and mechanical means. These techniques utilize RF switches like PIN diodes, varactor diodes, MEMS switches, optical switches, actuators, etc. Though these devices are economical but they are unable to provide best solutions. PIN diodes are inexpensive, easy to fabricate, reliable, and have high power handling capacity. Varactor diodes provide continuous and smooth tuning. Both these electronic components possess non linear characteristics and require DC biasing circuits for their operation, which may adversely affect the antenna's performance. MEMS switches provide good isolation and have low insertion loss but they are costly, unreliable, and have poor switching speed. Moreover, their fabrication is also complex. Though the optical switches provide faster switching, activation, and possess linear behavior but they require laser diodes for their operation, which in turn increases the cost and complexity of the system. Further, mechanically reconfigurable antennas comprise of movable parts such as motors, pulleys, actuators, etc. which led to the expensive and bulky structure. To enhance the performance, smart materials like metasurfaces have been proposed. These planar and ultrathin structures provide cost-effective solutions. So in this proposed research work, metasurface based planar frequency reconfigurable antennas have been designed for wireless applications, and their performance parameters are optimized for better results.

1.11 Problem Formulation

The rapidly rising requirements of today's users have enabled the wireless communication sector to develop at a faster pace. These technological advancements have stimulated the requirements of the modern market, thereby allowing the development of novel antennas possessing special functionalities. In the present era, frequency reconfigurable antennas have sparked a lot of interest in the research community because of their ability to incorporate various standards onto a single platform. This antenna can adjust its operating frequency over a wide bandwidth, thereby avoiding the requirement for several antenna devices dedicated to distinct wireless communication services. In comparison to broadband antennas, these special type of antennas has several advantages such as smaller size, effective utilization of electromagnetic spectrum, similar radiation patterns over all operating bands, and so on. Additionally, they provide frequency selectivity that helps to mitigate the negative impacts of co-site interference and jamming. Hence, the overall size and cost of the wireless system get lowered. As a result, they are used in wireless systems to enhance the overall performance and provide cost-effective solutions. Recent developments in this field have enabled researchers to design antennas at subwavelength scales. One of the recent developments at subwavelength in this domain is artificially engineered materials that provide controlled electromagnetic responses. Thus, the concept of metasurfaces has been introduced for the designing of frequency reconfigurable antennas. Further, the metasurface based designs not only minimize the cost and size but also provide high gain and efficient antenna structures. However, little work has been reported in the available literature on metasurface based reconfigurable antennas. Most of the previous work is based on general reconfiguration mechanisms. These mechanisms possess some drawbacks such as negative biasing to control switching, slow tuning, non-linearity, optical integration, and the device's physical reconfiguration effect. The present work is basically a step towards realizing compact metasurface based planar frequency reconfigurable antennas for wireless applications.

1.12 Research Objectives

The encompassing aim of the proposed research work is to design and implement a reconfigurable antenna for wireless applications and explore the viability of using a metasurface to introduce reconfigurability. This goal will be accomplished with the attainment of the following objectives:

- **To design and simulate a new structure for metasurface and analyze it for metamaterialistic characteristics.**
- **Design of planar reconfigurable antenna using the proposed metasurface structure.**
- **To evaluate and compare the performance of the proposed antenna with or without metasurface.**
- **Fabrication of the proposed antenna using metasurface and comparison of its performance with the simulated one.**

1.13 Organization of the Thesis

This thesis reports the analytical behavior of various frequency reconfigurable antennas designed for wireless applications. All the proposed antennas are designed with a two-layered approach. In these designs, new metasurface structures are incorporated onto the patch antenna so as to achieve a wide tuning range. Several important performance parameters are considered and discussed during the analysis. The whole thesis is broadly organized into six chapters:

The first chapter provides a brief introduction to reconfigurable antennas. A general description of different types of reconfigurable antennas based on reconfigured parameter and reconfiguration mechanism is presented. Some light has also been cast on the concept of artificially engineered materials: metamaterial and metasurface. The basic concept of the artificial neural network is also specified in this chapter. Following this, it gives a basic overview of the numerical methods employed for electromagnetic modeling and simulation tools for designing the proposed antennas. The motivation and research gaps behind this research work are also emphasized. Moreover, research objectives and thesis organization are covered in the concluding Section of this chapter.

The second chapter summarizes the theoretical background and emphasizes the major outcomes of a few frequency reconfigurable antennas that have already been developed. In addition to this, it also covers the selected design criteria and performance evaluation of various antennas designed for wireless applications. The antenna designs using soft computing techniques are also discussed. Thus, this comprehensive literature evaluation serves as a basis for the current research. It encourages the development of metasurface based frequency reconfigurable antennas for wireless applications.

The third chapter describes the electromagnetic modeling procedure for designing the left-handed material unit cell structure and the incorporating antennas. The finite element method is considered as one of the most efficient numerical methods. The adopted methodology for simulating antennas with the finite element method has also been covered in this chapter. The utility and the methodology of the employed High Frequency Structure Simulator tool is also briefly discussed. Further, it focuses on the metamaterial unit cell simulation methodology, which is followed by the Nicolson Ross Weir and Transmission Reflection approach for calculating the effective parameters.

The fourth chapter focuses on the design methodology and characteristic analysis of new metasurface structures. The extraction of complex factors such as permittivity and permeability is essential for characterizing the metamaterial behavior.

The fifth chapter presents the performance of planar frequency reconfigurable antennas using proposed metasurface structures. The modified metasurface structures provide wide bandwidth and fractional tuning range. Further, the structures are estimated using an artificial neural network approach. The simulated and measured results of the implemented antennas are also presented in this chapter.

The sixth chapter summarizes the entire thesis work in the form of a conclusion. Significant contributions and future scope are presented at the end of the chapter.

1.14 Concluding Remarks

This chapter provides an overview of reconfigurable antennas including their necessity and the classification based on the reconfigured parameter and mechanism. A brief history of the metamaterials and their classification based on constitutive parameters is presented. In addition, an exploration of the viability of the metasurface to introduce compact reconfigurable antennas is described. The use of artificial neural networks is presented further which describes how the parameters of antennas are estimated. Based on the foregoing, the primary objectives of this thesis are detailed as well as the organization of the whole work.

CHAPTER 2

LITERATURE REVIEW

Multifunctional behavior with myriad services on a single platform is the ultimate aim of every antenna designer. Nowadays, multiband, wideband, and frequency reconfigurable antennas are the likely candidates to fulfil these essential needs. The ideal alternative is tunable antennas or frequency reconfigurable antennas. These antennas open up new vistas and hence provide more functionality levels. This literature review represents the behavioral analysis of various types of frequency reconfigurable antennas, and their historical perspectives undertaken by several researchers. In order to meet the necessary requirements, several antenna designers put a huge effort in designing such types of antennas using specialized methodologies. It describes how the reconfiguration mechanism, substrate material, and structural shape affect the system's performance. In addition to this, it describes how the incorporation of metamaterials and metasurfaces yields optimal solutions and controllable properties. The issues faced by numerous antenna researchers are also highlighted. Afterwards, the proposed design problem is developed based on the defined challenges. Further, the artificial neural network based antenna structures are specified that effectively describe how the parameters of an antenna are estimated.

2.1 Review on the Frequency Reconfigurable Antennas

Around 1893-1901, the concept of reconfiguration capability came in with the contribution of Tesla and Marconi. Beginning years greatly demand that type of reconfigurable antennas that cover large frequency range without affecting the performance. A. N. Goldsmith proposed an FRA using variable inductor loading in 1926. This antenna can work at different frequencies. In 1942, E. Werndl introduced a frequency tunable antenna using liquid metal in his patent [58]. D. Schaubert's patent initially highlighted the designing approach of reconfigurable antennas. Afterwards, in 1983, he presented frequency and polarization reconfigurable antennas as well as frequency scanned arrays [59]. Also, in 1999, a Reconfigurable Aperture Program (RECAP) was started between various companies, research institutes, and twelve well-established universities by the United States based Defence Advanced Research Projects Agency (DARPA) [60]. Frequency reconfigurable antenna seems to be the most probable choice that switches its operating frequency to the desired level rather than employing several antennas operating at different frequencies. A wide review of FRAs has been reported in this Section. Several ideas were explored for frequency reconfiguration in later years.

Bernhard et al. (2001) demonstrated a two-layered electromagnetically coupled mechanically tuned rectangular microstrip patch antenna with a parasitic director. In the designed structure, displacement of the parasitic element was changed dynamically by the employed piezoelectric actuation system. The operating frequency band of the antenna was changed by varying the distance between the two components i.e. primary radiator and parasitic element. The authors mentioned that a good mechanical performance was achieved using mechatronic design. The actuated system control also helped in evaluating the performance [61].

Langer et al. (2003) presented a magnetically actuated micromachined reconfigurable microstrip antenna. A glass substrate with a thickness of 600 μm was employed for designing the suggested antenna structure. The resonance was observed at around 26 GHz using a micromachining process and magnetic actuation system. The plastic deformation of the antenna occurs with the application of a magnetic field. It was claimed that the whole arrangement can provide wide frequency coverage and suitable radiation characteristics to enhance the competence of planar arrays [62].

Peroulis et al. (2005) demonstrated a switchable slot antenna. The fabricated structure was based on RT/Duroid substrate (ε_r = 10.2). A combination of RF and PIN diode switches was used in the structure. The antenna tuning was accomplished by varying the electrical length of a single-fed resonant slot antenna. The structure showed good impedance matching with a tuning range of 540-890 MHz and a bandwidth of 1.7:1. In the design, no matching network was required. Further, the frequency tuning achieved from the designed antenna claimed no effect on the radiation characteristics [63].

Panagamuwa et al. (2006) enunciated the design of frequency and beam reconfigurable optically printed dipole antenna by suitably placing silicon photoconductive switches at the small gaps between dipole arms. This unique structure was constructed with a Taconic TLY-5 substrate. The silver-loaded epoxy was utilized for placing the silicon switches. For feeding the printed dipole, a transition from the coplanar waveguide to the coplanar stripline was used. Additionally, laser diodes were employed to enlighten the switch that offered a phase shift of around 40%. It was noticed that when the gaps in the dipole were bridged, the investigated antenna showed resonance at a lower frequency. Between the antenna and control circuitry, the optically controlled switches were responsible for thermal and electrical isolation [64].

Yang et al. (2008) realized a frequency tunable patch antenna incorporated with a U-slot. The proposed antenna geometry was simple and the control circuitry was hidden beneath the ground plane. The authors reported that antenna frequency can be varied by suitably placing a variable capacitor and an inductor at its input. Wider bandwidth along with flat input resistance and linear output reactance was observed. Results demonstrated that a tuning range within a 2.6 to 3.35 GHz span was achieved along with a frequency ratio of 1.28. It was claimed that the whole arrangement can also be used to reduce crosstalk between adjacent channels in multichannel systems [65].

Li et al. (2010) proposed a simple and compact reconfigurable antenna that offers a wide tuning range. The designed structure was constructed on Flame Retardant-4 (FR4) substrate using PIN and varactor diode. Deep analysis illustrated that the suggested slot antenna can resonate as a conventional slot or a half slot by toggling the PIN diode located at its open end. Further, it was stated that continuous tuning of frequency from 0.42 to 1.48 GHz can be attained by adjusting the reverse bias of the varactor diode inserted in the slot. It was stated that without introducing any lumped elements at the microstrip feed, adequate impedance matching may be obtained during the tuning of the varactor diode in both modes. The authors found that the structure works for radar and L-band applications [66].

Yu et al. (2011) mentioned the design of an electrically small FRA. In this, two structures having the same capacitively loaded loop, but with different feeding structures were designed. These designs were assembled on Rogers RO4350B substrate board with permittivity 3.4 and thickness 0.508 mm, respectively. The tunable capacitance was achieved by employing three varactor diodes. From the examined results, it was proved that the proposed antenna operates in the 457.5 to 894.5 MHz range and is applicable for radar and Ultra High Frequency (UHF) band communications. Moreover, the employed modified feeding structure was responsible for significant enhancement in the tuning range [67].

Erfani et al. (2012) introduced the concept of an elliptical monopole antenna integrated with a reconfigurable slot radiator for cognitive radio applications. A 0.667 mm thick Rogers RO4350B substrate of area 40 x 36 mm^2 was selected. The antenna impedance matching was improved by regulating the gap between the Ultra-WideBand (UWB) radiator and the ground plane along with some modifications in the ground. The results revealed that frequency reconfiguration in the 5 to 6 GHz range was achieved by deliberately inserting a varactor diode across the slot. A desired matching across the entire tuning band was achieved by an off-centered microstrip line. Therefore, it was stated that the small size antenna can perform sensing and communication operations [68].

Majid et al. (2012) proposed a compact and agile frequency reconfigurable microstrip slot antenna that claimed its resonance at six distinct frequency bands in the 2.2 to 4.75 GHz range. The narrowband antenna was designed on a Taconic RF35 substrate with 1.52 mm thickness. Frequency reconfiguration was obtained by positioning five PIN diodes in the slot. Thus, by using a slot and feed line bending, a reduction in the antenna size of 33% was noticed. The biasing circuit was built into the ground plane to reduce parasitic influences on the antenna's performance [69].

Sathi et al. (2012) designed an optically controlled FRA by employing an organic semiconductor polymer (P3HT). The antenna structure was mounted on an Ultralam 2000 substrate having a thickness of 1.8 mm. Square and square ring configurations of the antenna were designed for analysis purposes. Frequency reconfiguration was achieved by instantly changing the illumination intensity of the optical light source. The examined sweeping band associated with square P3HT structure was 950 MHz, whereas the examined sweeping band associated with square-ring P3HT geometry was 1.5 GHz. Hence, in both configurations of the antenna, shifting in the frequency between 1-2 GHz bands was noticed. The authors found that the proposed antenna performs admirably with low radiation efficiency [70].

Majid et al. (2013) demonstrated the frequency reconfigurable microstrip antenna that was designed on a 3.04 mm thick Taconic RF35 substrate. In the structure, five RF PIN diodes were effectively positioned in the slot and the effective length of the slot was varied. The antenna was successfully modeled, analyzed, and tested. Experimental verification showed that the antenna can switch between nine distinct frequency bands ranging from 1.98 to 3.59 GHz. Switching the employed PIN diodes resulted in a frequency ratio of 1.8:1. It was demonstrated that the suggested antenna structure is well-suited for cognitive radio applications [71].

Ge et al. (2014) presented the design of a low-profile frequency reconfigurable monopolar patch antenna. The design was constructed using four sector-shaped patches placed around a center-fed circular patch. The structure was mounted on a 6.34 mm thick Rogers dielectric substrate. Between these patches, varactor diodes were introduced to bridge the gap. The performed results showed that by altering the reverse bias voltage of the varactor diodes, the antenna can be shifted to operate in a continuous tunable frequency band of 1.64 to 2.12 GHz. Frequency-selective and stable radiation pattern features allowed its utility for wireless communication systems [72].

Majid et al. (2014) elucidated a FRA that exhibited a directional radiation pattern. The antenna structure was composed of a microstrip patch antenna and a slot antenna. A slot antenna with three switches was positioned beneath the ground plane. The design was structured on a Taconic RF35 substrate with a thickness of 3.04 mm. Six distinct frequency bands were successfully reconfigured from a 1.7 to 3.5 GHz frequency range. The authors revealed the suggested antenna provides a directional radiation pattern due to the installation of a reflector at the back side of the antenna [73].

Rajagopalan et al. (2014) introduced a wideband E-shaped optimized patch antenna with frequency reconfiguration property. Rogers RT Duroid 5880 was used for printing the designed structure. The addition of RF-MEMS switches to dynamically alter the dimensions of the slot, which allowed the bandwidth to nearly double than that of the original E-shaped patch. Recorded results illustrated that the design operates in a 2 to 3.2 GHz frequency range and works well for cognitive radio applications [74].

Liu et al. (2015) described a frequency reconfigurable patch antenna using reed switches. FR4 substrate was used for printing the designed antenna. The authors mentioned that a magnetic field that can easily penetrate through the ground plane controls these switches. The control circuit was positioned beneath the ground plane, away from the antenna's radiation performance. These switches were also responsible for the effect of bias lines and parasitic reduction. In it, 24 reed switches were utilized that connect the microstrip patch to the ground plane at various locations, which further increased the frequency reconfiguration from 0.3 to 3 GHz range. It was claimed that the antenna finds applications in wireless communications and tunable antennas [75].

Nassar et al. (2015) developed a mechanically tunable dual-band slot antenna. This operation was achieved by placing parallel slots of varying lengths. Afterwards, a rack and pinion mechanism was employed for realizing the tunability that slides the parasitic patches for the slot length variation. Two antenna designs were presented and motors were employed for achieving the reconfiguration. The first concept proposed the usage of two different motors for separate movement of the parasitic patches across each set of slots. A frequency band ratio of 1:2.6 was attained using this method. The second concept suggested a single motor to equally move the parasitic patches across both slot pairs while keeping the frequency band ratio unchanged. In this instance, the ratio was set to 2 to span the 2-3 GHz range associated with the lower band, and the 4-6 GHz range associated with the upper band, giving 40% tenability across each band [76].

Hussain et al. (2017) illustrated a miniaturized annular and circular slots based frequency reconfigurable MIMO antenna. A combination of annular and circular slots along with a varactor diode was utilized in the annular slot that allowed the antenna to be reconfigured. The structure was realized on Rogers RO4350B substrate with 0.76 mm thickness. A wide tuning range from 1.8 to 2.45 GHz was achieved with the help of a single varactor diode. This structure works well for different wireless hand-held devices and mobile terminals in cognitive radio applications [77].

Ali et al. (2018) designed frequency reconfigurable planar antenna by implementing highly resistive silicon switches. The deployed two silicon samples behaved like optical tunable resistors in the design that change the switching state from high to low resistance. The antenna structure was compact and its omnidirectional behavior makes it well-suited for numerous wireless applications [78].

Boukarkar et al. (2018) elucidated the frequency reconfigurability operation using a patch antenna. The operating frequency of the antenna was altered by suitably controlling the states of its six PIN diodes. All diodes were symmetrically positioned along non-radiating edges of the patch. F4B substrate was used for designing the antenna. Based on the obtained outcomes, it was stated that the prototype can effectively tune 36 different frequency channels in the 2.35 to 3.43 GHz frequency range and it may find utility in wireless applications [79].

Cai et al. (2018) designed a low-profile FRA using a grid-slotted patch and tunable varactors. Two stacked substrates and three metal layers were used in the design. The operational frequencies of the antenna were controlled by a single dc voltage applied to two different varactors. Experimental verifications revealed that the working frequency in the 2.45 to 3.55 GHz range was obtained by suitably controlling the capacitance of the varactor diodes. The designed structure offered high frequency selectivity. Moreover, it performs well for cognitive radio and wireless applications [80].

Performance comparison of various FRAs based on general reconfiguration mechanism is discussed in Table 2.1. All these antennas exhibit different size, design approach, and application type. In the table, the parameters considered for comparison are substrate type, size, frequency range, and application type.

Table 2.1 Comparison of different general reconfiguration mechanism based FRAs

Ref. No.	Substrate type	Antenna size (mm^2)	Frequency range (GHz)	Application type
[61]	Rogers RT/6002 (tm)	102 x 102	-	-
[62]	Glass	4.46 x 5	-	Planar arrays
[63]	Rogers RT/Duroid substrate	127 x 127	0.540 – 0.890	Wireless
[64]	Taconic TLY-5	-	2.26 - 3.15	-
[65]	Teflon	150 x 150	2.6 - 3.35	Wireless
[66]	FR4	35 x 20	0.42 - 1.48	Radar and L band
[67]	RO4350B	50 x 50	0.4575 – 0.8945	Radar and UHF band
[68]	RO4350B	36 x 40	5 - 6	Mobile systems
[69]	Taconic RF35	50 x 46	2.2 - 4.75	Wireless
[70]	Ultralam 2000	60 x 55	1 - 2	Frequency sweeping
[71]	Taconic RF35	50 x 50	1.98 - 3.59	Cognitive radio
[72]	Rogers dielectric	-	1.64 - 2.12	Cognitive radio
[73]	Taconic RF35	80 x 60	1.7 - 3.5	Wireless
[74]	Rogers RT Duroid 5880	100 x 120	2 - 3.2	Cognitive radio
[75]	FR4	220 x 150	0.3 - 3	Wireless
[76]	Acrylonitrile Butadiene Styrene	100 x 60	2 - 3 and 4 - 6 bands	Wireless
[77]	RO4350	60 x 120	1.8 - 2.45	Cognitive radio
[78]	RO4003	30 x 30	1.9 - 11	Cognitive radio
[79]	F4B	40 x 40	2.35 - 3.43	Wireless
[80]	F4B	70 x 70	2.45 - 3.55	Cognitive radio and wireless

Bronckers et al. (2019) demonstrated the design of an FRA using multiple tuning components. In it, three Barium Strontium Titanate (BST) capacitors, MEMS, and varactor diodes were employed for supporting an inverted L antenna. Results of the realized antenna confirmed that the design can effectively tune from 1.4 to 2.8 GHz range with a total efficiency of 35%. In both simulations and measurements, it was shown that the method can prevent instances such as combinations of tuning component values with a good input match. This novel technology simplifies the process of designing efficient FRAs [10].

Yuan et al. (2021) illustrated the behavior of a metasurface based FRA. In the structure, the patch antenna was covered with a metasurface. Circular-shaped Rogers 4350B dielectric substrate of radius 20 mm and thickness 1.524 mm was chosen for both the layers. Metasurface was consisted of elliptical patches that were placed periodically. The investigated resonance was about 5 GHz. An offset of 810 MHz was achieved. The structure worked at distinct frequency bands [81].

2.2 Review on the Material Change based Frequency Reconfigurable Antennas

Though a change in the type of conductor plays a significant role in antenna designing, the change in material characteristics also emerges as a promising technology to tune the antenna operating frequency. In general, the relative permittivity of material changes when a static electric field is applied to a ferroelectric material. Similarly, the permeability changes when a static magnetic field is applied to it. These changes can further assist in altering the operating frequency of the antenna. On this basis, the antennas are generally designed using smart materials such as metamaterials and metasurfaces [15].

2.2.1 METAMATERIAL

Mirzaei et al. (2011) investigated metamaterial inspired FRA using a coplanar waveguide line. The antenna structure was basically a printed monopole with an incorporated inbuilt lumped capacitor and an embedded slot. The possibility of independent tuning of the lower band over a wide frequency range was examined by employing a varactor diode, while the upper band (broadband) appeared virtually constant. The resonant frequency was tuned continuously in the range of 1.6-2.23 GHz by choosing different values of the capacitor. The designed structure exhibited a dual-band behavior. Further, it was found that the suggested reconfigurable antenna agreed well in terms of size, the number of tunable components, and tuning range [82].

Cheribi et al. (2013) designed metamaterial based FRA using a co-planar fed straight-line monopole and a pair of double SRRs. The benefit of this method was that the effect of the two cells may be simply deactivated by closing the double SRR's outer ring. Simulations proved that frequency reconfiguration was achieved by connecting a single switch that allowed the antenna to shift to four different resonant frequencies [83].

Rajeshkumar et al. (2015) presented a compact metamaterial inspired triple band antenna for reconfigurable Wireless Local Area Network (WLAN)/ Worldwide Interoperability for Microwave Access (WiMAX) applications. The structure of the antenna was incorporated with a rectangular slot and an SRR. The triple band antenna was highly compact due to the usage of SRR, as its size was very small in comparison to the resonant wavelength. A simple quarter wavelength rectangular slot was used to produce several resonances in the higher WLAN band. Tunability was accomplished with the use of a PIN diode. The antenna had an associated bandwidth of around 18.6%, 4.3%, and 40.3% at 2.4, 3.5, and 5 GHz bands. The structure exhibited small size, high gain of around 2.46 dB, and low cross-polarization [84].

Patel et al. (2018) designed an FRA loaded with switches and three metamaterial SRRs to achieve enhanced performance characteristics. Frequency reconfiguration was accomplished by changing the position of the switch. The experimentation revealed that frequency shifting and gain enhancement can be accomplished by putting switches in the patch geometry and loading metamaterial onto the patch surface. It was concluded that by employing a truncated corner patch in place of a simple patch and switches in place of loaded metamaterial, the reflection coefficient was enhanced from -21.36 to -38.24 dB. Moreover, a variation in gain from 4.47 to 16.71 dB was noticed [85].

Varamini et al. (2018) discussed the metamaterial metasurface based microstrip loop antenna for wireless applications. The metamaterial layer was composed of multiple equally extending rings. The proposed antenna offered radiations equally in all directions, thereby providing good quality gain and a superior axial ratio. The metamaterial layer also helped in antenna size reduction and down-shifting the frequency from 7 to 4 GHz. Moreover, circular polarization was achieved with the use of a metasurface [86].

Zhou et al. (2021) demonstrated the functional characteristics of an enhanced gain metamaterial-based FRA with large tuning range. The electrical size exhibited by the structure was $0.58\lambda \times 0.58\lambda$. The gain of the resultant structure was enhanced by utilizing the reconfigurable patch and upper layer reconfigurable negative-permeability metamaterial resonant loop. The wideband reconfigurability behavior was realized by tuning the associated capacitance values of the varactor diodes. Moreover, the proposed structure also discussed the effect of a different number of reconfigurable metamaterial units on the gain variations [87].

Abdelhadi et al. (2022) described the detailed procedure of a metamaterial-based reconfigurable antenna for wireless applications. A conventional square patch exhibited a size of 4.5 x 4.5 mm^2 and was surrounded by a controllable metasurface. In the entire design, cross-shaped metamaterial unit cell was selected. The metallic or dielectric behavior exhibited on the surface was responsible for the alteration in resonant frequency. The response of the unit cell was controlled electronically to switch between the metallic or dielectric behavior followed by the metasurface. The proposed structure offered 20 different resonances between 14.1 to 20.8 GHz [88].

2.2.2 METASURFACE

Zhu et al. (2014) designed an FRA using rectangular-loop unit cells that formed the metasurface. The designed structure was composed of a circular-shaped patch antenna and a metasurface. The whole structure became compressed and low profile by placing metasurface atop the patch antenna. This allowed the elimination of the air gap. The authors claimed that frequency tuning in the range of 4.76 to 5.51 GHz range can be achieved by rotating the metasurface from the center with reference to the patch antenna with a gain of more than 5 dB. The obtained results proved that the resonant frequency may be tuned continuously over a span of 750 MHz at roughly 5 GHz [6].

Zhu et al. (2014) presented a detailed design of slotted FRA using metasurface. The design was incorporated with a circular slot antenna and metasurface using planar technology. In the geometrical structure, the slot antenna and metasurface were in direct contact with each other to make the metasurface antenna more compact. The rectangular-loop unit cells were periodically placed to form the structure of the metasurface. The examined results revealed that frequency tuning was achieved from 2.78 to 3.2 GHz. Additionally, it offered a fractional tunable range of 14% along with high directivity and good radiation pattern [89].

Pavan et al. (2015) presented the design and analysis of FRA with overall dimensions of 30 mm and a total thickness of 3.048 mm. The structure was constructed on a RO4350B substrate that offered resonance from 5.2 to 5.9 GHz. The designed metasurface consisted of an array of properly arranged rectangular loop unit cells placed above the patch and rotated.

By doing this, the relative permittivity of the antenna changes, which in turn boosts up the resonant frequency of an antenna. Results demonstrated that the proposed antenna works for wireless applications that cover WLAN and Industrial, Scientific, and Medical (ISM) bands [90].

Zhu et al. (2015) illustrated the design of metasurface based frequency reconfigurable slot antenna with a wide tuning range. Both the slot antenna and metasurface were employed in the structure. The metasurface constituted a periodical arrangement of rectangular-loop unit cells having large value of length-to-width ratio. The authors claimed that the antenna can continuously tune its frequency over 860 MHz with a fractional tuning range of 28% [91].

Ma et al. (2016) presented the design of a mechanical reconfiguration based frequency tunable antenna using a new metasurface structure that utilized isosceles triangular loop unit cells. The antenna was designed on F4B-2 with a total thickness of 3 mm. The structure offered good performance results along with a tuning range of 2.51 to 3.70 GHz. The prototype was suitable for multistandard wireless communication applications and supported their varied requirements without increasing the volume. In the end, the designed antenna claimed easy tuning and offered a low profile and compact structure [92].

Majumder et al. (2016) proposed the design of frequency reconfigurable slot antenna in which thin anisotropic metasurface layers were used. The metasurface consisted of an array of I-shaped metallic inclusions arranged properly in both directions. Reconfiguration of frequency was achieved by effectively rotating the metasurface layers with reference to the center of slot antenna. The effective permittivity was altered by suitably rotating the metasurface layers, which further changed the loading of the slot antenna. Frequency tuning was achieved between 2.55 to 3.45 GHz with a fractional tuning of around 28%, an efficiency of more than 90%, and a gain between 5.3 to 8.3 dB [93].

Kumar et al. (2017) designed Swastika shaped low-profile FRA using a metasurface. The design was analyzed on an Arlan AD substrate of 1.3 mm height. It was examined that the investigated frequency can be continuously tuned from 4.48 to 4.60 GHz by suitably rotating its metasurface. In comparison to a typical microstrip patch antenna, the suggested structure demonstrated a gain boost of 1.96 dB in the E- and H-planes. It was proved that the antenna works for wireless and satellite applications that are employed in unmanned air vehicles [94].

Zhu et al. (2017) depicted the FRA with metasurface consisting of periodically arranged elliptical unit cells. The structure of the antenna was constructed on Rogers RO4350B substrate with a 40 mm diameter and a thickness of 3.048 mm. The authors stated that reconfiguration of frequency in the range of 4.52 to 5.31 GHz can be obtained by mechanically rotating the metasurface. The results showed that the projected prototype can provide higher gain and wider bandwidth [95].

Chen et al. (2018) designed a double-layer metasurface based frequency and polarization conversion antenna that can operate in 4 GHz band for LP mode and a 5 GHz band for circular polarization (CP) mode. Both the patch antenna and the metasurface were circular and exhibited the same value of radius for simplicity in mechanical rotation. The results demonstrated that operational frequency can be reconfigured continuously from 4 to 4.35 GHz by rotating the antenna while the polarization remains unchanged [96].

Ni et al. (2018) illustrated the design of frequency and polarization reconfigurable antenna. The metasurface, slot antenna and metallic reflector constituted the overall antenna structure and were fabricated on a 32 mm thick Rogers RO4003C substrate. The design of metasurface was made using 64 similar cells with serrated truncated corners. It was found that by properly adjusting the positions of metasurface and slot antenna, frequency and polarization reconfiguration can be achieved. A result showed that reconfiguration of polarization was achieved from 8 to 11.2 GHz range by adjusting the distance of three components i.e. metasurface, metallic reflector, and slot antenna [97].

Li et al. (2019) proposed metasurface enabled FRA designed using a radially homogenous model. Three metasurfaces representing elliptical-shaped unit cells were designed whose major axis was fixed while axial ratios differ. Experimental analysis revealed that the constructed prototype estimated the central operating frequency, thereby claiming improved accuracy, robustness, and simplicity [98].

Ulomi et al. (2021) projected a compact metasurface antenna with smooth dual-band frequency reconfiguration. In the structure, circular layers were placed next to each other in an upward direction. The lower layer exhibited a rectangular patch on one side and a ground plane on the other side. The upper layer atop the patch antenna incorporated a large number of unit cells. For the operation of frequency reconfiguration, the upper layer was rotated mechanically in the clockwise direction at an angle Θ_z along z-axis. Depending on the rotation angle, the scattering parameters associated with the antenna were changed that further affect the relative permittivity related to the upper layer. The designed structure can be functional for portable wireless communication systems [99].

Performance comparison of different types of material change mechanism based FRAs is done in Table 2.2. All antennas considered for this comparison have different size, substrate, frequency range, and application type.

Table 2.2 Comparison of various material change mechanism based FRAs

Ref. No.	Substrate type	Antenna design parameter (mm)	Frequency range (GHz)	Application type
[6]	Rogers RO4350B	D = 40	4.76 - 5.51	Wireless
[82]	FR4	L = 0.056 λ_0 W = 0.047 λ_0	1.6 - 2.23	-
[83]	-	-	-	Wireless
[84]	FR4	L = 27, W = 25	2.4, 3.5, 5.25 and 5.8 bands	Wireless
[85]	Rogers RT duroid	L = 136.4, W = 136.4	-	Radar systems & warfare antenna systems
[86]	FR4	L = 40, W = 40	2.7, 4.5 and 5.9 bands	Wireless
[89]	Rogers RO4350B	D = 50	2.78 - 3.2	Wireless
[90]	RO4350B	D = 30	5.2 - 5.9	-
[91]	Rogers RO4350B	D = 50	2.64 - 3.5	-
[92]	F4B-2	D = 50	2.51 - 3.70	Wireless
[93]	Rogers RT/duroid 5880	L = 100, W = 100	2.55 - 3.45	Wireless
[94]	Arlan AD	D = 60	4.48 - 4.60	Wireless and Satellite
[95]	Rogers RO4350B	D = 40	4.52 - 5.31	Wireless
[96]	Rogers RO4350B	-	4 - 4.35	Wireless
[97]	Rogers RO4003C	L = 80, W = 80	8 - 11.2	Wireless
[98]	Rogers RO4350B	D = 50	For ellipse type, 3.97 - 4.74 and for IM loaded ellipse type, 3.84 - 4.55	Wireless

L = Length, W= Width and D = Diameter

Ledimo et al. (2022) analyzed the functional characteristics of a metasurface antenna which was further utilized for the implementation of 4 x 4 array along with its reconfigurable counterpart. The entire procedure of FRA was based on the adjustment of operational frequency by incorporating PIN diodes instead of phase-shifters and power amplifiers. The implemented structure showed wide bandwidth from 28-40 GHz. The examined gain variations were from 27.33 to 28.8 dBi at different diode capacitances. The 16 element structure claimed to be a double negative metasurface. It was concluded that usage of diodes helped in the enhancement of gain and directivity [100].

2.3 Review on the ANN Approach based Antennas

Sivia et al. (2013) proposed an ANN approach for the designing and analysis of circular fractal antenna. The constructed antenna was built on chosen Rogers RT 5880 Duroid substrate. The authors suggested that this modeling technique can effectively predict the designed parameters under specified conditions, which in turn reduces the complex iterative process and designing cycles to shorten the product development time. The results achieved using ANNs were consistent with the simulated and measured outcomes [101].

Dhaliwal et al. (2016) developed an ensemble hybrid algorithm through the use of ANN and bacterial foraging optimization for designing a compact fractal antenna. The optimal dimensions of a pre-fractal antenna were calculated for the desired resonant frequency, thereby claiming bandwidth enhancement and size reduction. The developed antenna did not require a harmonic rejection filter, which in turn enhanced the conversion efficiency and can be employed for wide applications [102].

Kaur et al. (2019) applied an ANN and particle swarm optimization approach to evaluate the microstrip feed position of multi-fractals based antenna. The projected antenna was fabricated on chosen 1.6 mm FR4 substrate. The results clearly showed that the computed value of the feed position was close to the desired value. The average absolute error was calculated with the Feed-Forward Back Propagation Network (FFBPN) and generalized regression neural network. The projected antenna claimed excellent gain and high efficiency and is well suited for ISM frequency bands [103].

Rani et al. (2019) proposed the design and development procedure of a virtual instrument for fault diagnosis in the fractal antenna. The antenna was developed on a 1.6 mm thick FR4 epoxy substrate. In the designed structure, the radiation pattern values related to each fault were taken in Laboratory Virtual Instrument Engineering Workbench (LABVIEW) to obtain the fitted value. Hence, a neural network model was developed with Levenberg-Marquardt (LM) training algorithm to find out the faulty element in the designed array of an antenna from its damaged radiation pattern [104].

Kaur et al. (2020) designed and developed a hybrid fractal antenna using three widely used fractals such as Giuseppe Peano, Cantor Set, and Sierpinski Carpet. The material employed for designing this antenna was FR4 having 1.6 mm thickness. The performance verification was done by creating a data set of 58 samples. The position of its microstrip line feed was optimized using ANN and the firefly algorithm. Further, experimental evaluations claimed that the FFBPN model accurately estimates the resonant frequency of the projected antenna [105].

Sran et al. (2020) analyzed the behavior of a wearable hybrid fractal antenna using ANN and Iterative Function System. Various samples were created by varying ground plane dimensions. The outcomes of different algorithms such as Feed Forward Back Propagation and ELMAN Back Propagation were compared. The antenna based on Koch-Meander slot produced bandwidth of 178 MHz, 4.75 MHz and 334 MHz at the associated investigated resonance 2.53 GHz, 4.9 GHz and 7.6 GHz. The examined gain values at the respective resonances were 8.61 dB, 3.2 dB and 5.38 dB. The suggested geometry proved its functionality for S, C and X bands [106].

Sharma et al. (2021) illustrated the procedure of employing regression-based machine learning for the examination of operational frequency, slot dimensions and geometrical parameters associated with the chosen patch. In the design, two similar slots were incorporated at the opposite sides of the radiator. 3822 antenna structures having different slot size, substrate thickness, patch length and dielectric material were simulated and their responses were noted down. 20 different regression-based machine learning algorithms were compared and concluded that the Gaussian Process Regression model accurately predicted the physical or electrical parameters [107].

Sun et al. (2021) explored an ANN-based improved artificial bee colony technique for the realization of high performance L-shaped probe-fed antenna. Due to the complex internal relationship between the design performance and the desired performance standard, the employed deep learning approach effectively predicted the different antenna dimensional parameters. The designed L-shaped probe helped in achieving a wide operational band and improved the radiation efficiency. It was stated that the improved artificial bee colony algorithm had overcome the weak local optimization ability associated with the standard artificial bee colony algorithm [108].

Wei et al. (2021) utilized an ANN based optimization design method and convex optimization for antenna arrays. The purpose of using ANN was to design an antenna element and to optimize its radiation performance as well as the distance between the antenna elements. The convex optimization method was introduced for the optimal synthesis of main lobe direction and side lobe level associated with antenna arrays. It was concluded that with an inter-element coupling, the suggested synthesis method can effectively optimize the radiation pattern. Collaborative optimization of element pattern and the array factor helped in achieving optimal performance [109].

Tanguy et al. (2022) developed a neural network using effective parameters along with the GALERKIN function for the investigation of resonant frequency linked with the rectangular antenna. The designed rectangular antenna resonated at 6 GHz and its performance parameters were evaluated. The training errors were checked by generating error types on a 4 input 1 output model. This process helped in producing the final dimensions of the rectangular antenna [110].

2.4 Concluding Remarks

This chapter provides a comprehensive review on the design procedures and operational characteristics of various frequency reconfigurable antennas. The experimental observations of numerous antennas operating in the wireless communication domain have been reported. Additionally, a few antenna designs using an artificial neural network approach are discussed. Overall, the main purpose of this literature survey is to analyze the previous findings related to the current research problem.

CHAPTER 3
NUMERICAL MODELING PROCEDURE FOR DESIGNING ANTENNAS

Recent advancements in the computer industry have a significant impact on scientific research as well as on our daily lives. Nowadays, huge achievements have been made by fusing the advancing modern technology and computer-aided designs with deep-rooted research domains. This fruitful combination has given birth to a new field of research called Computational Electromagnetics (CEM) or electromagnetic modeling. This technique is beneficial in solving real-world electromagnetic problems such as asymmetrical geometries of real devices that cannot be solved analytically using numerical approaches.

3.1 Electromagnetic Modeling of the Antennas

Computational electromagnetics is a field that numerically solves Maxwell's equations using restricted computing resources. Numerical approaches break down complex arrangements into smaller parts. To show the medium's response to the Electromagnetic field (EMF) and boundary conditions, these techniques provide closed-form solutions. Thus, CEM becomes essential for antenna modeling using limited computational resources and time constraints. To evaluate basic antenna parameters, CEM formulates electric and magnetic fields. The physical interactions of EMFs with external objects and the environment are described in these solutions [111]. To retain high accuracy, physical approximations can be avoided. The particular discretized problem can be made similar to the original continuous problem by increasing the number of elements. As a result, the use of numerical approaches is limited only by the speed as well as by the storage capacity of employed computers [112].

The following steps are to be followed while computing the field using numerical methods [113]:

1. Define the approximate domain problem region where the governing equations need to be solved.

2. Formulation of discrete problems by splitting the defined problem domain into a specific number of sub-domains.
3. Derive a system of equations for general elements.
4. Gather all elements in the solution area.
5. Solve the resulting system of equations to provide a numerical estimation of the approximate field.

These fields connect across element boundaries to satisfy the general Maxwell's equations and formulate field solutions for the whole parent structure. Once a field solution is developed, there is a need to form the S-matrix. Therefore, other system performance parameters can also be obtained from the electromagnetic field and the S-matrix.

3.2 Finite Element Method

Finite element method, a numerical method, is used to obtain reasonably accurate solutions to abstract calculus equations that predict the response of the physical systems. From a mathematical standpoint, FEM appears as the most effective numerical method, and it may be seen as an extended version of Rayleigh-Ritz/Galerkin technique of formulating coordinate functions whose linear combination helps in approximating the unknown solutions [113]. In 1968, Peter P. Silvester published the first time usage of FEM in the electronics domain. By employing it for higher-order waveguide analysis, he demonstrated its utility in microwave engineering and EMF problems [114] and [115]. Better design quality, higher accuracy, better insight into important design parameters, result oriented, virtual prototyping, easier modeling, and increased productivity are all benefits of FEM.

To predict the EMF distribution, the problem area is broken into tiny regions or volumes depending on the size. For 2D problems, these tiny regions are usually polygons such as triangles and rectangles, but for 3D problems, tetrahedral elements are employed. Once the volume has been partitioned, well-labeled, and with relevant property values, an unknown field within each element is then approximated with the help of linear extrapolation. The main purpose of FEM is to formulate a specialized system of linear equations with adequate boundary conditions that may help to create an approximate solution to unspecified field intensity [116]. The field computation of FEM involves the following stages:

3.2.1 PRE-PROCESSING

This stage deals with the formulation of the problem in terms of defined parameters, limited nodes, and associated node equations. This step entails the creation of an initial model with well-specified material properties, appropriate boundary conditions, and the approximation/ discretization of a complicated geometry using appropriate mesh generation algorithms [117] and [118]. The following major functions are included in the pre-processing stage:

3.2.1.1 Geometric Modeling, Boundary, and Initial conditions

For modeling, design constraints and design specifications are taken into account. Before solving the specific PDE, appropriate boundary and initial conditions are required. The source of the electromagnetic model is necessary to specify the emission of electromagnetic waves [117].

3.2.1.2 Meshing of the Domain

Meshing refers to the process of subdividing a model into finite elements. These meshes are unified at the nodes or nodal locations that are shared by two or more elements, as well as boundary lines and/or surfaces. Mesh elements are generally discrete elements that are assessed at the nodes or edges in a system of PDEs. In the same solution area, different sorts of element forms might be used. The mesh is an integral part of any electromagnetic device numerical model [118].

(a) Elements for 1D geometries

The purpose of a mesh generator is to discretize the domains or intervals into distinct mesh elements. Mesh vertices are the terminal points of the mesh elements. The peripheral/boundary elements (or vertex elements) in the mesh represent the geometry's peripheries (boundaries/vertices) [116].

(b) Elements for 2D geometries

In 2D geometries, the mesh generator discretizes the domains into distinct triangular or quadrilateral mesh elements. If there is a curve then these elements effectively represent an approximation of the associated parent geometry. The mesh vertices are the corners of the geometry, and the mesh edges are the sides of triangles and quadrilaterals. The mesh vertices must not be present in the interior of a mesh edge. An approximate discretization is used to create mesh edges, and boundaries are determined. These borders are known as edge elements, and they must match the mesh elements of neighboring sectors. The vertex elements are used to represent the geometry vertices [117].

(c) Elements for 3D geometries

The mesh generator discretizes domains in 3D geometries into tetrahedral, hexahedral, prism, or pyramid mesh pieces. The mesh faces, mesh edges, and mesh vertices are the names given to the faces, edges, and corners of these elements, respectively. The discretization of boundary geometry produces triangular or quadrilateral boundary elements. The edge elements are created from the geometry edges. As in 2D geometries, the geometry vertices are represented properly by vertex elements [118].

(d) Pyramid elements

When the source and destination faces share an edge and the source face exhibits a triangular mesh, the pyramid elements emerge in the mesh [116].

3.2.1.3 Choice of Interpolation Function

The type of interpolation function to represent the deviation of the field variable over the element is assigned to each element's node. The interpolation function is just a trial function that provides an estimate of the element's unspecified solution. In computing the finite element solution, the choice of certain finite elements and the relevant approximation function is critical. The interpolation function is basically a polynomial of first (linear), second (quadratic), or higher order. These functions are fairly easy due to the smaller size of the sub-domains. As a result, linear interpolation is commonly employed [117] and [118].

3.2.2 PROCESSING

After the assignment of appropriate material characteristics, starting boundary conditions, and meshing for the geometry, a global equation system is produced, which is then solved using iterative or elimination methods. This stage uses a variety of processing approaches to compute the field variables at the individual nodes. The following functions are included at this stage.

3.2.2.1 Derivation of the Element Governing Equation

The unknown field quantity can be calculated as a linear combination of the shape functions belonging to each element as well as a linear combination of the domain's basic functions. The relationship involving the unknown field quantities at the nodes is then obtained from the problem formulation for the typical elements. The accuracy of the approximation can be improved by refining the mesh in the region or by using higher-order elements [117].

3.2.2.2 Assemble the Elemental Equations to obtain Equations for the Entire System

The governing equations are arranged into matrices and quantitatively solved during processing. To obtain the properties of the entire system depicted by the network of elements, all of the element properties are combined [118]. The fact that the field variable value is same for each element sharing a common node, thus forming the basis for the assemble method. The type of analysis, as well as the type and attributes of the elements, boundary conditions, and material properties, all influence the assembly process.

3.2.3 POST-PROCESSING

The results obtained in the previous stage match the analytical results calculated by the empirical formula. After that, an error analysis is performed. This phase involves the following steps:

3.2.3.1 Solving the Resulting Equations

This step begins with the systematic evaluation of possible problems in the solution. The FEM provides log files or warnings and provides a quantitative assessment of the efficiency of numerical methods used for solving. After that, the comparison is done between the results obtained in the processing phase and the analytical results calculated by the empirical formula [116].

3.2.3.2 Error Analysis

The error analysis presupposes to some extent that the acquired results match well with the intended results. The amount of interest can be analyzed once the solution has been confirmed. Depending on the mathematical and physical form of the quantity, many display options are there to describe the results properly [117].

The FEM possesses a lot of key benefits over other numerical techniques such as precise handling of complex geometries, ability to solve difficulties with eigenvalues and better frequency scaling. This numerical method can be employed for multiple applications. In general, using a large number of elements yields better outcomes [119]. The self-adaptive finite element mesh generators have been popular in recent years, intending to reduce computational and labor costs. These generators construct mesh structures from problem outline using the least amount of information from the user and provide a quick and accurate solution. The capacity to build unstructured meshes is strongly related to adaptive mesh creation. Extra vertices are added to the solution region by unstructured meshes [117].

3.3 Adaptive Finite Element Procedure

The term 'adaptivity' refers to a technique in which a finite element model and a solution are created at the same time. The numerical solution obtained from finite element discretization approximates only the system's true physical performance. But to confirm the results obtained from the FEM model, it is necessary to approximate the error in the particular solution [120].

Adaptive procedures, the finite element model, is built up step by step, starting with a rough problem approximation and gradually refining the approximation so that error in the solution gets reduced [121-123]. These methods can smartly develop and formulate the efficient distribution of degrees of freedom (DOF) over the problem domain by building solution error distributions. Afterwards, by altering or adding DOF to the discretization, it is possible to rectify them. The number of DOF is an important performance parameter that is concerned with the efficiency of numerical techniques. To ensure efficient distribution of DOF, the solver refines the problem domain mesh using tiny elements in the region of high variation and large elements in the regions of smaller variation [122]. Different methodologies can be used to discover faults in the solution at different phases of the field analysis to improve the quality of the discretization, such as:

a) A priori- before the field is examined
b) Posteriori- after the field solution has been computed and the error has been estimated

Error analysis assesses the effectiveness of the method by obtaining outcomes with the desired accuracy through mesh refinement [124]. The most efficient approach to evaluate errors is to compute them directly from the mesh structure and therefore as called prior estimates.

3.3.1 ERROR INDICATORS

The error estimate indicates that the elements in the mesh must be refined. The refinement technique is usually a combination of a priori, posterior error estimation, and a refinement algorithm. Error estimator based mesh refinement improves convergence compared to the uniform refinement of all elements. For a given number of node variables, an optimal mesh produces the least amount of inaccuracy [125]. The adaptive mesh works on the idea that the finite element program automatically finds out the areas that need refinement and uses error analysis calculations to adapt the mesh to the problem. After this, the mesh is modified to minimize the errors to an acceptable level.

The adaptive meshing algorithm looks for the E field for gradients and then breaks the mesh into the portions or regions with the largest gradients [126]. This verifies that the mesh has been sufficiently disrupted between each pass and true false convergence has occurred.

3.3.2 TYPES OF ADAPTIVE REFINEMENT

Adaptive refinement models are divided into three types: h-type, p-type, and hp-type. The main difference between both models is the finite element discretization techniques utilized within the adaptive feedback loop [127], which are provided as:

3.3.2.1 h-type refinement

In this method, the refinement of finite element discretization is accomplished by varying the size (h) of the mesh elements while keeping the order (p) of the approximation functions of the elements fixed. The accuracy of the finite element solution can be improved by increasing the number of parameters needed to compute the solution by reducing the overall element size [127].

3.3.2.2 p-type refinement

In this method, the refinement of the finite element discretization is achieved by adjusting the order of the approximation function on the elements while keeping the element size constant.

To generate an effective degree of freedom distribution, the polynomial order of the elements in the high-error parts of the mesh has to be increased while preserving the lower order of elements in the remaining sections of the mesh [127].

3.3.2.3 hp-type refinement

Finite element discretization refinement for hp-type adaptivity is performed by altering the size and order of elements belonging to the mesh. The hp-adaptive techniques employ both h-type and p-type modifications to benefit from both adaptive model advantages [127].

3.3.3 ERROR CONVERGENCE ANALYSIS AND ERROR OPTIMIZATION FOR IMPROVED SOLUTION ACCURACY

The convergence of the solution produced has a significant impact on the accuracy of numerical solutions for electromagnetic problems. The errors generated when solving the PDE must be analyzed to rectify the correctness of the numerical solution [121]. The accuracy of a model depends on how well the mesh resolves the system equations. Adaptive refinement is used to control meshing, and the appropriate solver settings are chosen to attain an effective and accurate solution [125]. Afterwards, the model's governing equations are solved with the help of an appropriate solver for the determination of error convergence. The adaptive solver automatically terminates after obtaining all possible solutions, based on the set maximum number of refinements [126]. Even if the maximum number of refinements is not attained, the solver will stop the process if the number of mesh elements reaches the maximum stated value. The FEM-based simulation tool i.e. HFSS is employed in this research work.

3.4 High Frequency Structure Simulator

High Frequency Structure Simulator, developed by Ansoft Corporation in 1990, was the first commercially available software package to use adaptive mesh refinement and was distributed by Hewlett-Packard Corporation for the first six years [128]. The HFSS is designed to simulate RF, microwave, and millimeter-wave devices such as printed circuit board interconnects, antennas, microwave components, etc. It offers a graphical user interface for simulation structural modeling, setting up solution configurations, parametric studies, and displaying the results. Its capacity to simulate very complicated geometric models, including models imported from 3D Computer Aided Design (CAD), has been significantly enhanced with a new fault-tolerant, high-quality finite element meshing algorithm. The HFSS parametric modeler allows defining variables instead of a defined position or size.

A finer mesh for a large structure involves multiple elements, which necessitates wide computer memory and processing power. As a result, caution should be exercised in selecting the mesh size, ensuring that it is neither too coarse nor too fine to overload the available computational resources. At the solution frequency, HFSS refines the mesh iteratively in the area of the largest error to optimize the mesh size. In the first iteration, HFSS generates a solution based on an initial unstructured, minimum mesh for the defined problem geometry. In the second iteration, the mesh is refined further using "Material Dependent Lambda Refinement" to provide a wavelength-based initial mesh density. Afterwards, the problem is solved on the existing mesh in the third phase to compute the error belonging to each mesh element, and the elements with the highest errors are refined. The mesh is refined again and a new solution is generated if the error tolerance is not met [128]. High Frequency Structure Simulator then exits from the loop when the error tolerance converges to a user-defined precision. The basic reason behind the material-dependent lambda refining is that in microwave applications, a low mesh density is needed to support wave propagation. As a result, for each object with a different material, HFSS starts with the development of a relatively uniform mesh. After then, the maximum number of iterations is set to a predetermined value. The simulator interrupts the loop with a warning stating that the error has not converged when this number is reached, even if the error has not converged. This mesh refinement is carried out at the chosen solution frequency. At the frequency that appears at the high end of the sweep range, a fixed density mesh can be employed as an alternative. This option produces a mesh that is more consistent and accurate than automated mesh refinement. It employs adaptive mesh generation and refinement to generate the best possible combination of hierarchical basis functions [129]. It employs a direct solver that can manage the memory. After applying excitations and boundary conditions, it calculates the electric and magnetic fields. After that, an S-matrix is constructed for the EM problem [129].

3.5 Design Methodology

The fundamental properties of metamaterials must be properly understood to create the LHM structure. The shape and distribution of certain patterns included in metamaterial define its properties. Therefore, it is important to consider how the constituent elements are designed and modeled using numerical methodologies. The structure is modeled using FEM or 3D full-wave platform for simulation. Afterwards, the results are evaluated. All simulations have been carried out on a computer with an Intel Core TM i5 7th Generation CPU running at 2133 MHz and 4 GB of random access memory.

Metamaterial must be realized first for the extraction of S-parameters. This process necessitates an infinite number of repeating unit cell elements in the direction of lattice vectors. For achieving this, boundary conditions should be imposed on the unit element. To attain periodicity, two different types of boundary conditions are used. The periodic boundary conditions are simulated using a combination of Perfect Electric Conductor (PEC) and Perfect Magnetic Conductor (PMC) boundary conditions by using the symmetry inherited by the metamaterial due to the periodicity property followed by the unit elements. The excitation ports are necessary to excite the structure after the boundary conditions have been set. The incident wave is guided from the top to the bottom of the unit element by the excitation ports. For this purpose, wave port is used generally [22].

3.5.1 METHODS TO DETERMINE RELATIVE PERMITTIVITY AND PEAMEABILITY

Extraction of the basic parameters from the composite materials is one of the most challenging tasks to do. Therefore, it has attracted significant attention among researchers. All materials can be electrically characterized in the frequency domain by the complex permittivity and permeability. The response to electromagnetic radiation is mainly determined by these parameters. There are various methods available in the literature for calculating the values of these effective parameters including Nicolson Ross Weir, Transmission Reflection, direct retrieval, Drude, Lorentz model, etc. [40]

3.5.1.1 Nicolson Ross Weir Approach

The Nicolson Ross Weir (NRW) approach is an analytical and standard method that determines the effective parameters of homogenous, isotropic materials [130]. It is widely popular due to its simplicity as it does not require any kind of determination of the cosine branch index or any other complex term. Following are the mathematical Equations (3.1– 3.4) that are employed for extracting the effective parameters.

$$V_1 = S_{21} + S_{11} \tag{3.1}$$

$$V_2 = S_{21} - S_{11} \tag{3.2}$$

$$\mu_r = \frac{2}{jk_o d}\frac{1 - V_2}{1 + V_2} \tag{3.3}$$

$$\varepsilon_r = \frac{2}{jk_o d}\frac{1 - V_1}{1 + V_1} \tag{3.4}$$

where, V_1 and V_2 are the composite terms consisting of the sum and difference of transmission and reflection coefficients, respectively. μ_r represents the effective permeability, ε_r indicates the effective permittivity, d specifies the substrate thickness, and k_0 signifies the wave number.

3.5.1.2 Transmission Reflection Method

The Transmission Reflection (TR) method is one of the popular methods that are used for determining the refractive index and wave impedance directly from the transmission and reflection coefficients. This method directly calculates the value of permittivity and permeability from scattering parameters [18]. The simplified Equations (3.5 - 3.8) of this method are shown below:

$$z = \sqrt{\frac{(1 + S_{11})^2 - S_{21}^2}{(1 - S_{11})^2 - S_{21}^2}} \tag{3.5}$$

$$n = \frac{1}{k_o d}\cos^{-1}[\frac{1}{2S_{21}}(1 - S_{11}^2 + S_{21}^2)] \tag{3.6}$$

$$\varepsilon = \frac{n}{z} \tag{3.7}$$

$$\mu = nz \tag{3.8}$$

here, S_{11} and S_{21} represent the scattering parameters for reflection and transmission, respectively. The literal k_o signifies the free space wave vector, n represents the refractive index, z denotes the wave impedance, and d the thickness of the substrate.

3.6 Concluding Remarks

In this chapter, the numerical modeling procedure for designing antennas is described. It has been observed that the finite element method provides the best fit for complicated geometric shapes and inhomogeneous materials, as well as reduces the computational effort. The basic design methodology is also described. Moreover, a brief overview of the general methods to calculate the relative permittivity and relative permeability is given for easy understanding.

CHAPTER 4

DESIGN AND CHARACTERISTIC ANALYSIS OF NOVEL METASURFACE STRUCTURES

This chapter focuses on the design methodology and electromagnetic characteristics of novel metasurface structures. Permittivity and permeability are considered as the primary characteristics that determine the progress of electromagnetic waves through matter. These are the parameters associated with the substance that is present in the dispersion equation. The computation of these parameters is essential for the characterization of the metamaterials. These complex factors must be measured both for scientific and industrial purposes. With the rapidly growing importance of metamaterial, the extraction of effective parameters has attained huge attention from the antenna community. In this chapter, three distinct metasurface structures: dual split-ring shaped resonator, H and I shaped resonator, and compounded double split-ring resonator have been designed and their operational characteristics have been investigated.

4.1 Dual Split-Ring Shaped Resonator

4.1.1 INTRODUCTION

The proposed new metasurface structure of the unit cell described in this Section is composed of an orthogonally placed Dual Split-Ring Shaped Resonator (DSRR). Additionally, a thin wire is used to join them. The material used for the structure is 1.524 mm thick Rogers RO4350B. The chosen material provides excellent thermal stability and a low dissipation factor. With proper adjustments of all design parameters, the proposed unit cell structure shows DNG properties in the desired frequency regime. The behavior is examined from the reflection and transmission coefficients of the proposed metasurface structure. The phase reversal related to the reflection and transmission coefficient validates these intriguing metamaterialistic characteristics. The real value belonging to the refractive index offers negative values in this examined 4.0 to 4.81 GHz frequency range. The projected 3 x 3 array of DSRRs behave like a left-handed material.

4.1.2 GEOMETRICAL DESIGN PROCESS OF PROJECTED DSRR

A unit cell is a very critical and fundamental element while implementing the structure of an antenna. The unit cell of the suggested new metasurface structure is generated by employing orthogonally placed DSRRs connected with a thin wire. The substrate material selected for designing the whole array is 1.524 mm thick Rogers RO4350B (dielectric constant = 3.48). This material is chosen as it provides excellent thermal stability and a low dissipation factor. Moreover, it provides tight control of the dielectric constant and helps in maintaining low losses.

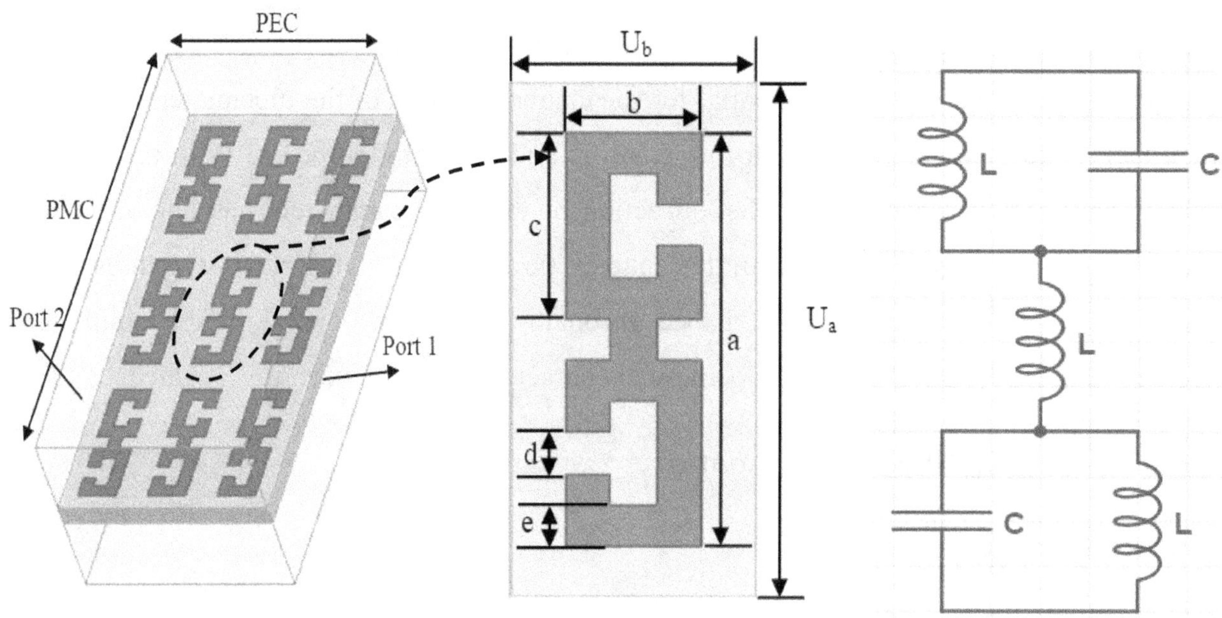

(a) **(b)** **(c)**

Figure 4.1 (a) 3 x 3 DSRR array in a waveguide medium **(b)** Enlarged unit cell **(c)** LC equivalent structure

Table 4.1 Geometrical description of projected DSRR unit cell (Units : mm)

U_a	U_b	a	b	c	d	e
12.4	5.4	10	3	4.5	1	1

In a waveguide, a small block containing 3 x 3 cells has been arranged properly and the associated boundary conditions and excitations are well-defined. The whole setup represents an infinite number of unit cells in order to investigate the metasurface. The boundary conditions such as the PEC and the PMC are assigned along the z and y-axis of the medium, respectively.

The waveports 1 and 2 are allocated along the x-axis. As a result, a triad of E-H and k is generated [131-133]. The electromagnetic behavior of metamaterials is identified by analyzing the phase reversal characteristics associated with the reflection coefficient (S_{11}) and transmission coefficient (S_{21}).

Basically, the equivalent circuit of an SRR employs two metallic rings along with a split or gap. A magnetic dipole moment is created whenever current flows continuously inside the coil. The resulting dipole moment vector acts in the perpendicular direction to the coil plane. The combination of coil and capacitor offers an LC circuit at the resonance. Hence, the SRR performs just like an LC circuit. Here, the metallic ring depicts the inductance (L) and the gap illustrates the capacitance (C) [134] and [135]. The 3 x 3 simulation model is represented in Figure 4.1 (a). The enlarged unit cell is represented in Figure 4.1 (b). The LC equivalent circuit associated with the designed DSRR is effectively illustrated in Figure 4.1 (c). The detailed geometrical description related to DSRR unit cell is revealed in Table 4.1.

4.1.3 DETERMINATION OF METAMATERIALISTIC CHARACTERISTICS OF PROJECTED DSRR

For a better and more convenient understanding, the suggested new metasurface structure is well-introduced and its electromagnetic behavior is carefully investigated. The performed analysis gives an insight into the DNG properties.

The extracted S_{11} and S_{21} parameters of the projected DSRR structure are specified in Figure 4.2. From the obtained plot, it has been noticed that a strong reflection of -47.67 dB is observed at the realized resonance i.e. 4.76 GHz. This indicates that the proposed LHM structure has a resonance frequency of 4.76 GHz. The magnitude and phase responses associated with these coefficients are illustrated in Figure 4.3. These curves represent their respective group velocity and phase velocity. The metamaterialistic behavior of the DSRR array is depicted from the phase reversal response of S_{11} and S_{21} at a particular frequency [134]. The real and imaginary parts corresponding to these coefficients are displayed in Figure 4.4. These values are further employed to examine the behavior of permeability and permittivity. The effective values of the fundamental parameters are extracted by utilizing the four Equations (3.1-3.4) of the NRW method given in Section 3.5 of chapter 3.

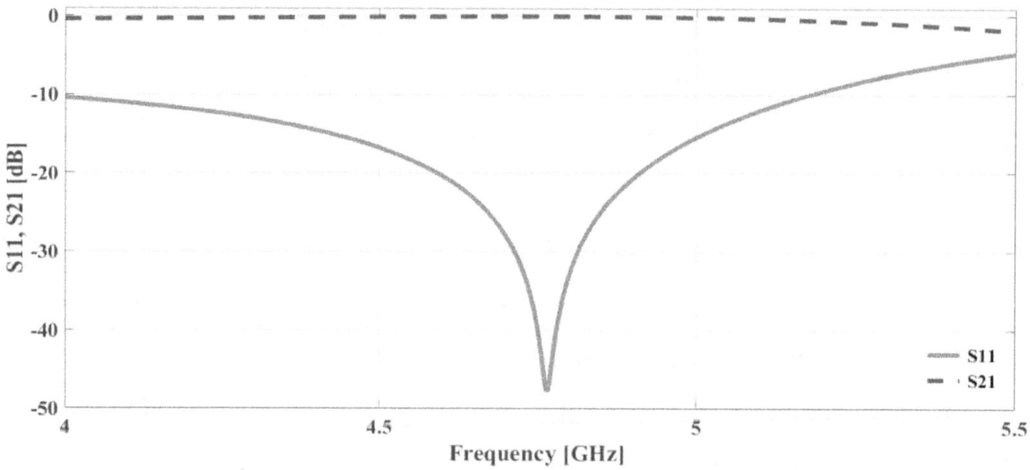

Figure 4.2 Extracted S_{11} and S_{21} parameters of the projected DSRR

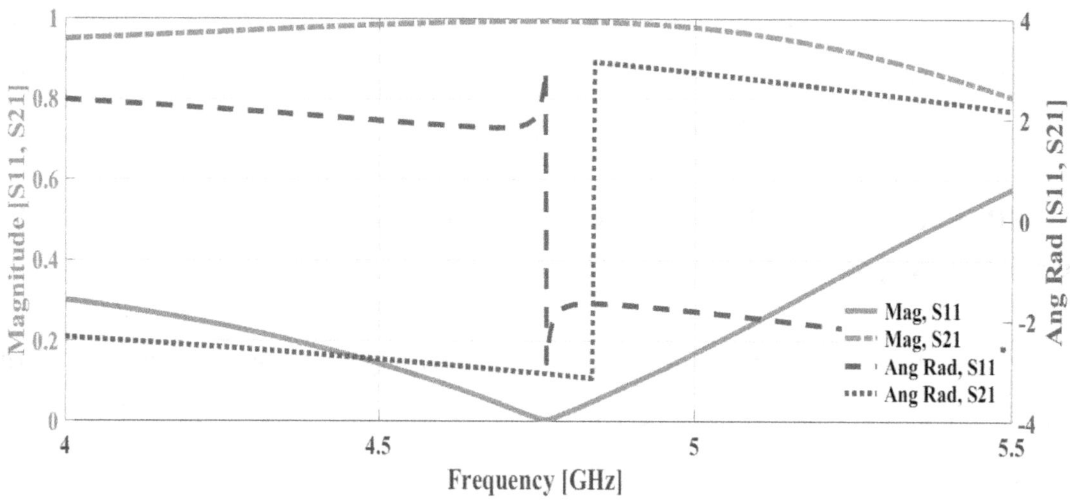

Figure 4.3 Magnitude and phase response of S_{11} and S_{21}

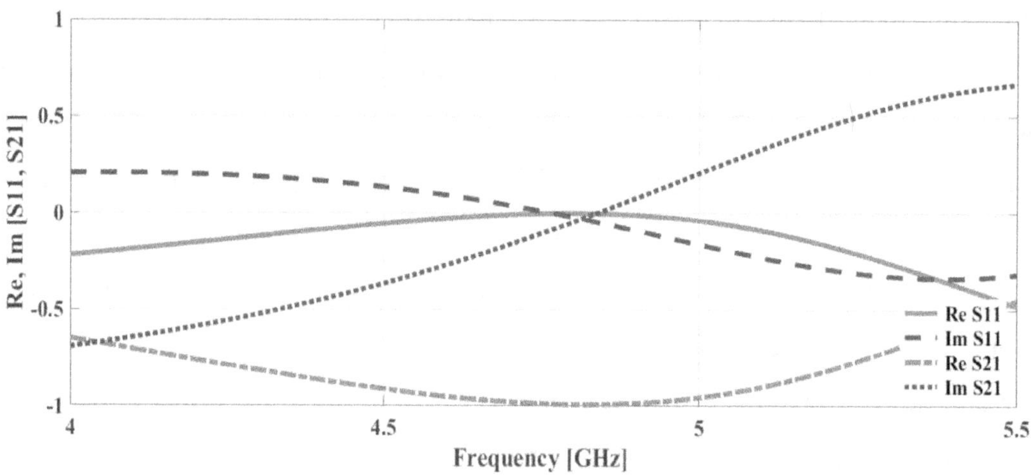

Figure 4.4 Real and imaginary parts of S_{11} and S_{21}

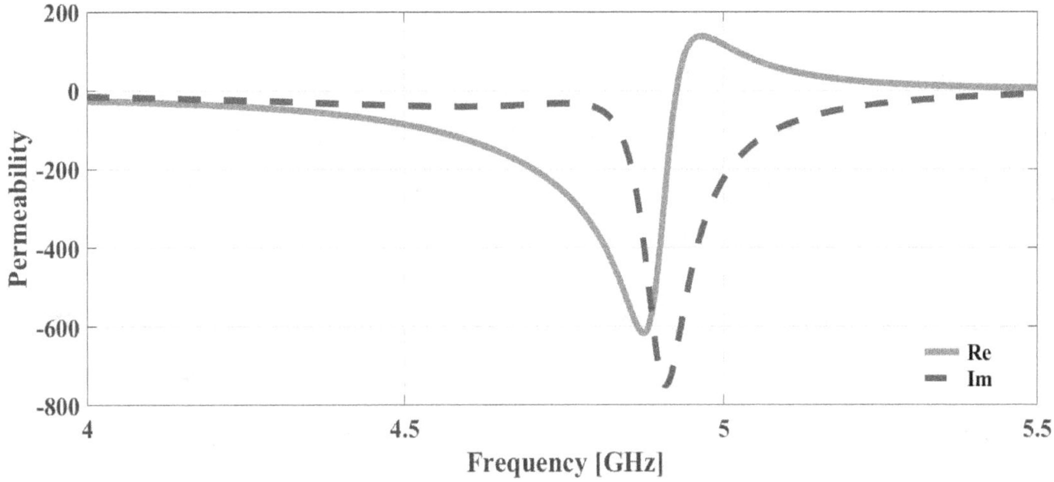

(a)

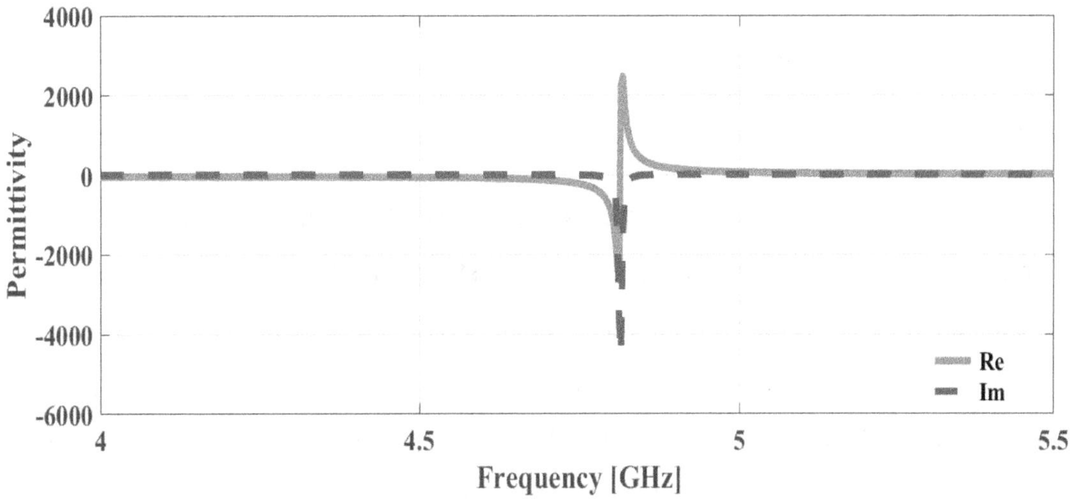

(b)

Figure 4.5 Real and imaginary parts of **(a)** Permeability **(b)** Permittivity

Metamaterials have negative permittivity and permeability. Therefore, their refractive index is also negative. The group and phase velocities associated with the electromagnetic waves appear in the opposite direction as a result of the negative refractive index i.e. the propagation direction is reversed with reference to the directional flow of energy. The reversal of phase associated with the reflection and transmission coefficient at specific resonances validates these intriguing metamaterialistic characteristics. The real and imaginary parts i.e. the fundamental variables associated with the effective material parameters are effectively revealed in Figure 4.5. This figure depicts that the effective permeability and permittivity have negative values in the frequency span of 4.0 to 4.92 GHz and 4.0 to 4.81 GHz, respectively. Table 4.2 illustrates the negative index frequency region corresponding to the effective parameters of the projected DSRR. These computed parameters show simultaneous negative values in the 4.0 to 4.81 GHz operational span. In the examined range, the real value corresponding to the refractive index also shows a negative value. Hence, the projected 3 x 3 array of DSRRs performs as a left-handed material.

Table 4.2 Negative index frequency region of effective parameters of the projected DSRR

Parameter	Negative index frequency region (GHz)
Permeability (μ_r)	4.0 - 4.92
Permittivity (ε_r)	4.0 - 4.81

4.2 H and I Shaped Resonator

4.2.1 INTRODUCTION

In this Section, a novel H and I Shaped Resonator (HISR) based metasurface structure is demonstrated that exhibits double negative metamaterialistic properties. The projected structure is inscribed on the Rogers RO4350B substrate and its behavior is analyzed with High Frequency Structure Simulator tool. Nicolson Ross Weir approach described in Section 3.5 of chapter 3 has been considered for calculating the complex permittivity and permeability associated with these materials. The designed 3 x 3 array structure acts like a tank circuit having resonant frequency corresponding to the inductance and capacitance values.

4.2.2 DESIGN CONFIGURATION OF PROJECTED HISR

In a waveguide, a small block containing 3 x 3 cells has been oriented properly and the associated boundary conditions and excitations are well-defined. The whole arrangement approximates an infinite number of unit cells for the evaluation of metasurface [131]. The symbolic representation of the 3 x 3 HISR array and the extended version of the single unit cell is illustrated in Figure 4.6 (a) and Figure 4.6 (b), respectively. The structure is composed of a repeating array containing H shaped and I shaped structures. The entire structure is embedded on the Rogers RO4350B substrate. The characteristics of the material are dielectric constant whose ε_r = 3.48 and height h = 1.524 mm. The gap chosen between the adjacent cells is 2.4 mm. The loop and gap represent the corresponding inductance and capacitance values. The PEC and PMC boundary conditions are applied on the appropriate surface of the 3 x 3 array [132]. Apply waveports along the x-plane. To properly excite electromagnetic waves, suitable waveports and well-defined boundary conditions are applied [131]. The simulation is performed in the specified frequency range i.e. 4 to 6 GHz. In the defined range, the transmission and reflection behavior of the projected HISR is evaluated. Table 4.3 illustrates the dimensional parameters of projected HISR.

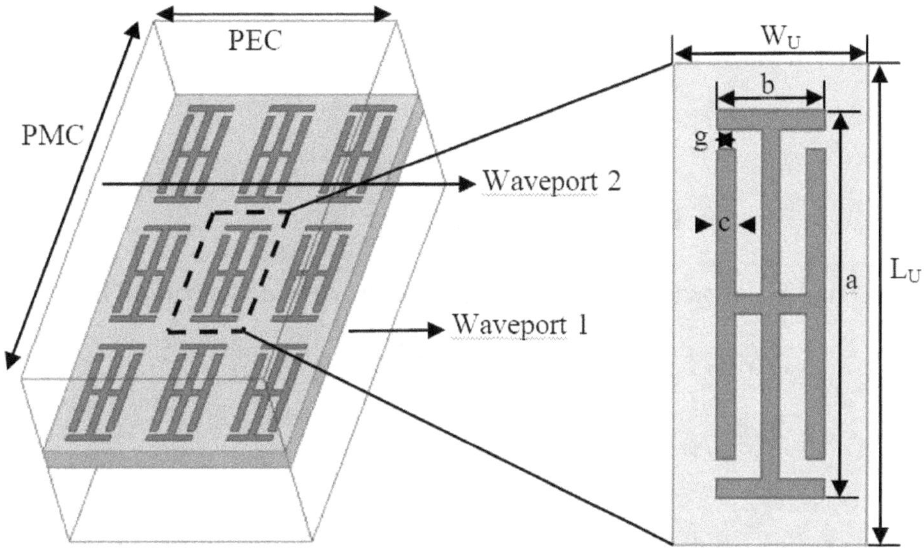

(a) **(b)**

Figure 4.6 Geometrical framework of **(a)** Waveguide set up **(b)** Zoomed unit cell

Table 4.3 Dimensional parameters of projected HISR (Units: mm)

L_U	W_U	a	b	g	c
12.4	5.4	10	3	0.5	0.5

4.2.3 DETERMINATION OF METAMATERIALISTIC CHARACTERISTICS OF PROJECTED HISR

To present several proofs of the reliability and effectiveness of the projected prototype, results obtained through simulations are described. The extracted S_{11} and S_{21} parameters of the projected HISR are specified in Figure 4.7. For the analysis purpose, the selected frequency range is 4.0–6.0 GHz. From the observations, it has been depicted that at 5 GHz frequency, the S_{11} value examined is -46.47 dB. Therefore, it has been stated that the projected HISR structural array exhibits resonance at the 5 GHz claimed frequency. The magnitude and phase of S_{11} and S_{21} are shown in Figure 4.8. Hence, it can be stated that the phase reversal characteristics of S_{11} and S_{21} confirm the metamaterial behavior.

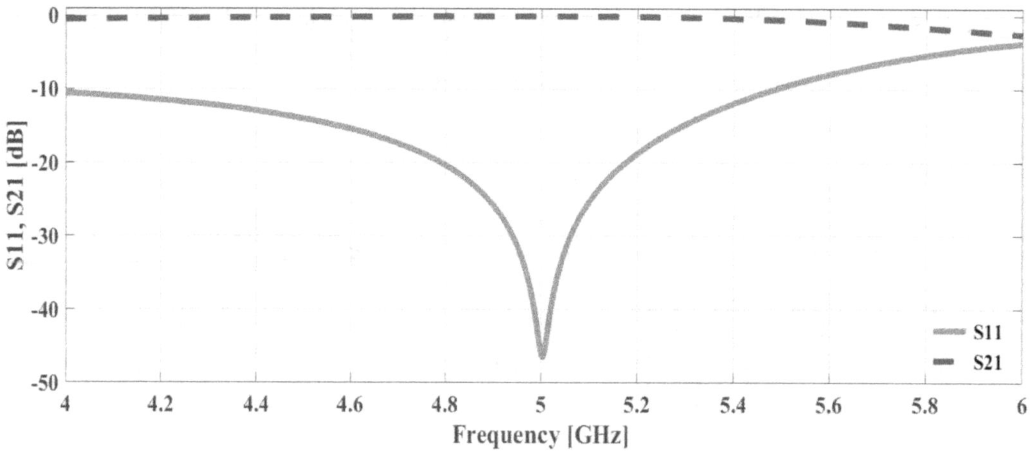

Figure 4.7 Extracted S_{11} and S_{21} parameters of the projected HISR

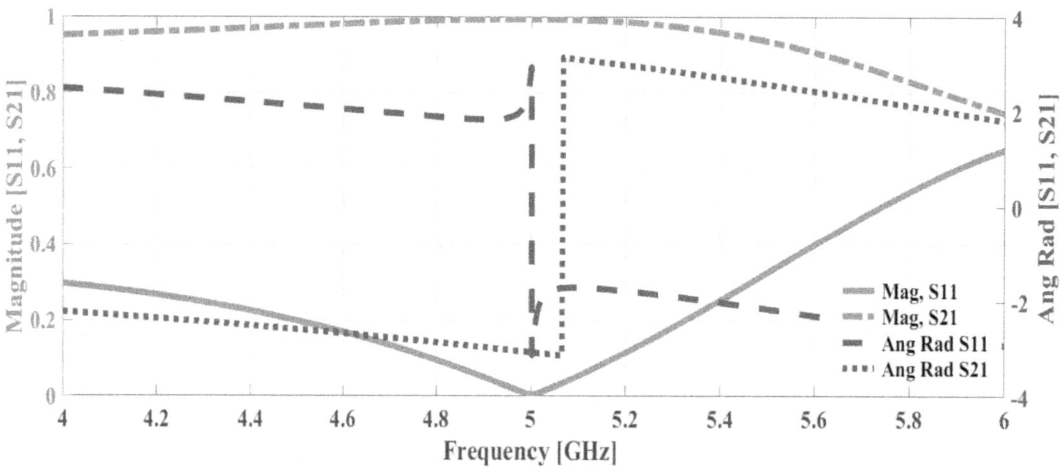

Figure 4.8 Magnitude and phase of S_{11} and S_{21}

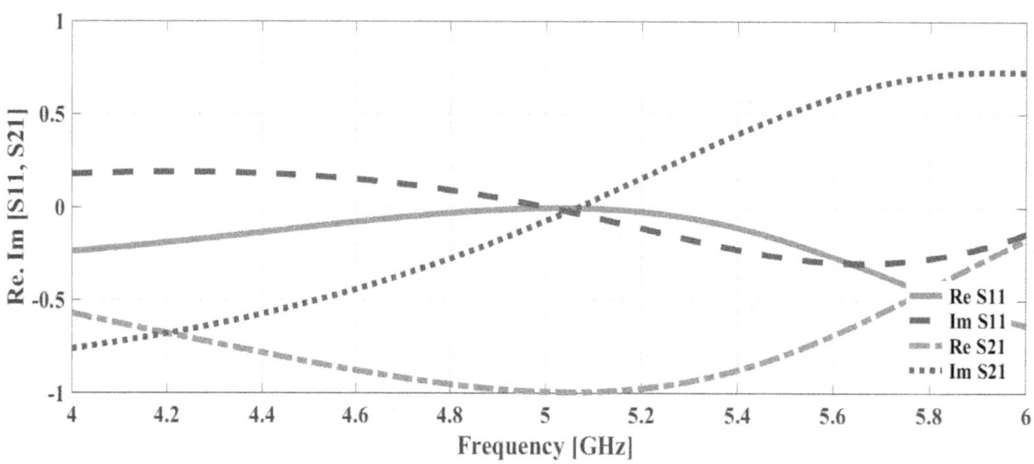

Figure 4.9 Real and imaginary parts of S_{11} and S_{21}

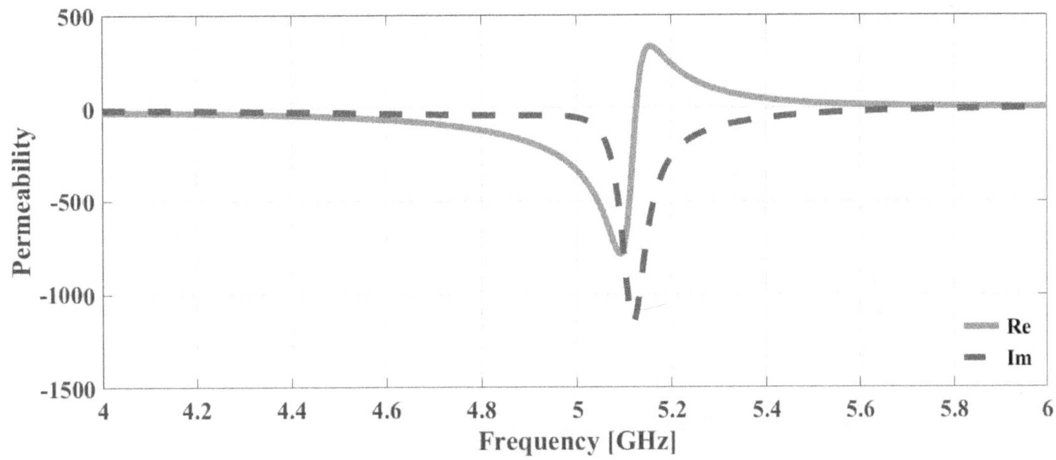

(a)

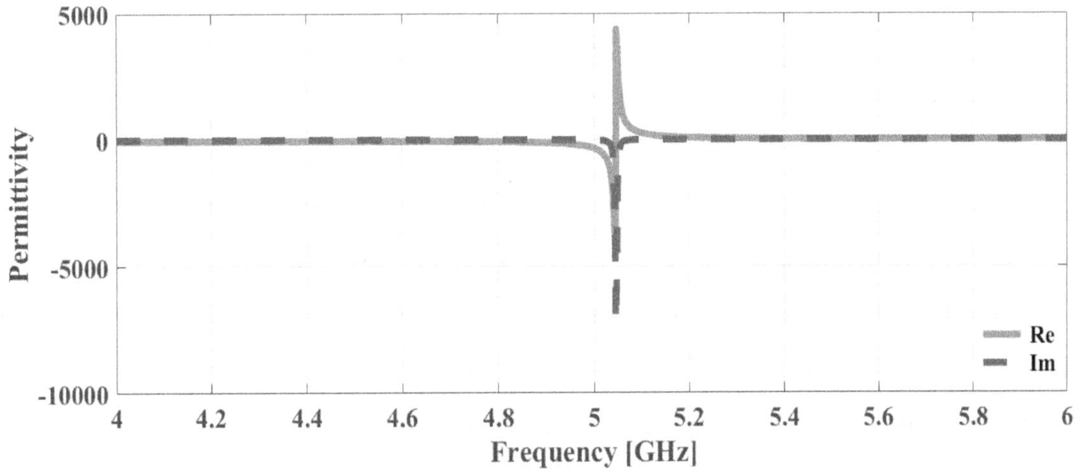

(b)

Figure 4.10 Extracted real and imaginary parts of **(a)** Permeability **(b)** Permittivity

The real and imaginary parts associated with S_{11} and S_{21} are described in Figure 4.9. Based on these values, the negative characteristics of permittivity and permeability are calculated possibly. The four Equations (3.1-3.4) of NRW method described in Section 3.5 of chapter 3 are utilized for the retrieval of the effective parameters [134-136]. Figure 4.10 (a) and 4.10 (b) show the corresponding real and imaginary parts associated with effective permeability and permittivity. Here the thick line is used to depict real value and the dashed line represents the imaginary value corresponding to the associated parameter. The effective permeability and permittivity have a negative value ranging from 4 to 5.04 GHz. Table 4.4 depicts the negative index frequency region of effective parameters of the projected HISR. Hence, it is stated that in the observed resonating span, the projected HISR array behaves like a DNG metamaterial. The simulation results of the above-mentioned metasurface structure demonstrate the characteristics of LHMs.

Table 4.4 Negative index frequency region of effective parameters of the projected HISR

Parameters	**Negative index frequency region (in GHz)**
Permeability (μ_r)	4.0 - 5.125
Permittivity (ε_r)	4.0 - 5.045

4.3 Compounded Double Split-Ring Shaped Resonator

4.3.1 INTRODUCTION

In this Section, the electromagnetic characteristics of new metasurface structure comprising of Compounded Double Split-Ring Shaped Resonator (CDSRR) shaped unit cell have been analyzed. A 1.524 mm thick flexible Rogers RO4350B substrate is employed for the designing. The investigation of the desired electromagnetic properties of the projected structure is carried out using the Transmission Reflection method. From the evaluated results, a strong reflection of -29.2 dB is noted at the claimed resonance i.e. 7.7 GHz. This specifies the existence of the LHM band. Thus, the occurrence of a double negative medium region is responsible for the negative refractive index with backward wave propagation that is present within the transmission band.

4.3.2 GEOMETRICAL DESIGN PROCESS OF PROJECTED CDSRR

The structure is created by using a flexible and affordable Rogers RO4350B substrate having a dielectric constant (ε_r) of 3.48. The unit cell structure is formed by using three double SRRs placed next to each other. This structure works like an LC resonator. The gap and metal strip act like corresponding capacitive and inductive elements. The effective electromagnetic parameters of the unit cell structure (permittivity ε_{eff}/permeability μ_{eff}/refractive index n_{eff}) are determined by using scattering parameters. For this purpose, the whole arrangement is put effectively in a waveguide environment with ports, electric field, and magnetic field applied properly along the respective axis, representing an infinite number of unit cells. Thus, for the representation of infinitely large periodic geometry, a single unit cell is used. Overall, it represents the metasurface [131-133]. For simplicity, this waveguide medium is shown in Figure 4.11 (a). The detailed dimensions of the unit cell are illustrated in Figure 4.11 (b). The LC equivalent circuit of the unit cell is shown in Figure 4.11 (c). The detailed geometrical parameters of the unit cell are elucidated in Table 4.5.

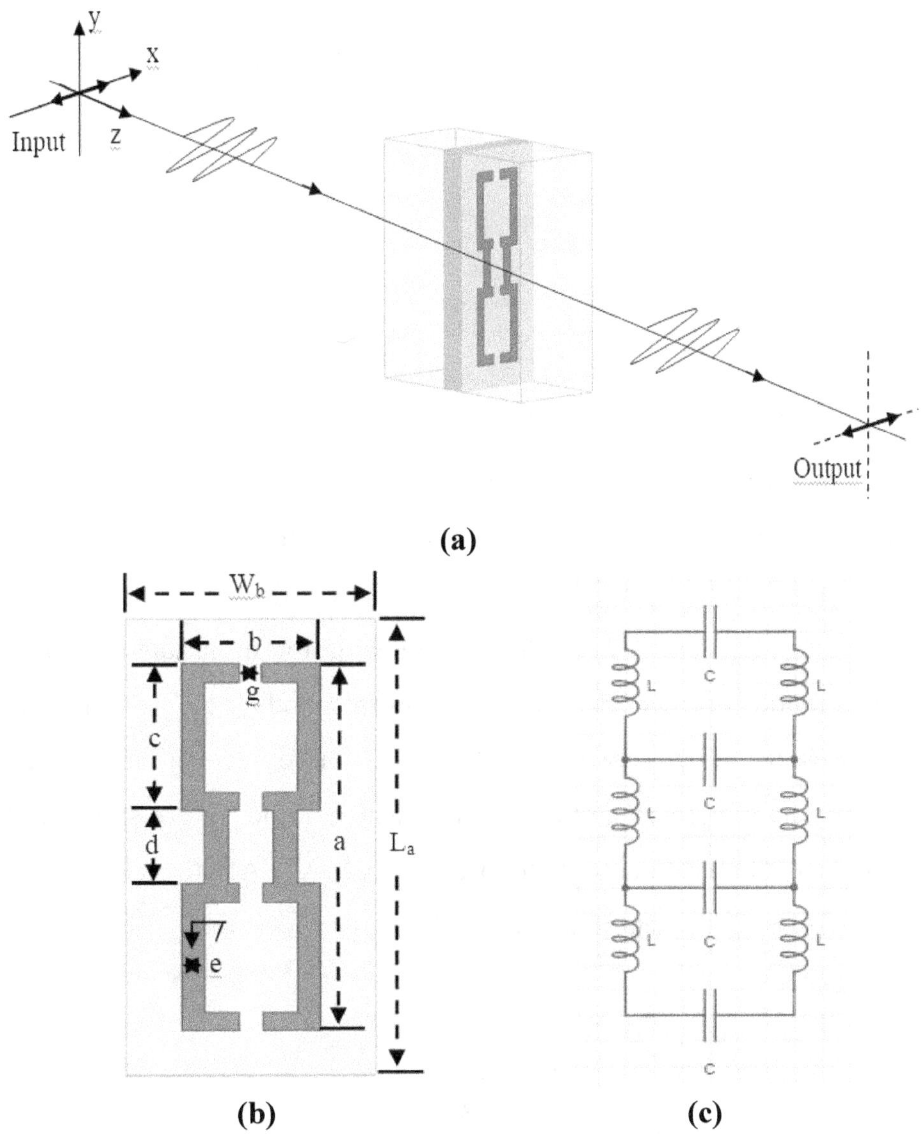

Figure 4.11 Projected CDSRR **(a)** Waveguide medium for extracting the S-parameters **(b)** Unit cell **(c)** Equivalent circuit of the unit cell

Table 4.5 Dimensional parameters of the projected CDSRR (Units: mm)

L_a	W_b	a	b	c	d	e	g
12.4	5.4	10	3	4	2	0.5	0.5

4.3.3 DETERMINATION OF METAMATERIALISTIC CHARACTERISTICS OF PROJECTED CDSRR

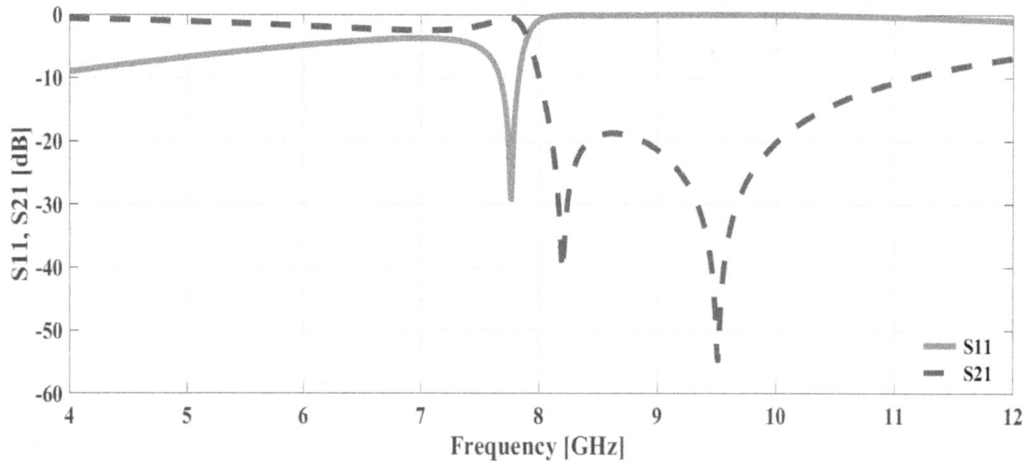

Figure 4.12 Extracted S_{11} and S_{21} of projected CDSRR

Figure 4.12 demonstrates the extracted scattering parameters (S_{11} and S_{21}) associated with the projected CDSRR. The results illustrate that a strong reflection of -29.2 dB is observed at investigated resonance 7.7 GHz. At the examined resonance, there is a coexistence of electric and magnetic resonances [134] and [138]. The first transmission minimum of -40.7 dB is found at 8.2 GHz. The magnitude and phase characteristics corresponding to S_{11} and S_{21} are shown in Figure 4.13. These results effectively demonstrate the phase reversal characteristics of the metamaterial. The real and imaginary parts associated with S_{11} and S_{21} are shown in Figure 4.14. After this, the examined observations are imported into MATLAB to determine the essential electromagnetic properties of the metamaterial.

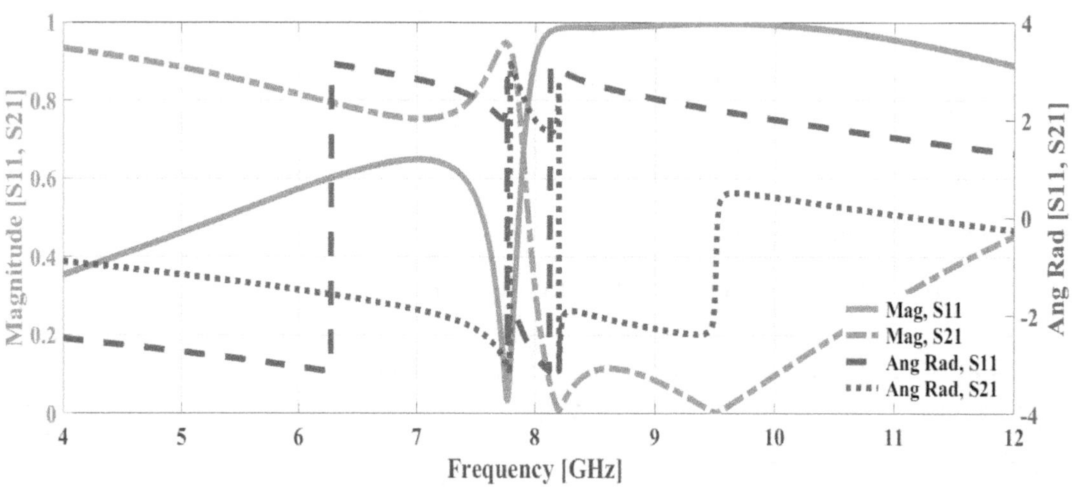

Figure 4.13 Magnitude and phase characteristics of S_{11} and S_{21}

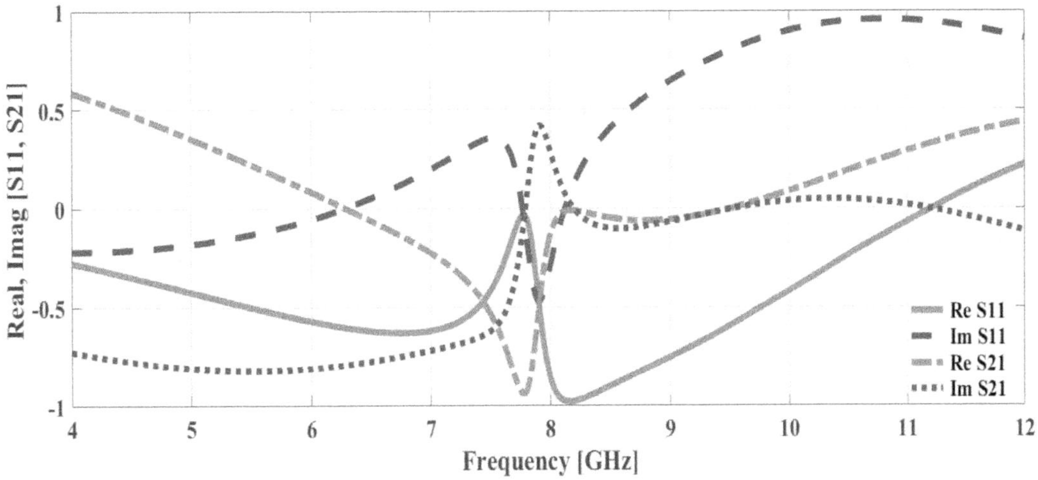

Figure 4.14 Real and imaginary parts of S_{11} and S_{21}

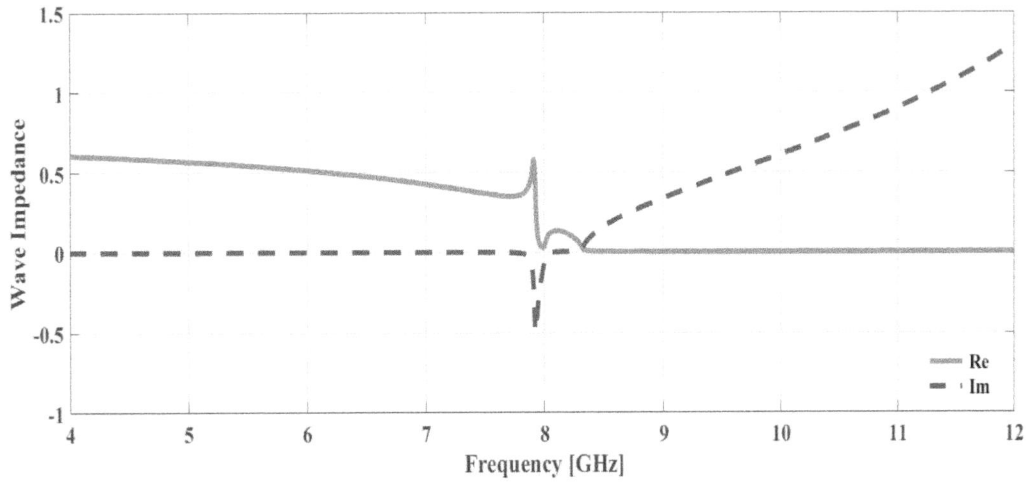

(a)

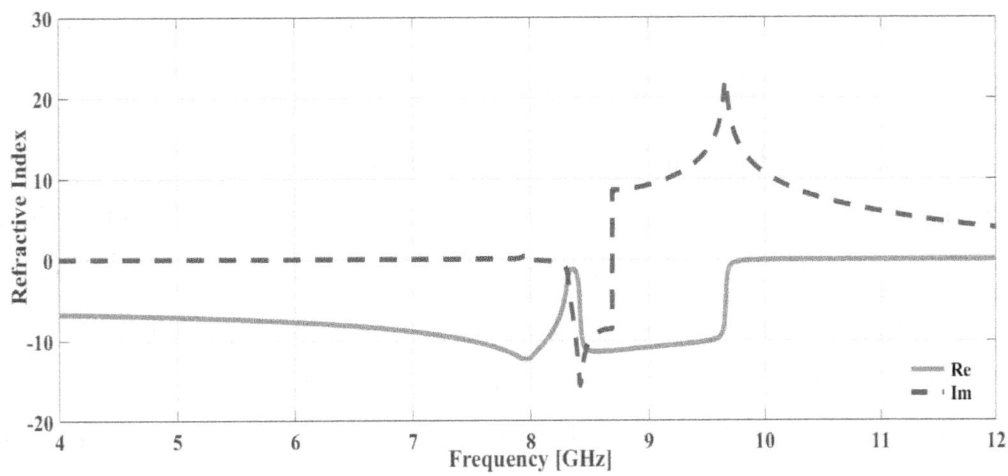

(b)

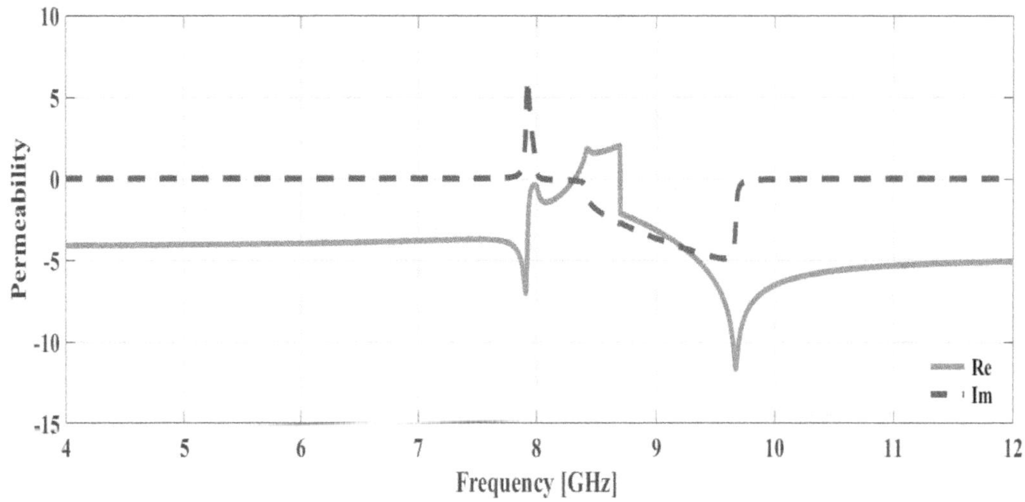

(c)

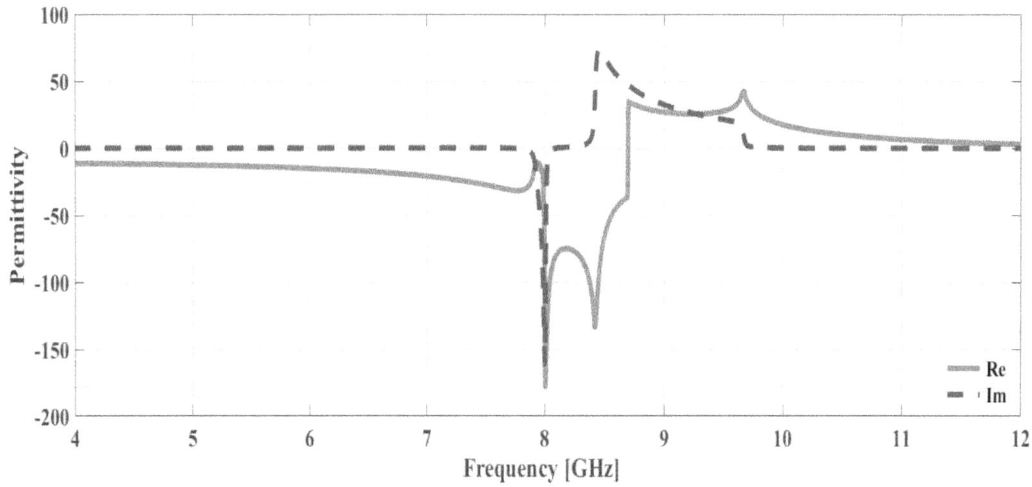

(d)

Figure 4.15 Real and imaginary parts of parameters **(a)** Wave impedance **(b)** Refractive index **(c)** Permeability **(d)** Permittivity

In this work, the TR method is used because it offers an easy and simple way to determine the wave impedance. The respective values of wave impedance and refractive index are determined using Equations (3.5-3.6) given in Section 3.5 of chapter 3. The permittivity and permeability values can be determined using Equations (3.7-3.8) given in Section 3.5 of chapter 3. The negative parts of permeability and permittivity play a crucial role in determining the material characteristics of the metamaterial. Therefore, reflection and transmission coefficients are the important components of this method. The real and imaginary parts of the homogenous parameters are illustrated in Figure 4.15. For the associated parameter, the thick red line depicts the real element, whereas the dashed blue line depicts the imaginary element. In the case of wave impedance, the positive real value is examined in the range of 4 to 8.32 GHz. Similarly, for permittivity, negative real value exists in 4 to 8.7 GHz, and the magnetic permeability exists in the range of 4 to 8.31 GHz and 8.7 to 12 GHz. These values are shown in Table 4.6. The permittivity and permeability values show the frequency of electric and magnetic plasma. The results of successful retrieval in the frequency range of 4 to 8.31 GHz confirm that the above structure exhibits the left-handed characteristics of the metamaterial.

Table 4.6 Negative index frequency region of effective parameters of the projected CDSRR

Parameters	Negative index frequency region (in GHz)
Permeability (μ_r)	4.0 - 8.31, 8.7 – 12
Permittivity (ε_r)	4.0 - 8.7

4.4 Concluding Remarks

In this chapter, three distinct novel metasurface structures have been designed and analyzed. The structure described in Section 4.1 comprises of orthogonally placed DSRRs. Nicolson Ross Weir approach has been applied to determining the metamaterialistic characteristics. The negative index frequency span associated with the effective parameters lies in 4.0 to 4.81 GHz.

In Section 4.2, the designed structure is based on the H and I shaped resonators. For the analysis of double negative properties of metamaterial, the NRW approach has been employed. The desired parameters associated with the structure are found negative in the 4.0 to 5.04 GHz range.

The structure described in Section 4.3 consists of CDSRR shaped unit cells in which the transfer matrix method is employed for the determination of the homogenous properties. The effective parameters show negative values in the 4.0 to 8.31 GHz range. Numerical analysis proved that these designed structures exhibit the left-handed properties of the metamaterial in the specified domain.

To gain superior performance characteristics, the suggested metasurface structures can be introduced onto the microstrip antennas for achieving the frequency selective surface and reconfigurability operation.

CHAPTER 5

DESIGN OF PLANAR FREQUENCY RECONFIGURABLE ANTENNAS USING METASURFACE STRUCTURES

This chapter concentrates on the design methodology of planar frequency reconfigurable antennas using novel metasurface structures. Metasurfaces are composed of regularly ordered metallic unit cells with homogenous or inhomogeneous subwavelengths. In this chapter, three distinct planar frequency reconfigurable antennas using metasurface structures have been designed and developed that showed enhanced performance metrics. In these antennas, two circularly shaped stacking layers are used. Both layers are fabricated on Rogers RO4350B. Due to the ease of integration and low fabrication cost, the designed planar antennas are largely utilized in various applications belonging to wireless communication systems. Further, FFBPN approach has been applied to determine the output parameters of these antennas. For this, the network is trained with a sufficient number of samples. Once the network is trained, the specific dimensions of the antenna are estimated effectively.

5.1 Dual Split-Ring Shaped Resonator based Planar Frequency Reconfigurable Antenna

5.1.1 INTRODUCTION

The proposed Dual Split-Ring Shaped Resonator based Planar Frequency Reconfigurable Antenna (DSRR-PFRA) is implemented using two circularly shaped stacking layers. The metasurface is designed using an array of DSRRs. The designed radiating patch and metasurface are placed above the 1.524 mm thick Rogers RO4350B substrate (dielectric constant, $\varepsilon_r = 3.48$). The dielectric loss tangent, tan δ of the associated material is = 0.0037. As the Rogers RO4350B is electrically thin, it possesses excellent dimensional stability and low loss. All the geometrical dimensions belonging to the antenna are interlinked with each other. By properly adjusting the designed antenna parameters, desired frequency reconfiguration with sufficient bandwidth has been achieved. Results illustrate that frequency reconfiguration attained is from 4.40 to 5.34 GHz and fractional tuning range of 19.3%.

5.1.2 DESIGN CONFIGURATION OF PROPOSED DSRR-PFRA

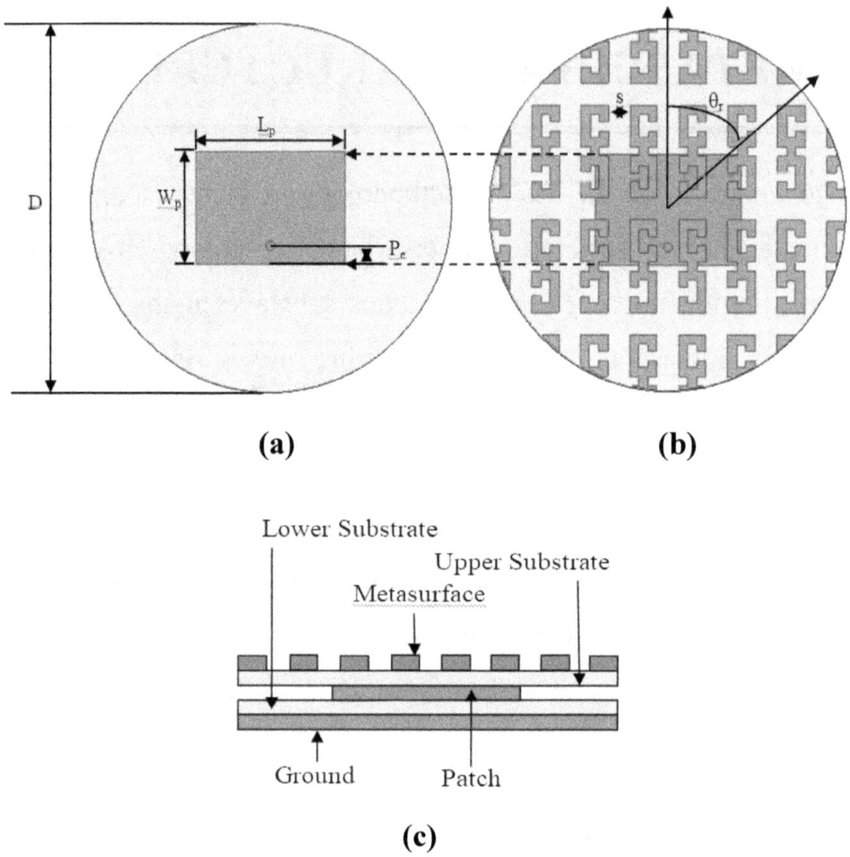

Figure 5.1 Geometrical configuration of proposed DSRR-PFRA **(a)** Patch antenna **(b)** Metasurface **(c)** Side view

Table 5.1 Parametric description of proposed DSRR-PFRA (Units: mm)

D	L_p	W_p	P_e	s
39	16	12	2	2.4

The configuration scheme of the proposed DSRR-PFRA is elucidated in Figure 5.1. The design structure of the suggested DSRR-PFRA consists of two circularly-shaped stacking layers having a diameter of 39 mm. The top view of the lower substrate represents a rectangular-shaped patch antenna fed by a coaxial feed. The bottom view of the lower substrate represents the ground plane with same size as that of the lower substrate. The geometrical view of the patch antenna is illustrated in Figure 5.1 (a). The top side of the upper substrate is an array of orthogonally placed DSRRs that are connected by a thin wire at the center, thus forming the entire metasurface. The geometrical structure of the metasurface is demonstrated in Figure 5.1 (b). Frequency reconfigurability is achieved by properly rotating the metasurface physically around its center with respect to the patch antenna. The rotation angle (θ_r) is evaluated along the y-axis. It possesses equal similarity both in horizontal as well as in vertical directions. Thus, it has been found that $\theta_r = - \theta_{r,}$ and the largest value adopted without repetition is 90^0. During the manufacturing process, the radiating side belonging to the lower substrate and the non-radiating side belonging to the upper substrate are placed in closed contact, thus eliminating the existing gap and making the whole structure compact [6]. The side view representing the two-layered structure of the projected DSRR-PFRA is revealed in Figure 5.1 (c). For the implementation of the designed antenna, Rogers RO4350B substrate material is chosen. A 50Ω SubMiniature Version A (SMA) connector is selected for appropriate impedance matching. The optimized parameters associated with the proposed DSRR-PFRA are tabulated in Table 5.1.

5.1.3 ANN FRAMEWORK FOR THE PROPOSED DSRR-PFRA

The selected FFBPN model for evaluating the proposed DSRR-PFRA is illustrated in Figure 5.2. The suggested network has 2 input, 10 hidden, and 2 output layer neurons. The unit cell dimensions 'a' and 'b' are considered as inputs, and the corresponding 'f_r' and 'S_{11}' are considered as outputs. A data set containing 41 samples is created to examine the process in which 29 samples are present in the training set, 6 in the validation, and the rest 6 in the testing set.

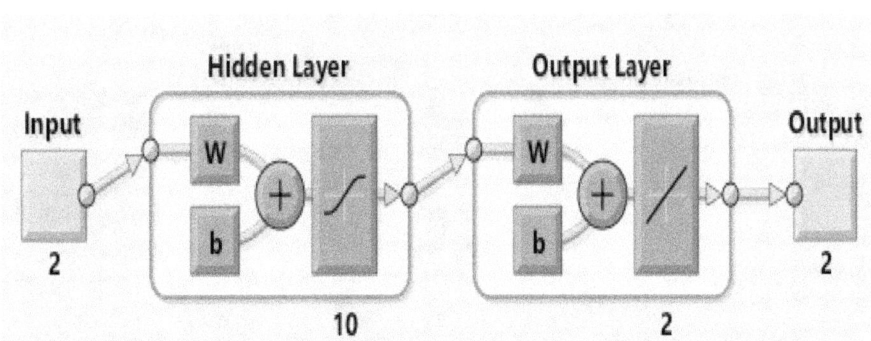

Figure 5.2 FFBPN model for the proposed DSRR-PFRA

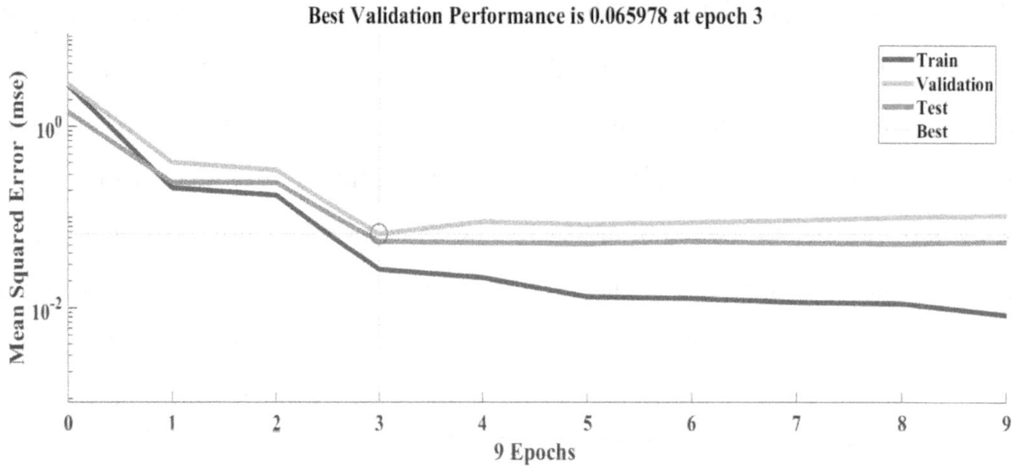

Figure 5.3 Performance plot during the analysis of the proposed DSRR-PFRA

Table 5.2 Performance parameters during the analysis of proposed DSRR-PFRA

	Samples	MSE	Regression
Training	29	2.66172e-2	9.99906e-1
Validation	6	6.59775e-2	9.99767e-1
Testing	6	5.45709e-2	9.99813e-1

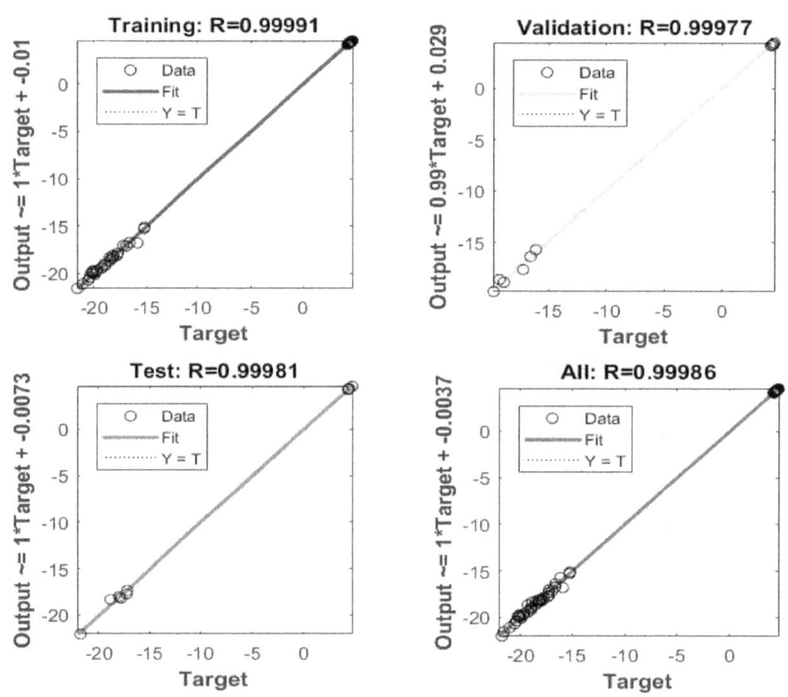

Figure 5.4 Scatter plot showing regression values for training, validation, testing, and total output during the analysis of proposed DSRR-PFRA

In this work, LM based ANN model is chosen so as to achieve the desired accuracy level and proper estimation of output parameters. Tansig and purelin are the transfer functions used at the hidden and output layers, respectively. The three statistical performance parameters such as Mean Squared Error (MSE), number of epochs taken, and the maximum absolute error are determined to evaluate the proposed model's performance. Mean Squared Error is defined as the average of squared differences between the presented ANN model and the simulated software outcomes [105]. Figure 5.3 illustrates the performance plot in which MSE is plotted against 9 epochs. The graph showed that the best validation performance of 0.065978 is found at epoch 3. The performance parameters examined during the analysis of the designed DSRR-PFRA are presented in Table 5.2. Regression (R) is a statistical measure used to evaluate the degree of correlation between the target value and the ANN model output. Its value should be close to 1, which indicates good modal performance [105]. The regression plot for training, validation, testing, and total output obtained during the analysis phase of the proposed DSRR-PFRA is presented in Figure 5.4. The total value of regression obtained during this process is 0.99986.

Table 5.3 Absolute error estimation during analysis of proposed DSRR-PFRA

Inputs		**HFSS outputs**		**ANN outputs**		**Absolute error**	
a	**b**	**f_r**	**S_{11}**	**f_r**	**S_{11}**	**f_r**	**S_{11}**
10	3.1	4.321	-18.506	4.3350	-18.289	-0.013	-0.217
10	3.7	4.265	-17.259	4.3151	-17.354	-0.050	0.094
10	2.9	4.345	-19.267	4.3193	-18.629	0.026	-0.637
10	2.4	4.409	-19.776	4.4203	-19.828	-0.010	0.052
10	2	4.480	-20.053	4.4858	-19.728	-0.005	-0.324
10.1	3	4.305	-18.855	4.3074	-18.332	-0.002	-0.523
11	3	4.136	-15.260	4.1196	-15.280	0.016	0.019
9.7	3	4.433	-19.296	4.4309	-19.433	0.002	0.137
9.3	3	4.546	-20.534	4.5395	-20.713	0.006	0.179
9	3	4.618	-21.744	4.5814	-22.043	0.037	0.299
Average Absolute Error						0.002	0.008

The examined values of Average Absolute Error (AAE) corresponding to 'f_r' and 'S_{11}' are illustrated in Table 5.3. In this table, a random set of 10 samples is taken and for these samples, values of AAE corresponding to 'f_r' and 'S_{11}' are computed. The estimated value of the average absolute estimated error corresponding to 'f_r' is 0.002, whereas the average absolute estimated error corresponding to 'S_{11}' is 0.008. It has been noticed that both the estimated values are positive.

5.1.4 PROPOSED DSRR-PFRA RESULTS

Full wave electromagnetic solver HFSS is employed for the designing of the proposed DSRR-PFRA. Vector Network Analyzer (VNA) Anritsu MS46322A has been utilized for the testing of the fabricated structure. For easy understanding, the photographic view of the patch antenna and the generated metasurface is illustrated in Figure 5.5 (a), whereas the pictorial view of the proposed DSRR-PFRA is shown in Figure 5.5 (b).

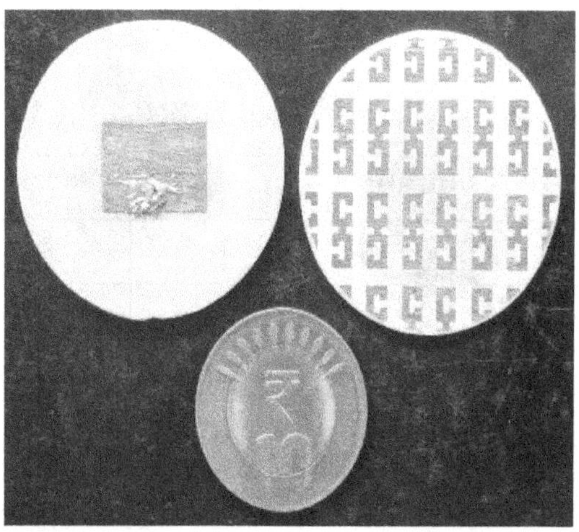

(a)

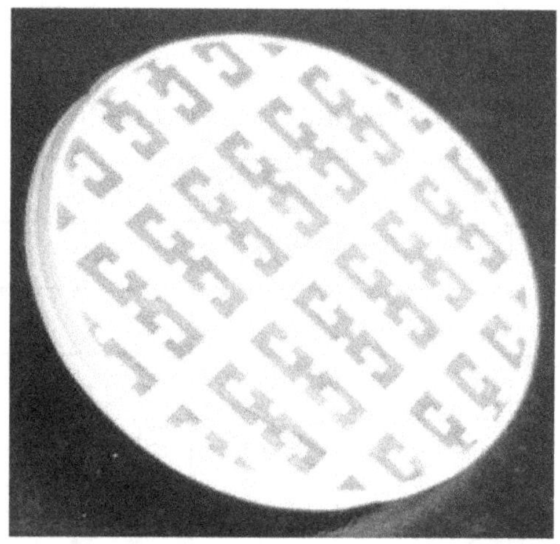

(b)

Figure 5.5 Fabricated prototype of **(a)** Patch antenna and metasurface **(b)** DSRR-PFRA

5.1.4.1 Proposed Patch Antenna

The patch antenna serves as a source antenna that radiates an electromagnetic field towards the metasurface. The simulated (bold red line) and measured (dashed blue line) S_{11} characteristics of the patch antenna are shown in Figure 5.6. From the Figure, it is noted that the simulated resonance frequency is 6.12 GHz and the associated S_{11} value is -10.27 dB, whereas the measured resonance is 6.50 GHz with a corresponding S_{11} value of -16 dB. Minor variations seen in the results are due to impedance mismatch and fabrication tolerances.

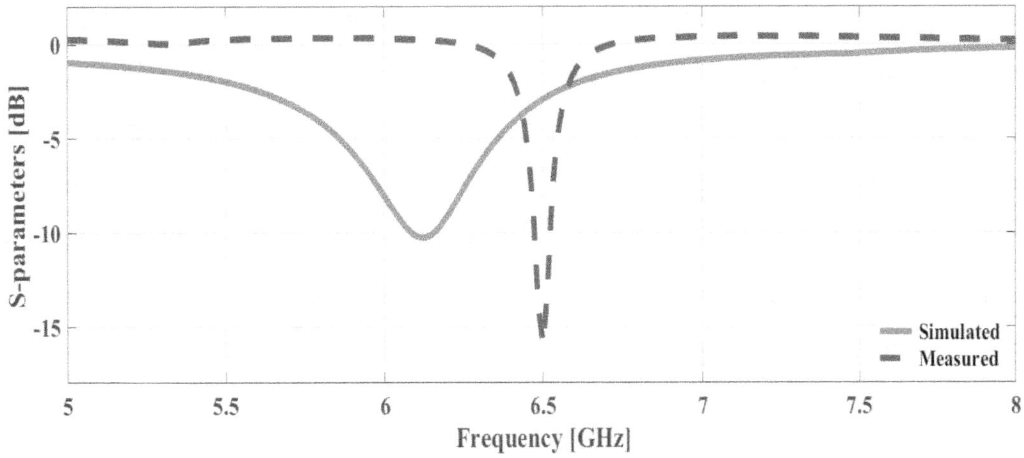

Figure 5.6 Simulated and measured S_{11} values of the patch antenna

5.1.4.2 Proposed DSRR based Frequency Reconfiguration

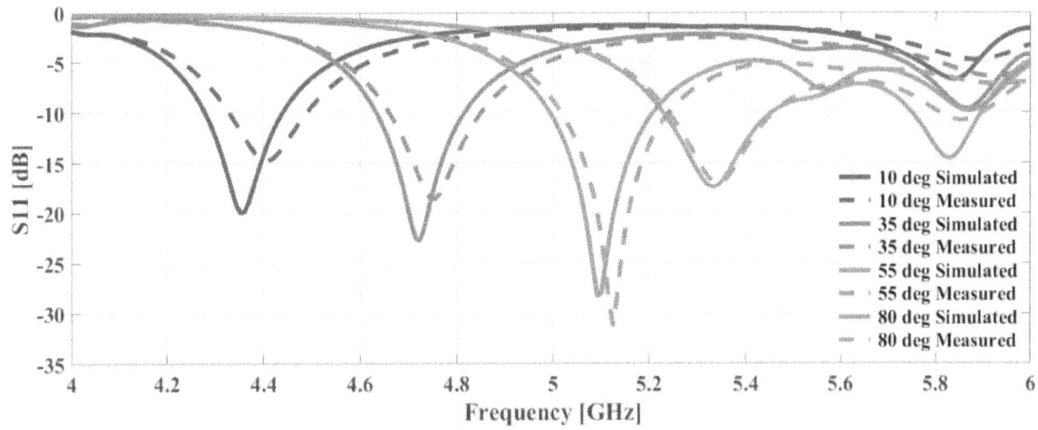

Figure 5.7 Simulated and measured S_{11} characteristics of the proposed DSRR-PFRA

Table 5.4 Simulated and measured outcomes of the proposed DSRR-PFRA

Rotation angle	Simulated		Measured	
	Frequency (GHz)	S(11) (dB)	Frequency (GHz)	S(11) (dB)
10^0	4.35	-19.96	4.40	-14.72
35^0	4.72	-22.73	4.75	-18.56
55^0	5.09	-28.19	5.12	-31.14
80^0	5.33	-17.40	5.34	-17.09

In Figure 5.7, the simulated and measured outcomes associated with the S_{11} parameter reveal a noble trend over all frequencies. As the rotation angle enhances from 10^0 to 35^0, 55^0, and 80^0, continuous upgradation of resonant frequency from 4.35 to 4.72, 5.09, and 5.33 GHz has been examined, respectively. The best matching condition is obtained at 5.09 GHz with reference to the rotation angle of 55^0. With a further increase in the rotation angle, the resultant condition degrades. The simulated and measured outcomes of the proposed DSRR-PFRA obtained at four different rotation angles are revealed in Table 5.4. A suitable agreement has been noticed among these values. Minor differences are there among these values. These are mainly due to fabrication inconsistencies, minor faults in cables, environmental factors, and SMA connector losses.

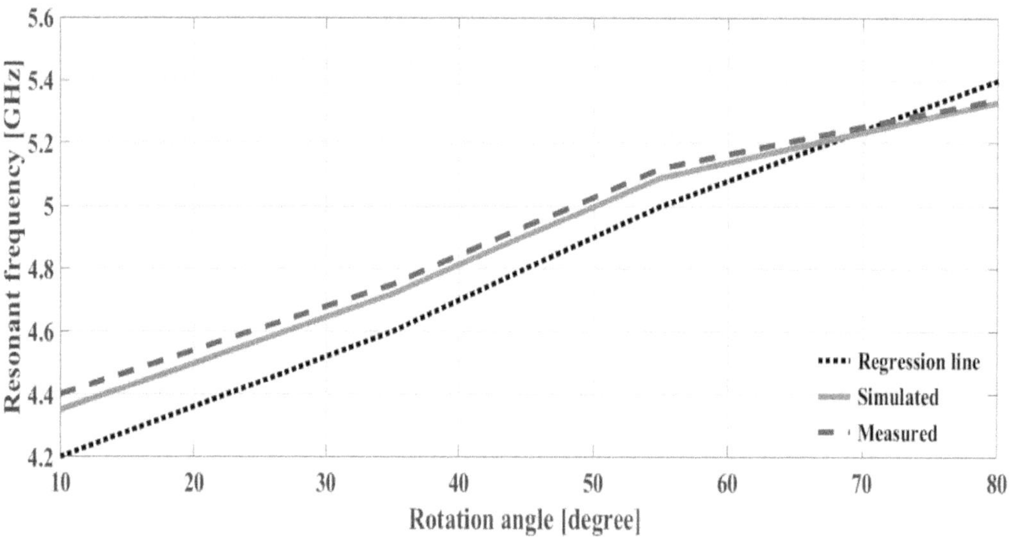

Figure 5.8 Resonant frequency versus rotation angle of the proposed DSRR-PFRA

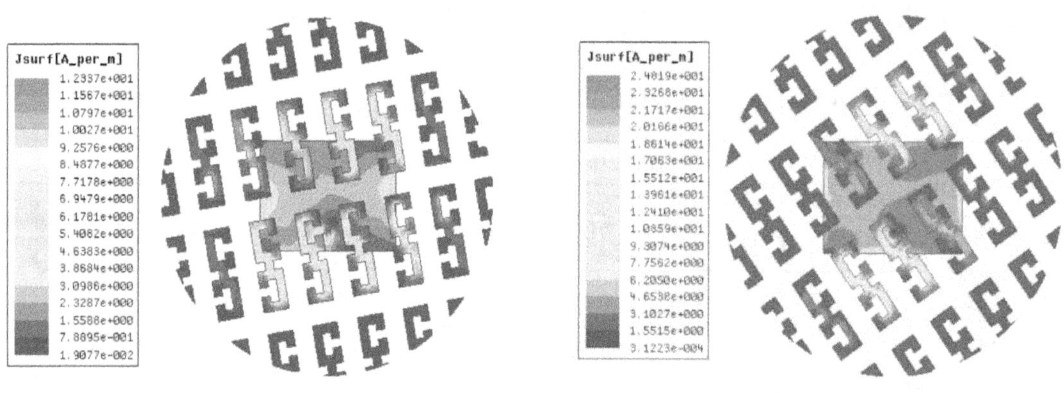

(a) **(b)**

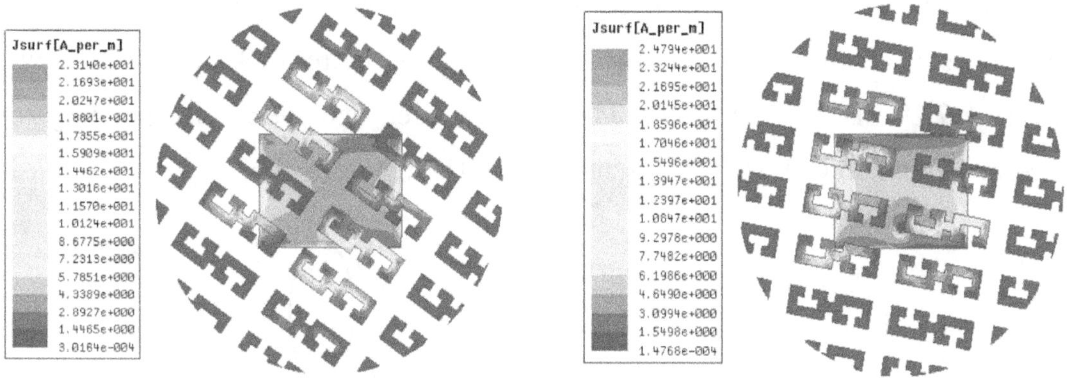

(c) **(d)**

Figure 5.9 Surface current distributions of the proposed DSRR-PFRA at **(a)** 10^0 **(b)** 35^0 **(c)** 55^0 **(d)** 80^0

The relationship that exists between the rotation angle and the resonant frequency can be best analyzed from the graph when there is an increase in θ_r from 10^0 to 80^0. This relation can be approximated using linear regression analysis. Figure 5.8 reveals that the resonant frequency exhibits a linear relationship with the rotation angle. The simulated and measured outcomes depict appreciable agreement. Results reveal that as the rotation angle extends from 10^0 to 80^0, the resonant frequency increases smoothly from 4.35 to 5.33 GHz, thus offering a fractional tuning range of about 20.2%. The simulated surface current distribution plot of the proposed DSRR-PFRA at different rotation angles is depicted in Figure 5.9. From Figure 5.9 (a), it is observed that surface current density is very strong at the left and right edge of the patch, and on the unit cells that are placed just above these positions. At angle 35^0, the surface current is least distributed on the patch and on the four unit cells that are elongated along the right diagonal of the metasurface. At rotation angle 55^0, the current density is concentrated more along the right and left edge of the patch, and on the unit cells that are placed along the left diagonal of the metasurface. At rotation angle $80^{0,}$ the current density is concentrated on the extreme left/ right end and center of the patch, and on the center part of the unit cells that are placed right above the patch.

5.1.4.3 Gain and Radiation Pattern of the Proposed DSRR-PFRA

Here, important antenna parameters such as gain and radiation pattern obtained at the fundamental resonances correspondence to rotation angle 10^0, 55^0, and 80^0 are described. Gain is a critical parameter that properly describes the antenna behavior. The graph showing simulated and measured values of gain versus frequency is elucidated in Figure 5.10. These results clearly show that gain of 7.29 dB, 7.33 dB, and 7.02 dB has been achieved corresponding to the fundamental resonances 4.35 GHz, 5.09 GHz, and 5.33 GHz, respectively.

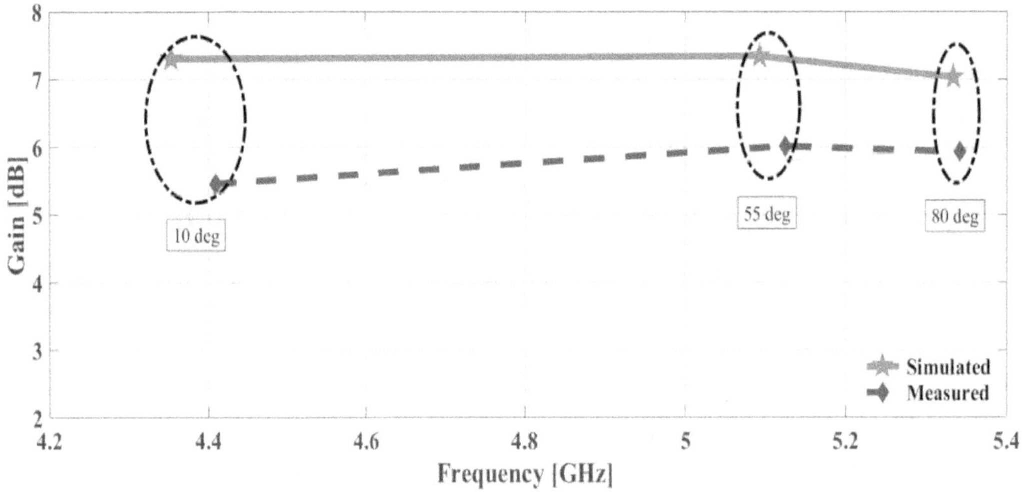

Figure 5.10 Gain versus frequency plot of the proposed DSRR-PFRA

Figure 5.11 Proposed DSRR-PFRA placed in an anechoic chamber

The pictorial view of the proposed DSRR-PFRA placed in an anechoic chamber of a microwave laboratory is shown in Figure 5.11. The simulated and measured radiation patterns at resonances 4.35 GHz, 5.09 GHz, and 5.33 GHz examined in xz and yz planes are illustrated in Figure 5.12 and Figure 5.13, respectively. From these plots, it has been examined that the co-polarization observed along the y-axis radiates largely in comparison to cross-polarization observed along the x-axis. When the DSRR gaps are placed orthogonally to each other, the cross-polarization component offers the largest value. Thus, a gradual increase in cross-polarization transmission amplitude is observed with the variation of θ_r from 10^0 towards 80^0 [137]. At all angles, the front to back ratio value is > 20 dB. Thus, the metasurface only alters the operational frequency without much affecting the shape associated with the radiation pattern and polarization at different rotation angles. The performance parameters of the proposed DSRR-PFRA are compared with the other reported antennas in Table 5.5. Hence, it is claimed that the proposed structure offers better performance regarding fundamental parameters such as size, tuning range, gain, and bandwidth.

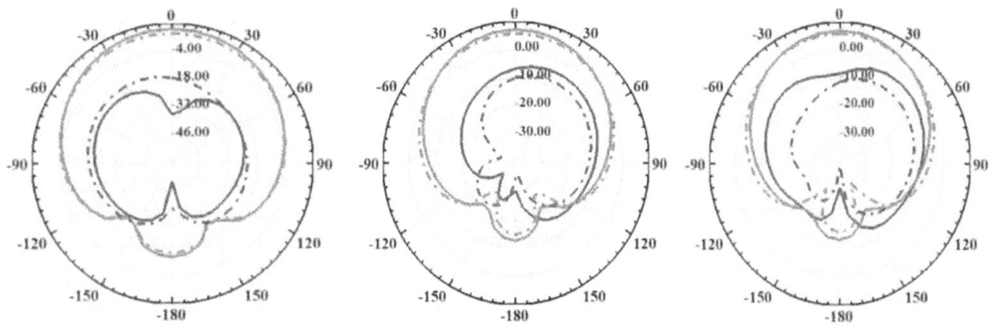

(a) (b) (c)

Figure 5.12 Simulated (bold line) and measured (dot-dashed line) radiation patterns of proposed DSRR-PFRA in xz plane at rotation angle **(a)** 10^0 **(b)** 55^0 **(c)** 80^0 (Red line indicates co-polarization whereas the blue line signifies cross-polarization)

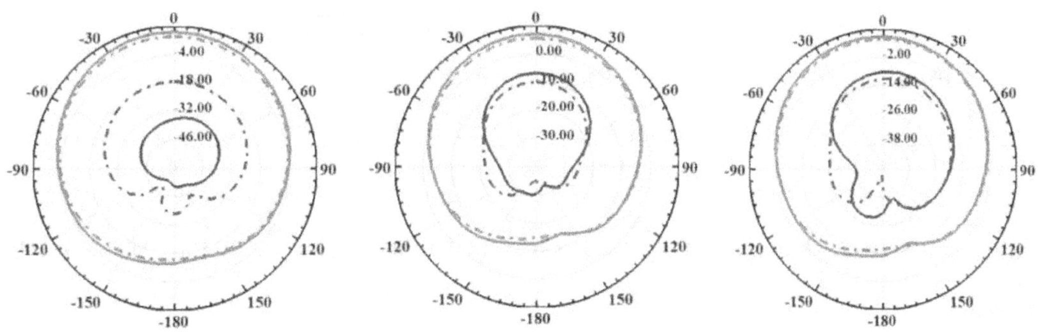

(a) (b) (c)

Figure 5.13 Simulated (bold line) and measured (dot-dashed line) radiation patterns of proposed DSRR-PFRA in yz plane at rotation angle **(a)** 10^0 **(b)** 55^0 **(c)** 80^0 (Red line indicates co-polarization whereas the blue line signifies cross-polarization)

Table 5.5 Performance comparison of proposed DSRR-PFRA with few existing FRAs

Ref. No.	[6]	[89]	[138]	[96]	[98]	Proposed antenna
Antenna Design Parameter (mm)	D = 40	D = 50	L = 105 W = 105	-	D = 50	D = 39
Tuning Range (GHz)	4.76 - 5.51	2.78 - 3.2	1.9 - 2.3	4 - 4.35	3.97 - 4.74, 3.84 - 4.55 (ellipse) and 3.82 - 4.87 (wire)	4.35 - 5.33
Bandwidth (MHz)	750	420	-	350	-	980
Fractional Tuning Range (%)	14.6	14	19	8.4	21.1, 18.9 (ellipse) and 24.2 (wire)	20.2
Realized Gain	> 5 dBi	4.8 dBi	5 dBi	5 dBi		> 7 dB
Reconfigur-ability type	Frequency	Frequency	Frequency	Frequency and polarization	Frequency	Frequency

5.2 H and I Shaped Resonator based Planar Frequency Reconfigurable Antenna

5.2.1 INTRODUCTION

In this Section, the proposed H and I Shaped Resonator based Planar Frequency Reconfigurable Antenna (HISR-PFRA) is designed by placing two substrate layers one above the other. The patch antenna is designed on the upper side associated with the first layer, whereas the H shaped and I shaped metallic inclusions in the form of an array are placed on the upper side associated with the second layer. The radiating structures are constructed on a 1.524 mm thick Rogers RO4350B substrate. The basic dimensions are estimated by creating a data pool of 40 samples using ANN. The fabricated prototype is also experimentally verified. The practically evaluated results verify that the projected antenna can effectively tune from 4.86 to 5.89 GHz. The estimated, simulated and experimental results elucidate the validity of the reconfiguration concept.

5.2.2 DESIGN METHODOLOGY OF THE PROPOSED HISR-PFRA

The projected antenna structure has two layers i.e. patch antenna and metasurface. These layers are mounted one above the other, and there is no air gap between them. The whole arrangement is shown in Figure 5.14 (a). The substrate used for these two layers is Rogers RO4350B along with a thickness of 1.524 mm. A rectangular patch is incorporated on the upper side associated with the first layer, and a circular ground is printed on its lower side. A 50 Ω impedance matching is achieved by appropriately adjusting the dimensional parameters associated with the feedline ('L_f' and 'W_f'). The metasurface is designed as a periodic array of H shaped and I shaped metal inclusions, which is incorporated on the upper side associated with the second layer. For simplicity, both the chosen layers are circular bearing a diameter of 36 mm. The configured models belonging to the patch and metasurface are shown in Figure 5.14 (b) and Figure 5.14 (c), respectively. In order to achieve the frequency reconfigurability of the constructed antenna, the metasurface is spinned with reference to the center of the rectangular patch antenna. During the measurements, the angle of rotation (θ_r) changes along the y-axis. Since the symmetry (horizontal and vertical) of the metasurface is equal, it is assumed that $\theta_r = -\theta_r$, and for performance evaluation, the highest value of the rotation angle adopted is 90^0. The optimal geometrical design parameters of the proposed HISR-PFRA are revealed in Table 5.6.

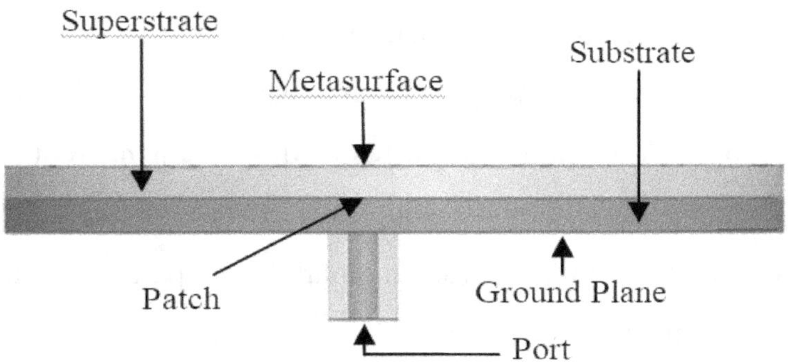

(a)

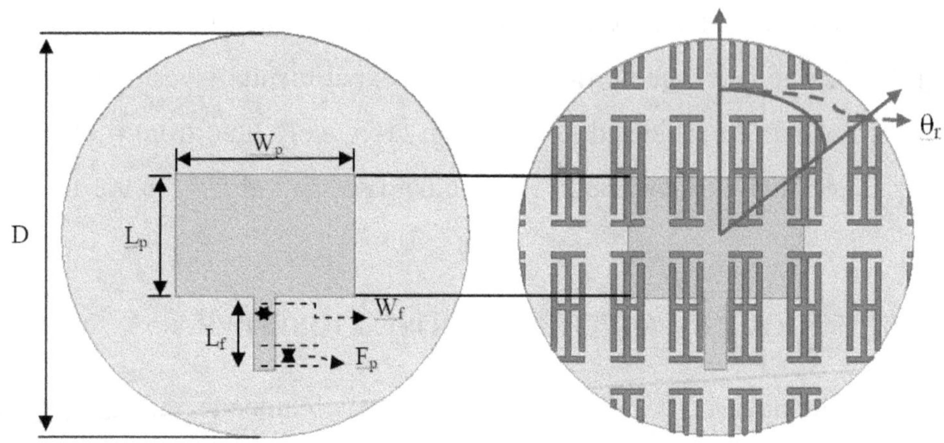

(b) **(c)**

Figure 5.14 Proposed HISR-PFRA **(a)** Side view **(b)** Patch **(c)** Metasurface

Table 5.6 Optimized parameters of the proposed HISR-PFRA

Parameter	Description	Value (mm)
D	Diameter	36
L_p	Length of patch	11
W_p	Width of patch	16
L_f	Length of feedline	6.5
W_f	Width of feedline	2
F_p	Feed position from edge	2

5.2.3 ANN MODEL FOR THE PROPOSED HISR-PFRA

The projected FFBPN model for the analysis of the proposed HISR-PFRA is shown in Figure 5.15. The model contains 2 input layer neurons, 10 hidden layer neurons, and 2 output layer neurons. The fundamental dimensional parameters associated with the unit cell are taken as the input of the analysis model. Afterwards, the corresponding resonant frequency and S_{11} values are noted accordingly. A data pool holding 40 samples is created for the entire process. All the samples are designed by suitably varying the fundamental design parameters associated with the unit cell. In the whole arrangement, training set holds 28 samples, validation set holds 6 samples and the testing set holds the remaining 6 samples. In this work, LM based ANN model is chosen so as to achieve the desired accuracy level and proper estimation of output parameters. Tansig and purelin are the transfer functions used at the respective hidden and output layers. The performance of the model is analyzed by considering the important statistical parameters that include MSE, number of epochs taken, and the maximum absolute error. Figure 5.16 illustrates the performance plot in which MSE is plotted against 9 epochs. The graph showed that the best validation performance of 0.065099 is found at epoch 3. Table 5.7 describes the performance parameters evaluated during the analysis of the proposed antenna.

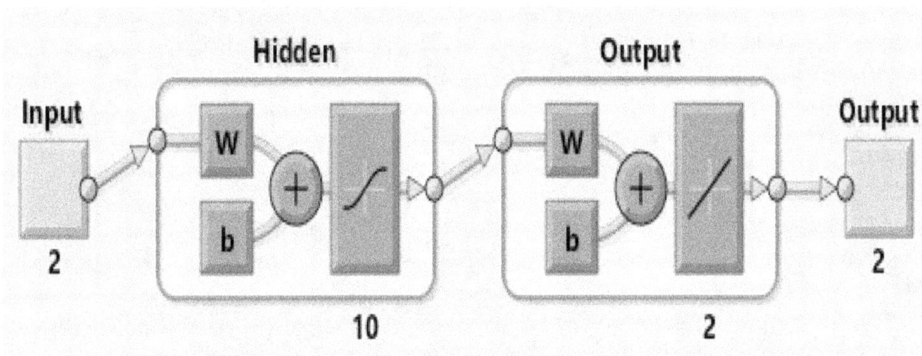

Figure 5.15 FFBPN model for the proposed HISR-PFRA

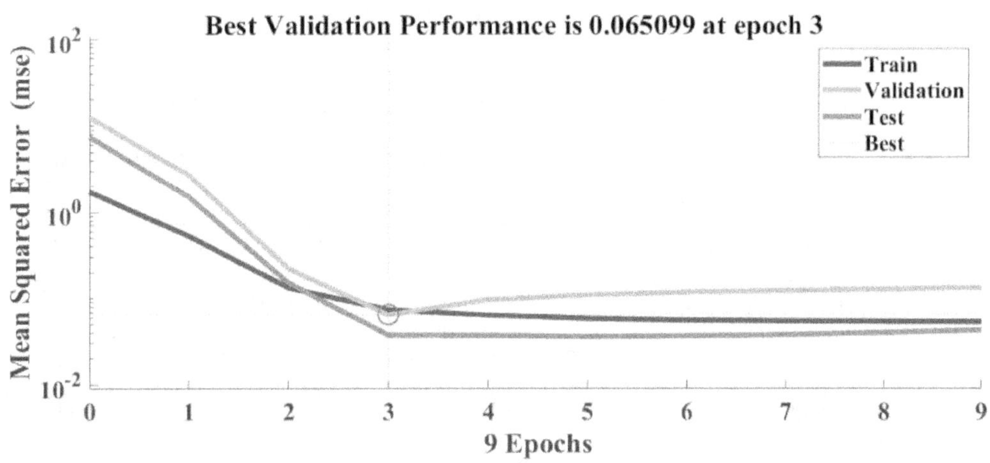

Figure 5.16 Performance plot during the analysis of proposed HISR-PFRA

Table 5.7 Performance parameters during the analysis of proposed HISR-PFRA

	Samples	MSE	Regression
Training	28	7.43209e-2	9.99810e-1
Validation	6	6.50986e-2	9.99853e-1
Testing	6	3.75510e-2	9.99923e-1

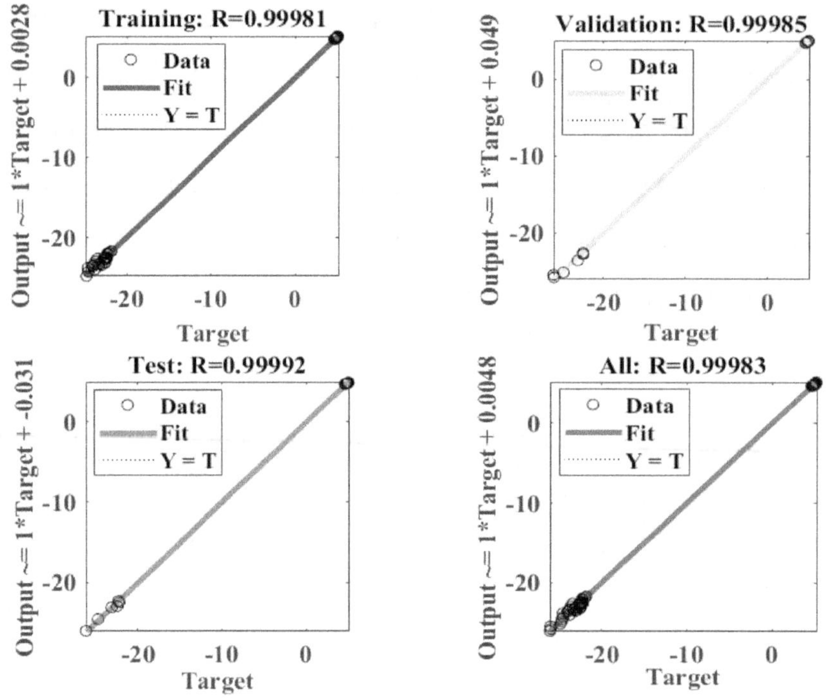

Figure 5.17 Scatter plot showing regression values for training, validation, testing and total output during the analysis of the proposed HISR-PFRA

Table 5.8 Absolute error estimation during the analysis of the proposed HISR-PFRA

S. No.	Inputs		HFSS Outputs		ANN Outputs		Absolute error	
	a	b	f_r	S_{11}	f_r	S_{11}	f_r	S_{11}
1	10	3	4.869	-22.952	4.849	-23.460	0.020	0.508
2	10	3.5	4.821	-22.657	4.839	-22.812	-0.018	0.155
3	10	4	4.797	-22.459	4.793	-22.586	0.003	0.127
4	10	2.7	4.909	-23.100	4.855	-23.116	0.053	0.015
5	10	2	5.014	-22.423	5.012	-22.433	0.002	0.009
6	11	3	4.604	-26.107	4.726	-26.045	-0.122	-0.062
7	9.6	3	4.973	-22.495	4.888	-22.769	0.085	0.273
8	9.2	3	5.102	-22.277	5.065	-21.978	0.037	-0.298
9	10.3	3	4.797	-23.806	4.831	-24.026	-0.034	0.219
10	9.7	3	4.957	-22.438	4.872	-22.976	0.085	0.537
Average Absolute Error							0.011	0.148

During the analysis phase of the proposed DSRR-PFRA, the examined regression plot for training, validation, testing, and total output is presented in Figure 5.17. The total regression value obtained from the analysis phase of the proposed DSRR-PFRA is 0.99983. The obtained values of AAE corresponding to 'f_r' and 'S_{11}' are illustrated in Table 5.8. In this table, a random set of 10 samples is taken and for these 10 samples, values of AAE corresponding to 'f_r' and 'S_{11}' are estimated. The estimated value of the average absolute estimated error corresponding to 'f_r' is 0.011, whereas the average absolute estimated error corresponding to 'S_{11}' is 0.148. The value of AAE corresponding to 'f_r' is less than the value of AAE.

5.2.4 PROJECTED HISR-PFRA RESULTS

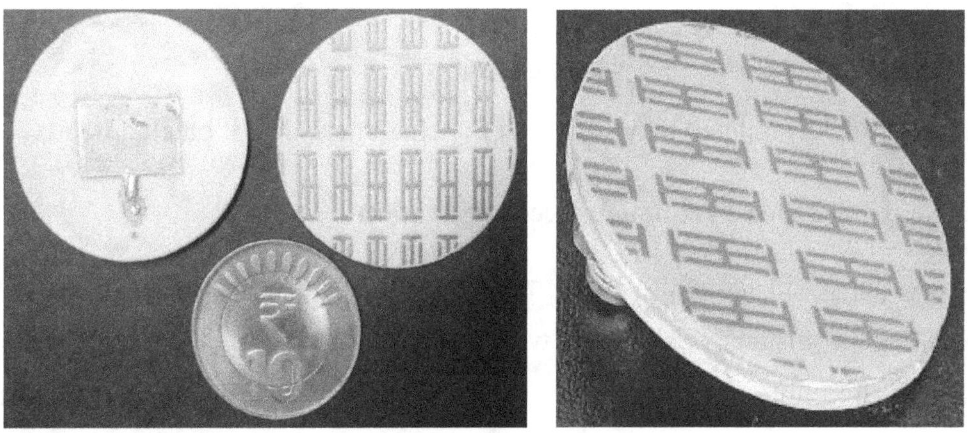

(a) **(b)**

Figure 5.18 Pictorial view of fabricated **(a)** Patch antenna and metasurface **(b)** HISR-PFRA using Rogers RO4350B

In order to effectively validate the projected HISR-PFRA performance, the fabricated prototype is practically analyzed. The pictorial view of the fabricated HISR-PFRA is shown in Figure 5.18. The prototype is tested in the microwave laboratory with VNA MS46322A manufactured by Anritsu Company.

5.2.4.1 Patch Antenna Results

The simulated and measured outcomes associated with parameter S_{11} corresponding to the patch antenna are illustrated in Figure 5.19. Both the outcomes are in good accord. It has been observed from this Figure that the simulated and measured values corresponding to the patch antenna are found at 6.86 GHz and 7.1 GHz with respective S_{11} value -10.24 dB and -29.50 dB.

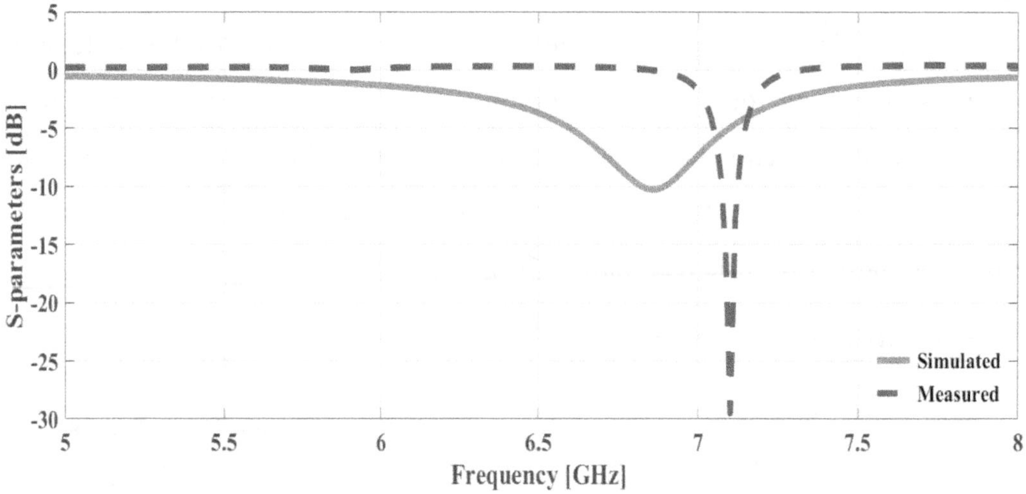

Figure 5.19 Simulated and measured S_{11} characteristics of patch antenna

5.2.4.2 Proposed HISR based Frequency Reconfiguration

S_{11} is an important antenna performance parameter that shows the input-output relationship between the terminals associated with an electrical system. This parameter illustrates the frequency reconfigurable operation. The parameter S_{11} is calculated by considering four different rotation angles i.e. 0^0, 30^0, 60^0, and 90^0. The simulations and measurements corresponding to the fundamental resonances are carried out during the rotation from 0^0 to 90^0. For this purpose, the incremental value of the rotation angle taken is 30^0. Extensive parametric analysis is carried out in the 4.5 to 6.5 GHz span. The simulated and measured values belonging to S_{11} obtained at four different rotation angles are revealed in Table 5.9. The S_{11} characteristics belonging to the proposed HISR-PFRA at different rotation angles are drawn in Figure 5.20. It has been observed that as the value of θ_r increases, the resonance frequency shifts towards the higher side. At rotation angle $\theta_r = 60^0$, the best matching condition is noticed. As the rotation angle further increases, the matching condition decreases. Thus, the resonant frequency enhances smoothly from 4.86 to 5.90 GHz offering fractional tuning of 19.3% and a bandwidth of 1.04 GHz. The relationship that exists between the rotation angle and the resonant frequency can be best analyzed from the graph when there is an increase in θ_r from 0^0 to 90^0. Figure 5.21 reveals that the resonant frequency exhibits a linear relationship with the rotation angle. It has been found that as the rotation angle increases from 0^0 to 90^0, the resonance shifts steadily from 4.86 to 5.90 GHz, yielding a 19.3% fractional tuning range.

Table 5.9 Simulated and measured S_{11} characteristics of proposed HISR-PFRA at $0^0 < \theta_r < 90^0$

Rotation angle 'θ_r'	Simulated		Measured	
	Resonant frequency 'f_r' (GHz)	S_{11} (dB)	Resonant frequency 'f_r' (GHz)	S_{11} (dB)
0^0	4.86	-22.95	4.86	-26.53
30^0	5.19	-17.58	5.18	-19.72
60^0	5.74	-52.36	5.72	-27.72
90^0	5.90	-11.91	5.89	-11.93

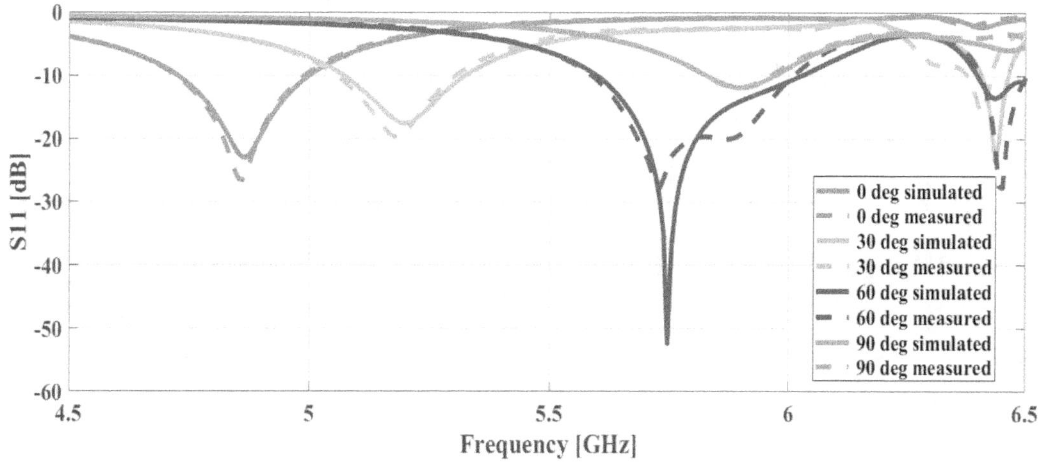

Figure 5.20 Simulated and measured S_{11} characteristics of the proposed HISR-PFRA

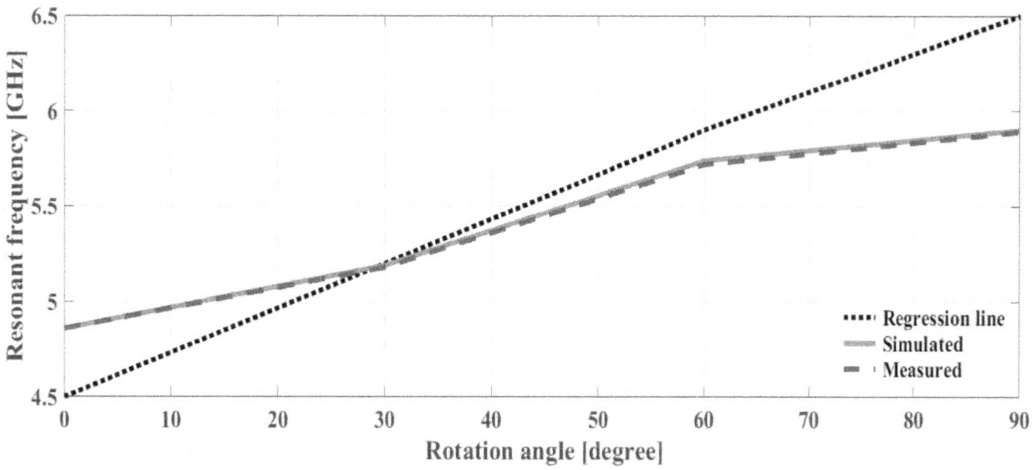

Figure 5.21 Rotation angle versus frequency of the proposed HISR-PFRA

The surface current distribution of the proposed structure is properly illustrated in Figure 5.22. This distribution is evaluated under different rotation angles. These plots are helpful in describing the variations in the current density on the surface of the structure. It can be seen from Figure 5.22 (a) that at rotation angle 0^0, the current concentrates on left/right edge of the patch and the stripline. In the case of metasurface, the current mainly flows at the centre of those unit cells that are positioned above the patch area. At rotation angle 30^0, the current mainly distributes along the centre of the patch and on the middle portion of the unit cells that are placed diagonally on the right side of the metasurface. At rotation angle 60^0, the current density is large near the right edge of the patch and on the metasurface unit cells above this position. At rotation angle 90^0, the current density is concentrated on the extreme left and right end of the patch and on the centre part of the unit cells that are placed right above the patch.

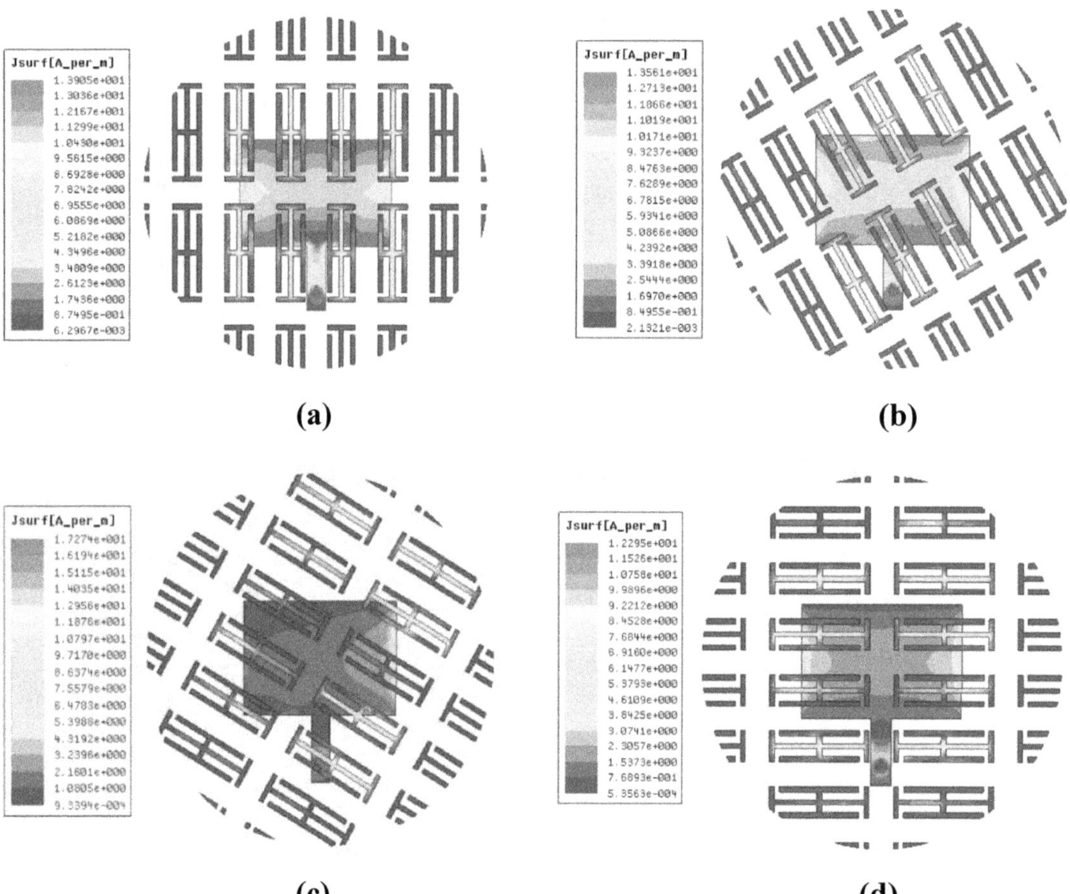

(a) (b) (c) (d)

Figure 5.22 Surface current distribution of proposed HISR-PFRA at **(a)** 0^0 **(b)** 30^0 **(c)** 60^0 **(d)** 90^0

5.2.4.3 Gain and Radiation Pattern of the Proposed HISR-PFRA

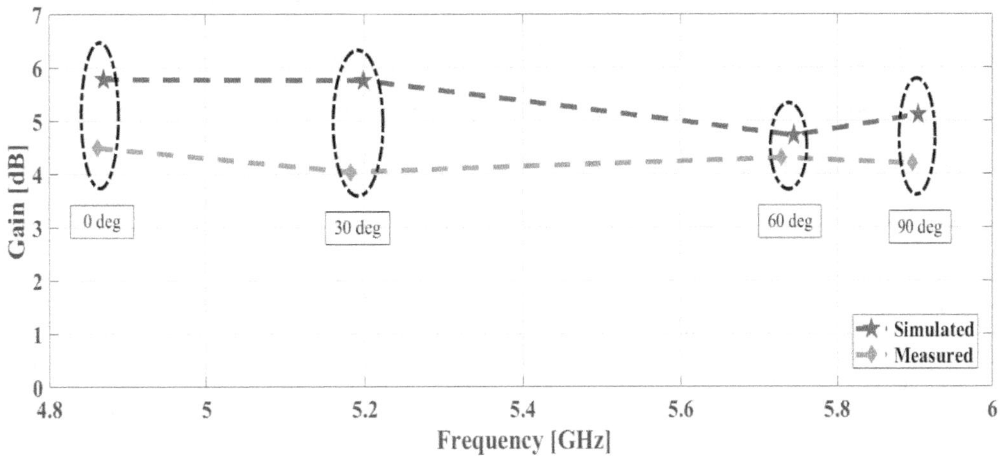

Figure 5.23 Simulated and measured gain values of the proposed HISR-PFRA

Figure 5.24 Proposed HISR-PFRA placed in an anechoic chamber

Figure 5.23 depicts the simulated and measured gain values associated with the proposed HISR-PFRA at four different rotation angles. A positive agreement is observed between the values. For experimental analysis, the proposed HISR-PFRA antenna is tested in an anechoic chamber placed in the microwave laboratory. The pictorial view of the proposed HISR-PFRA is revealed in Figure 5.24. The radiation pattern plots are drawn that effectively illustrate the far-field radiation characteristics. The 2D simulated and measured radiation patterns of the implemented HISR-PFRA at $\theta = 0^0$, 30^0, 60^0, and 90^0 in xz plane are shown in Figure 5.25, whereas the patterns corresponding to yz plane are shown in Figure 5.26. The patterns reveal the co-polarization and cross-polarization components in the respective planes. At all angles, the examined value of front to back ratio is > 19 dB. From the figure, it has been clearly seen that patterns are well-matched. Therefore, the designed metasurface based antenna successfully reconfigures the resonant frequency while keeping the polarization and radiation pattern characteristics constant.

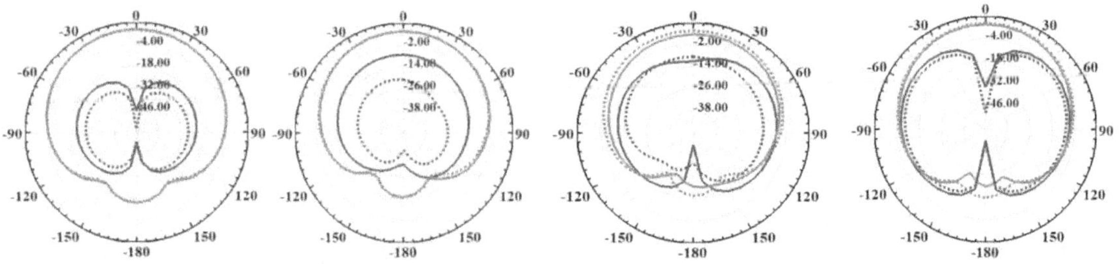

(a) **(b)** **(c)** **(d)**

Figure 5.25 Simulated (solid line) and measured (dot-dot line) radiation pattern of the proposed HISR-PFRA in xz plane **(a)** 0^0 **(b)** 30^0 **(c)** 60^0 **(d)** 90^0 (red line indicates the co-polarization and the blue line indicates the cross-polarization)

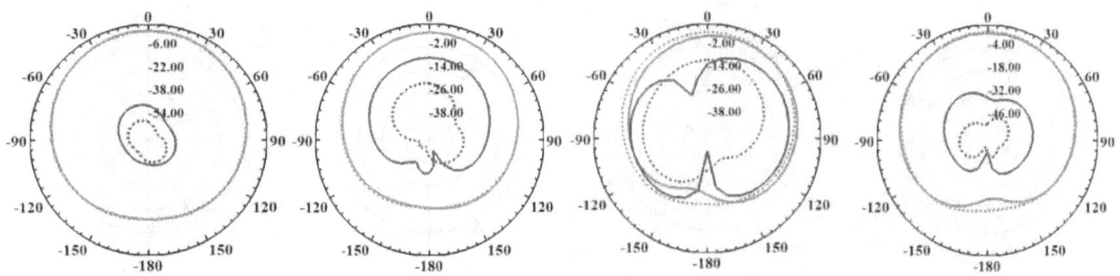

(a) **(b)** **(c)** **(d)**

Figure 5.26 Simulated (solid line) and measured (dot-dot line) radiation pattern of the proposed HISR-PFRA in yz plane **(a)** 0^0 **(b)** 30^0 **(c)** 60^0 **(d)** 90^0 (red line indicates the co-polarization and the blue line indicates the cross-polarization)

Table 5.10 summarizes the comparison of the overall performance of the proposed HISR-PFRA with other existing antennas. From the comparison results, it has been observed that the projected design shows significant improvement in area, tunable range, bandwidth, efficiency, and front to back ratio. The performance parameters are estimated by the ANN approach. Therefore, it is confirmed that the antenna is very suitable for wireless applications.

Table 5.10 Comparison of proposed HISR-PFRA with few existing designs

Reference No.	[6]	[91]	[96]	[98]	Proposed antenna
Design Parameter (mm)	D = 40	D = 50	-	D = 50	D = 36
Operating frequency	5 GHz	3 GHz	-	-	5.4 GHz
Antenna	Patch	Slot	Patch	Slot	Patch
Metasurface	Rectangular loop unit cells	Rectangular loop unit cells	Rectangular loop unit cells	Ellipse and wire type unit cells	HISR unit cells
Tuning range (GHz)	4.76 - 5.51	2.64 - 3.5	4 - 4.35	3.97 - 4.74 and 3.84 - 4.55 bands (ellipse) and 3.82 - 4.87 (wire)	4.86 - 5.90
Bandwidth (MHz)	750	860	350	-	1040
Fractional Tuning Range	14%	28%	8.4%	21.1%, 18.9% (ellipse) and 24.2% (wire)	19.3%
Efficiency	> 80%	> 85%	-	-	> 90%
Front to back ratio	> 15 dB	-	-	-	> 19 dB
Gain	5 dBi	-	5 dBi	-	Around 5 dB
Technique used	-	-	-	Radially homogenous model	ANN approach

5.3 Proposed Compounded Double Split-Ring Shaped Resonator based Planar Frequency Reconfigurable Antenna

5.3.1 INTRODUCTION

Dual layer module is selected for designing the Compounded Double Split-Ring Shaped Resonator based Planar Frequency Reconfigurable Antenna (CDSRR-PFRA). The rectangular shaped patch antenna is printed on the upper side associated with the first layer, whereas CDSRR shaped unit cells are imprinted on the upper side associated with the second layer. The selected Rogers RO4350B substrate has a thickness of 1.524 mm and a loss tangent of 0.0037. The basic parameters of the antenna are estimated by creating a data pool of 36 distinct samples using

ANN. The proposed antenna is fabricated and tested. From the experimental results, it is observed that by increasing the rotation angle from 0^0 to 90^0, the resonant frequency rises steadily from 5.03 to 6.13 GHz, giving a fractional tuning range of 19.7%.

5.3.2 DESIGN CONFIGURATION OF PROPOSED CDSRR-PFRA

The proposed work uses a dual layer approach The schematic diagram of the proposed CDSRR-PFRA is shown in Figure 5.27. The dual layer module consisting of two substrate layers is properly illustrated in Figure 5.27 (a). The rectangular-shaped patch antenna and circular ground plane are printed on the upper and lower side associated with the first layer, respectively. A periodical array containing CDSRR shaped unit cells illustrating the metasurface is printed on the upper side associated with the second layer. The module uses a flexible Rogers RO4350B substrate. For both layers, a fixed thickness of 1.524 mm is chosen, so the total thickness is 3.048 mm. A feedline having a width of 2 mm is used, which offers a characteristic impedance of 50 Ω. For input purposes, the antenna uses a coaxial feed type, and an SMA connector is used for connection purposes. For proper matching conditions, both layers are chosen circular. The angle θ_r, the rotation angle associated with the metasurface is measured with respect to the y-axis in a clockwise and anticlockwise direction and the maximum rotation angle assumed is 90^0. The schematic of the patch antenna and metasurface is demonstrated in Figure 5.27 (b) and Figure 5.27 (c), respectively. The optimized geometrical specifications of the proposed CDSRR-PFRA are presented in Table 5.11.

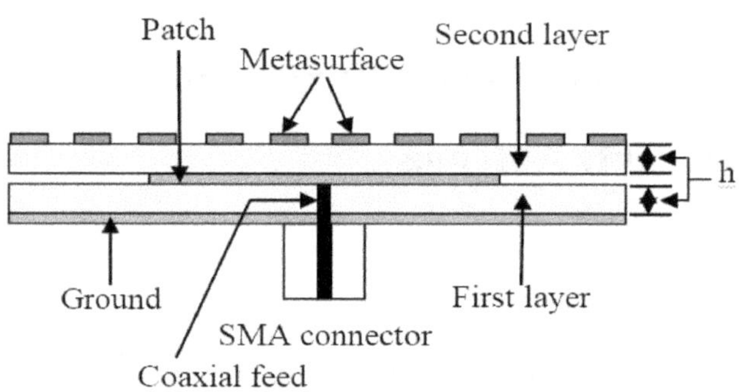

(a)

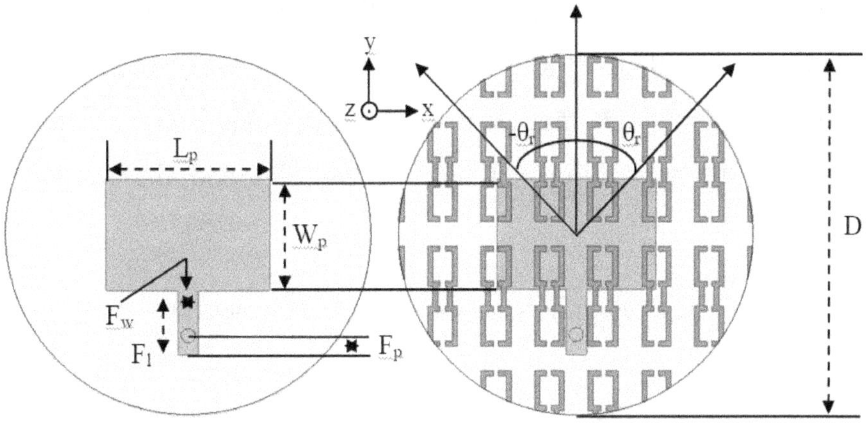

(b) **(c)**

Figure 5.27 Design schematic of proposed CDSRR-PFRA **(a)** Dual layer module **(b)** Patch antenna **(c)** Metasurface

Table 5.11 Proposed CDSRR-PFRA design specifications (Units: mm)

D	**h**	**L_p**	**W_p**	**F_l**	**F_w**	**F_p**
36	1.524	11	16	6.5	2	2

5.3.3 ANN MODEL FOR PROPOSED CDSRR-PFRA

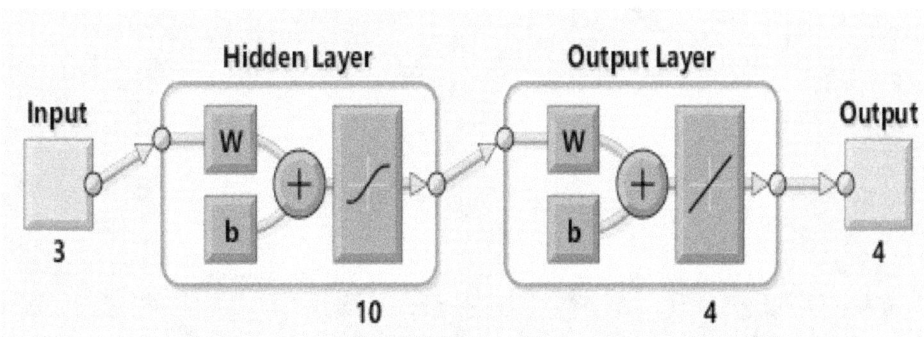

Figure 5.28 FFBPN model for proposed CDSRR-PFRA

The metasurface unit cell must be designed properly because the metallic loop represents inductance L and the gap between them represents capacitance C, which determines the resonating frequency associated with the unit cell. As a result, control of the resonance can be done by changing the structure. Thus, an ANN model for the analysis of metasurface has been developed and utilized in an antenna for reconfiguration purposes. Figure 5.28 depicts the FFBPN model for the proposed CDSRR-PFRA. This model has 3 input layer neurons, 4 output layer neurons, and 10 hidden layer neurons. The unit cell dimensions (a,b) and rotation angle (θ_r) associated with the proposed CDSRR-PFRA are taken as inputs, while the resonant frequencies (f_{r1}, f_{r2}, f_{r3}, f_{r4}) are taken as outputs. A data set holding 36 samples is constructed. Out of these, training set holds 26 samples, validation set holds 5 samples and the testing set holds the remaining 5 samples.

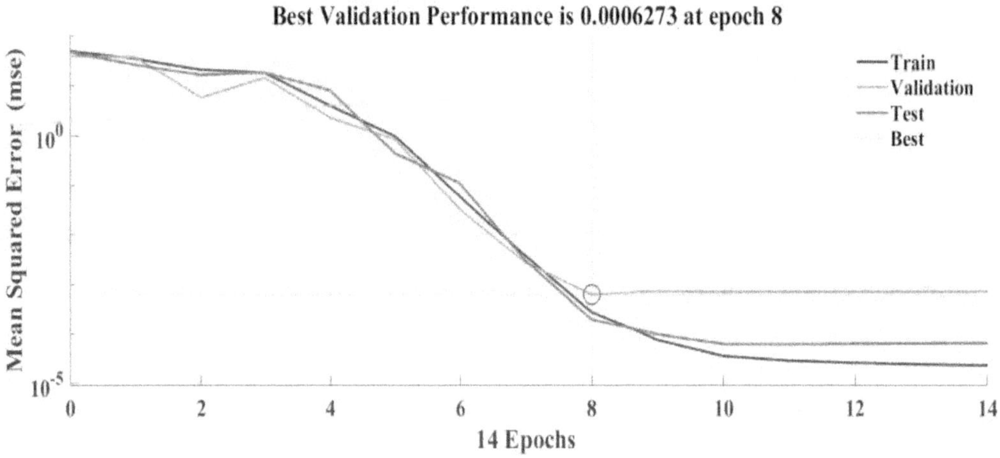

Figure 5.29 Performance plot during the analysis of proposed CDSRR-PFRA

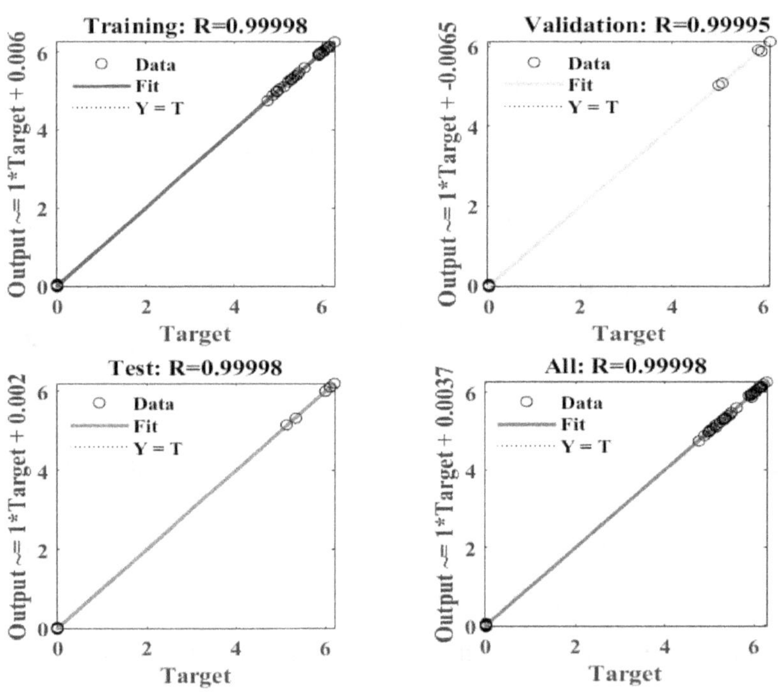

Figure 5.30 Scatter plot showing regression values for training, validation, testing and total output during the analysis of the proposed CDSRR-PFRA

Table 5.12 Performance parameters during the analysis of proposed CDSRR-PFRA

	Samples	MSE	Regression
Training	26	2.76710e-4	9.99979e-1
Validation	5	6.27304e-4	9.99952e-1
Testing	5	1.95663e-4	9.99984e-1

Table 5.13 Absolute error estimation during analysis of the proposed CDSRR-PFRA

Inputs			**HFSS outputs**				**ANN outputs**				**Absolute error**			
a	**b**	θ_r	f_{r1}	f_{r2}	f_{r3}	f_{r4}	f_{r1}	f_{r2}	f_{r3}	f_{r4}	f_{r1}	f_{r2}	f_{r3}	f_{r4}
10	2	0	5.08	0	0	0	5.07	-0.00	0.02	-0.01	0.01	0.00	-0.02	0.01
10	3.5	0	4.99	0	0	0	4.99	-0.00	0.00	0.01	-0.01	0.00	-0.01	-0.01
9.5	3	0	5.13	0	0	0	5.15	-0.00	0.01	-0.01	-0.01	0.00	-0.01	0.01
10.5	3	0	4.88	0	0	0	4.88	-0.00	0.01	0.02	0.00	0.00	-0.02	-0.02
10	2.5	30	0	5.39	0	0	-0.00	5.38	-0.01	-0.02	0.00	0.01	0.02	0.02
10	3.5	30	0	5.34	0	0	-0.00	5.32	-0.02	-0.01	0.01	0.01	0.02	0.02
9	3	30	0	5.60	0	0	0.01	5.59	-0.01	0.01	-0.01	0.00	0.00	-0.00
11	3	30	0	5.14	0	0	0.01	5.10	-0.03	-0.01	-0.01	0.04	0.03	0.01
10	2	60	0	0	6.00	0	-0.00	-0.00	6.00	-0.00	0.00	0.00	-0.00	0.00
10	3	60	0	0	5.94	0	-0.00	-0.02	5.97	0.01	0.01	0.02	-0.03	-0.01
9	3	60	0	0	6.10	0	0.00	-0.00	6.11	0.01	-0.01	0.00	-0.01	-0.01
10.5	3	60	0	0	5.87	0	-0.01	-0.02	5.90	0.01	0.01	0.02	-0.04	-0.01
10	3.5	90	0	0	0	6.10	-0.01	-0.01	-0.02	6.10	0.01	0.01	0.03	0.00
10	4	90	0	0	0	6.07	-0.01	-0.00	-0.02	6.07	0.01	0.00	0.03	-0.00
9.5	3	90	0	0	0	6.20	-0.00	-0.00	-0.02	6.20	0.00	0.00	0.03	0.00
11	3	90	0	0	0	5.92	-0.00	-0.01	-0.05	5.92	0.01	0.01	0.05	0.01
Average Absolute Error											0.04	0.19	0.08	0.01

Figure 5.29 illustrates the performance plot of the proposed CDSRR-PFRA. A LM algorithm is used to obtain the appropriate level of accuracy. Trainlm is the employed training function. The transfer functions utilized at the respective hidden and output layers are Tansig and Purelin. The best validation performance of 0.0006273 is found at epoch 8. During the analysis phase of the proposed CDSRR-PFRA, the regression plot for training, validation, testing, and total output is presented in Figure 5.30. The obtained value of regression is 0.99998. The performance parameters obtained during the analysis of the designed CDSRR-PFRA are presented in Table 5.12. At first, the ANN is trained with a sufficient amount of samples. After the completion of ANN model training, the output frequency in each case is calculated. The AAE values corresponding to the resonant frequencies are illustrated in Table 5.13. For the chosen 16 samples, the calculated AAE values corresponding to f_{r1}, f_{r2}, f_{r3}, and f_{r4} are 0.04, 0.19, 0.08, and 0.01, respectively. Hence, the value of frequency achieved at the ANN output is in good agreement with the simulated value.

5.3.4 PROPOSED CDSRR-PFRA RESULTS

The antenna prototype is simulated using a 3D full-wave HFSS support tool based on the FEM. Figure 5.31 depicts a photographic view of the constructed CDSRR-PFRA. The experimental results are evaluated using an Anritsu MS2028C VNA.

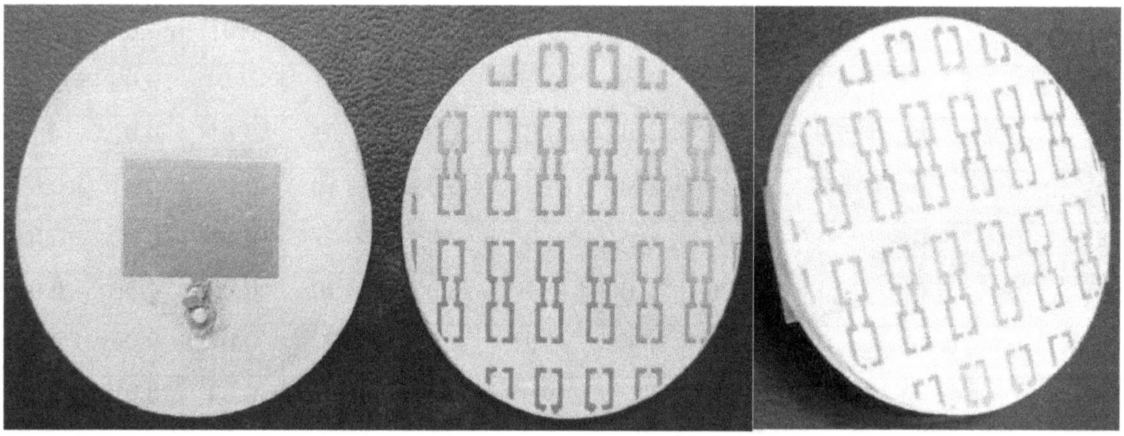

(a) (b)

Figure 5.31 Photographic view of the fabricated CDSRR-PFRA **(a)** Patch antenna and metasurface **(b)** CDSRR-PFRA

5.3.4.1 S_{11} of Patch Antenna

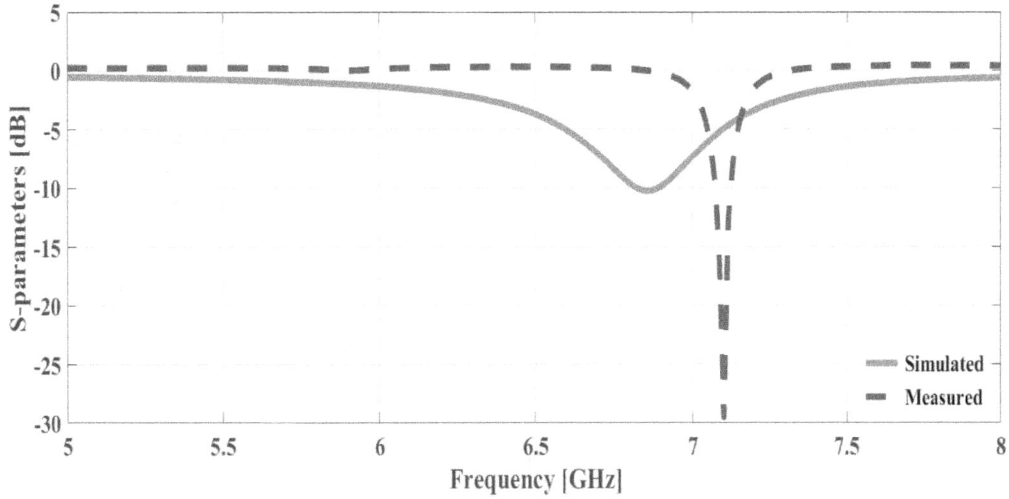

Figure 5.32 Simulated and measured S_{11} characteristics of patch antenna

The simulated and measured S_{11} values associated with the patch antenna are illustrated in Figure 5.32. Both values are in good accord. Figure 5.32 reveals that the simulated and measured resonances belonging to patch antenna appear at 6.86 GHz and 7.1 GHz with S_{11} value -10.24 dB and -29.50 dB, respectively.

5.3.4.2 S_{11} of Proposed CDSRR-PFRA

The simulated and measured S_{11} values associated with the proposed CDSRR-PFRA are illustrated in Figure 5.33. In both cases, the obtained results showed good agreement. It has been anticipated from the Figure that by rotating the metasurface from 0^0 towards 30^0, $60^{0,}$ and 90^0 corresponding to the fixed patch antenna, the resonant frequency continuously upgraded from 4.99 to 5.35, 5.93, and 6.12 GHz, respectively. The best matching condition occurs at a rotation angle of 60^0. Further rotation of metasurface causes decay in matching. Therefore, metasurface plays an indispensable role in realizing frequency reconfiguration property. The simulated and measured values belonging to frequency and S_{11} obtained at four different rotation angles are revealed in Table 5.14. The simulated results are slightly different from the measured ones. This difference is mainly due to the solder joints, fabrication, and measurement tolerances.

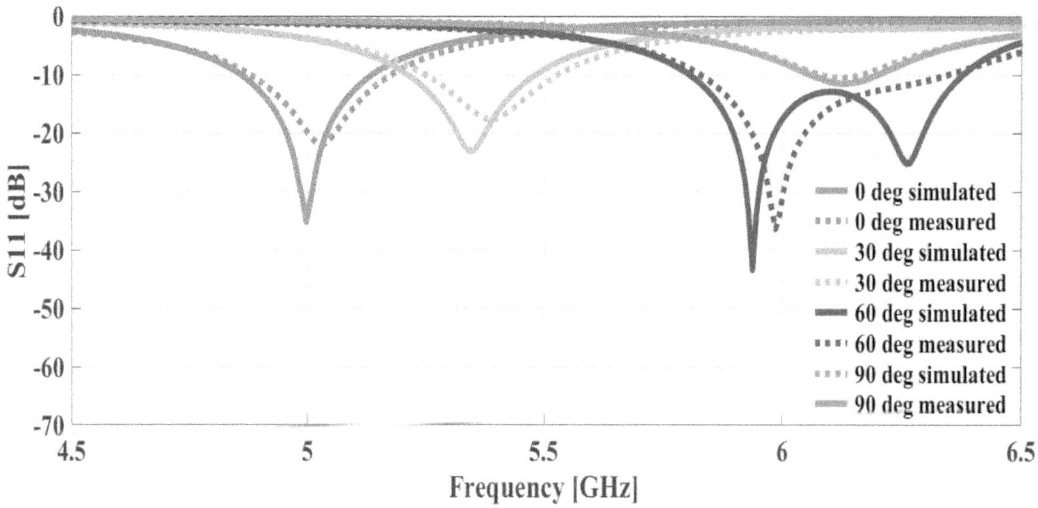

Figure 5.33 Simulated and measured S_{11} values of the proposed CDSRR-PFRA

Table 5.14 Summarized results of the proposed CDSRR-PFRA

Rotation angle	Simulated		Measured	
	Resonant Frequency (GHz)	S_{11} (dB)	Resonant Frequency (GHz)	S_{11} (dB)
0^0	4.99	-35.17	5.03	-21.99
30^0	5.35	-23.05	5.39	-17.71
60^0	5.93	-43.39	5.98	-36.33
90^0	6.12	-10.51	6.13	-11.46

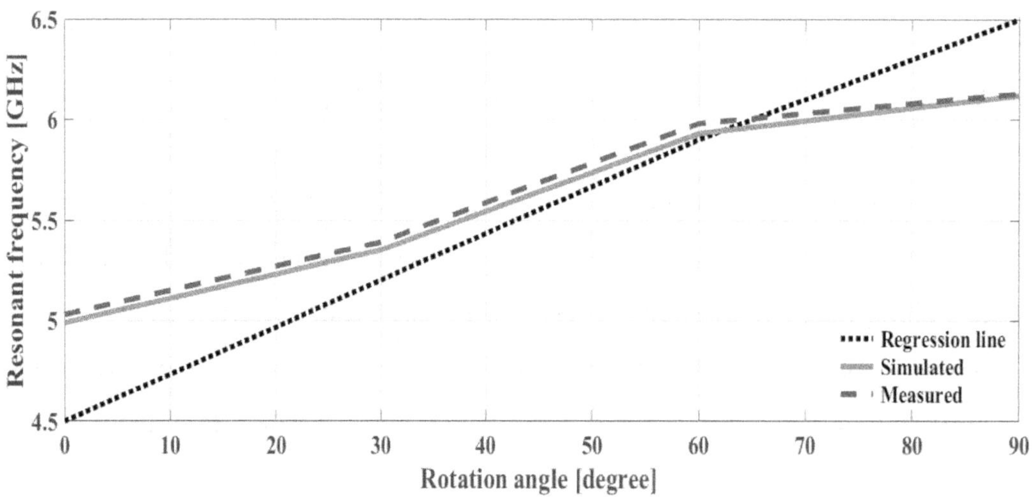

Figure 5.34 Resonant frequency versus rotation angle of proposed CDSRR-PFRA

The graph showing the relationship between resonant frequency and rotation angle is illustrated in Figure 5.34. With the increase in the rotation angle from 0^0 to 90^0, the relationship between the rotation angle and the resonance frequency is examined. It has been noticed that the resonant frequency exhibits a linear relationship with the rotation angle. The simulated and measured results show a good match. As the rotation angle increases from 0^0 to 90^0, the resonant frequency rises steadily from 4.99 to 6.12 GHz, thus offering a fractional tuning range of 20.3%. The surface current distribution on the proposed CDSRR-PFRA at different rotation angles is shown in Figure 5.35. It has been revealed from these figures that at 0^0 rotation angle, the large current distribution is concentrated around the center of metasurface, and at the patch edges. At 30^0 rotation angle, the current is strongly distributed at the right part of the metasurface, and the left/right edges of the patch. Corresponding to 60^0 rotation angle, there is large flow of current near the extreme right end of the metasurface, and at the patch. When the rotation angle is 90^0, the current distribution is intensively accumulated along the center of the metasurface, and at the patch edges.

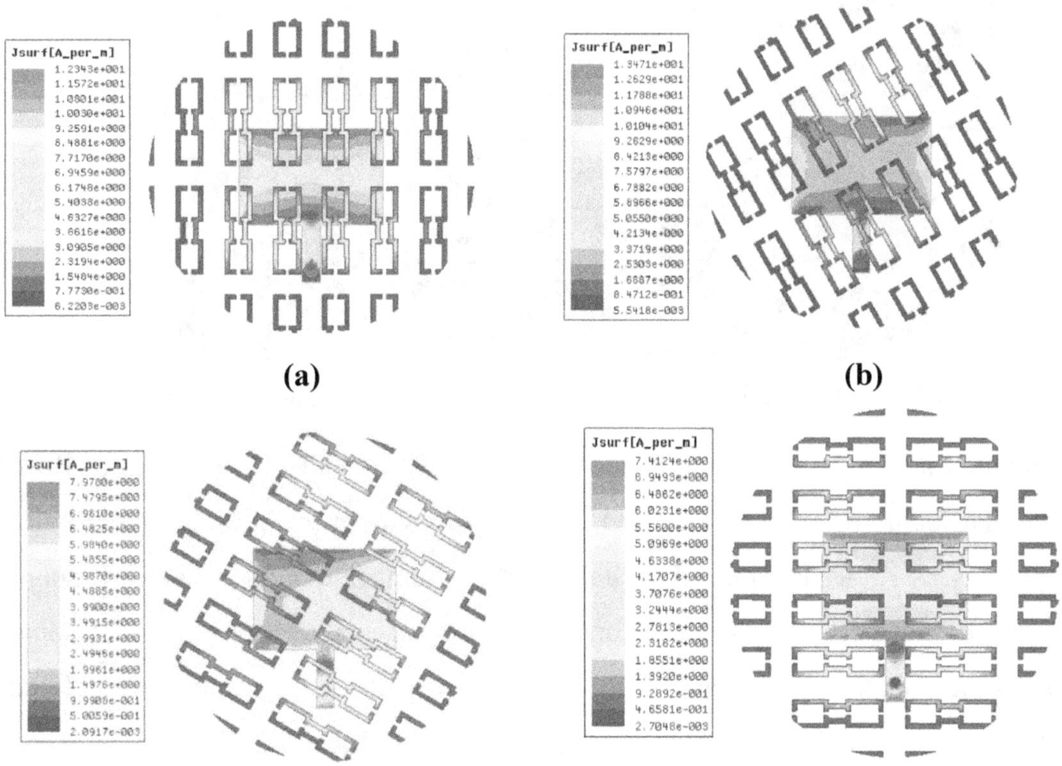

(a) (b) (c) (d)

Figure 5.35 Surface current distribution of proposed CDSRR-PFRA at rotation angle **(a)** 0^0 **(b)** 30^0 **(c)** 60^0 **(d)** 90^0

5.3.4.3 Gain and Radiation Pattern of the Proposed CDSRR-PFRA

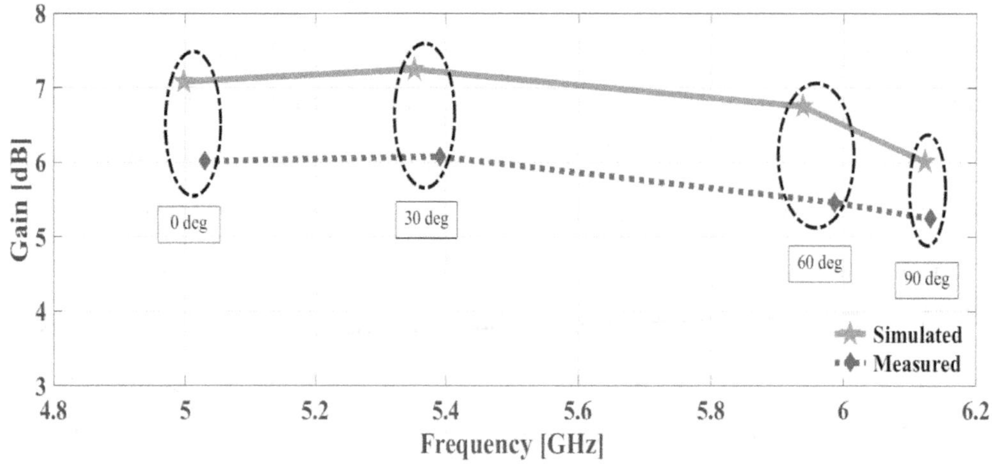

Figure 5.36 Simulated and measured gain of the proposed CDSRR-PFRA

Figure 5.37 Proposed CDSRR-PFRA placed in an anechoic chamber

The simulated and measured gain of the proposed CDSRR-PFRA obtained at different rotation angles that including 0^0, 30^0, 60^0, and 90^0 [20] are shown in Figure 5.36. Figure 5.37 show the proposed CDSRR-PFRA placed in the anechoic chamber. Figure 5.38 and Figure 5.39 show the simulated and measured 2D radiation characteristics analyzed at claimed resonances corresponding to the selected rotation angles in xz and yz planes. These patterns are defined for two main planes ($\varphi = 0^0$ and $\varphi = 90^0$). When $\varphi = 0^0$, the bidirectional pattern is examined whereas, at $\varphi = 90^0$, the omnidirectional behavior shape is examined. It is examined from the patterns that the co-polarized radiation observed along the y-axis is higher than the cross-polarization observed along the x-axis. At all rotation angles, the value of front to back ratio examined is > 20 dB. Therefore, the metasurface only reconfigures the operating frequency of the antenna and does not have much influence on the radiation pattern and shape of the polarization at different rotation angles.

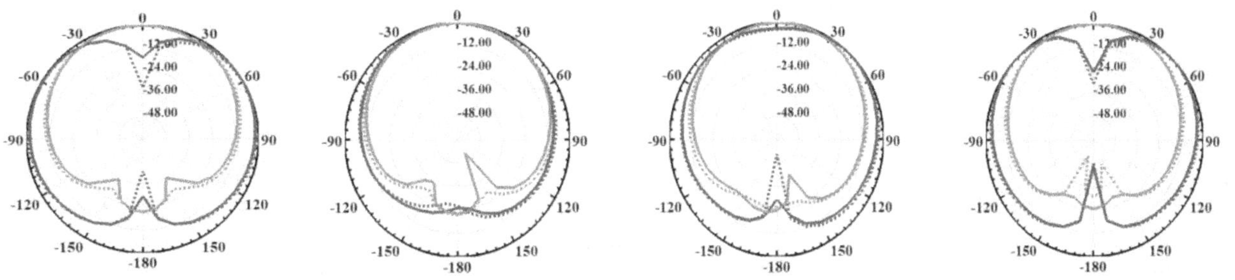

(a) (b) (c) (d)

Figure 5.38 Simulated (solid line) and measured (dot-dot line) radiation pattern of proposed CDSRR-PFRA at rotation angles **(a)** 0^0 **(b)** 30^0 **(c)** 60^0 **(d)** 90^0 in xz plane

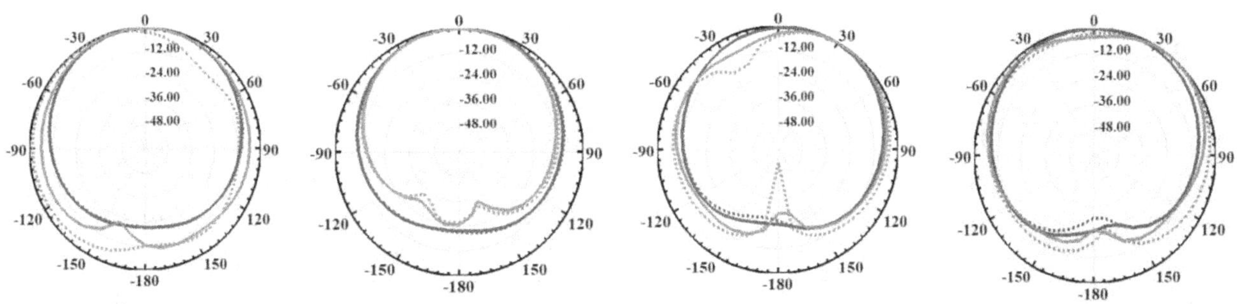

(a) (b) (c) (d)

Figure 5.39 Simulated (solid line) and measured (dot-dot line) radiation pattern of proposed CDSRR-PFRA at rotation angles **(a)** 0^0 **(b)** 30^0 **(c)** 60^0 **(d)** 90^0 in yz plane

Table 5.15 compares the performance parameters of the proposed CDSRR-PFRA with the examined parameters associated with a few existing FRAs. It can be clearly seen from the Table that, in comparison to [6], [138], [89], and [98], the proposed antenna's size is reduced by 19%, 88.2%, 48.16%, and 48.16%, respectively. Upon considering the bandwidth, a 50.66% and 169% hike is observed in comparison to [6] and [89], respectively. When the tuning range is considered, 6.3% 1.3%, and 6.3% rise is examined in comparison to [6], [138], and [89], respectively. It can be suggested that the proposed antenna has a smaller size, acceptable gain, wide bandwidth, and tuning range at all rotation angles.

Table 5.15 Comparison of proposed CDSRR-PFRA with few existing FRAs

	[6]	[128]	[86]	[95]	Proposed work
Antenna design parameter (mm)	D = 40	L = 105, W = 105	D = 50	D = 50	D = 36
Electrical size	0.67λ	0.735λ*0.735λ	0.5λ	-	0.66λ
Operating frequency	5 GHz	-	3 GHz	-	5.55 GHz
Antenna	Patch	Slot	Slot	Slot	Patch
Metasurface	Rectangular loop unit cells	Meandered unit cells	Rectangular loop unit cells	Ellipse type and wire type unit cells	CDSRR unit cells
Tuning range (GHz)	4.76 - 5.51	1.9 - 2.3	2.78 - 3.2	3.97 - 4.74 and 3.84 - 4.55 (ellipse) and 3.82 - 4.87 (wire)	4.99 - 6.12
Bandwidth	750 MHz	-	420 MHz	-	1.13 GHz
Fractional tuning range	14%	19%	14%	21.1%, 18.9% (ellipse) and 24.2% (wire)	20.3%
Gain	5 dBi	5 dBi	4.8 dBi	-	> 6 dB
Technique used	-	-	-	Radially homogenous model	ANN

5.4 Concluding Remarks

In this chapter, three different planar frequency reconfigurable antennas have been designed using metasurface structures. The artificial neural network approach is applied to all these designs for estimating their performance metrics and the minimum value of absolute error is observed in all three cases.

The design given in Section 5.1 is constructed using an array of dual split-ring resonators and rectangular-shaped patch antenna. 41 samples are created by varying the fundamental design parameters associated with the antenna. The frequency reconfiguration is observed by changing the rotation angle from 10^0 to 80^0. The resonant frequency boosts up from 4.35 to 5.33 GHz and thus, offering a fractional tuning range of 20.2%.

H and I shaped resonator based planar frequency reconfigurable antenna is described in Section 5.2. In it, 40 samples are created by changing the fundamental design parameters of the unit cell associated with the antenna. On increasing the rotation angle from 0^0 to 90^0, the resonant frequency rises steadily from 4.86 to 5.90 GHz, yielding a 19.3% fractional tuning range.

In Section 5.3, planar frequency reconfigurable antenna is described which is designed by incorporating the compounded double split-ring resonator shaped cells forming the metasurface. A data pool holding 36 samples is constructed for estimating its output parameters. As the rotation angle increases from 0^0 to 90^0, the resonant frequency rises steadily from 4.99 to 6.12 GHz, giving a fractional tuning range of 20.3%.

CHAPTER 6

CONCLUSION AND FUTURE SCOPE

This thesis presents the design and optimization of a single antenna that can operate at different frequencies. Therefore, an extensive search of the archived literature on reconfigurable antenna technology and its applications was conducted for a successful, low-cost, miniaturized reconfigurable antenna design. The modeling and performance of three different antenna designs with the reconfiguration concept utilizing metasurface have been demonstrated. This chapter compiles the entire research work, summarizes the main findings in the form of a conclusion, and also presents some future directions associated with this research work. This thesis details my contribution to technical innovation in the realm of reconfigurable antennas. Significant contributions are also listed.

6.1 Conclusion

Reconfigurable antennas have drawn widespread attention in the wireless domain for their multifunctional behavior and additional degrees of freedom. This research work embodies the investigations on the adopted design procedure, simulation, characterization, and development of planar frequency reconfigurable antenna using metasurface. Three distinct frequency reconfigurable antennas have been designed based on novel metasurface structures. Rogers RO4350B substrate with $\varepsilon_r = 3.48$ has been chosen. Two circular substrate layers have been adopted in the design. Reconfigurability has been achieved by arranging an array of unit cells that are placed atop the second substrate. Different metasurface structures have been designed and analyzed to validate their metamaterialistic characteristics. The chosen antenna shape and design of the unit cells make it compact and adaptable over a wide range. An artificial neural network approach is utilized for estimating the important dimensions of an antenna. The High Frequency Structure Simulator is a 3D EM simulation tool that provides valuable support in designing these antennas. A multi-paradigm programming software, MATLAB is used for analyzing the left-handed metamaterial properties of metasurface structures.

The main aim of the current research work is to design planar FRAs for wireless applications. The behavior of all the designed antennas has been thoroughly investigated. The major contributions of the proposed research work are enumerated as follows:

In the first phase, three different novel metasurface structures have been designed and their metamaterialistic characteristics have been analyzed. Rogers RO4350B substrate material with a thickness 1.524 mm is chosen for designing the structures. These structures are placed in a waveguide medium with apposite boundary conditions and excitations applied along the respective axis. The electromagnetic behavior is examined from the phase reversal characteristics at a particular frequency response. The first structure has been constructed using an array of dual split-ring shaped resonators. The effective parameters of this structure exhibit negative real values in 4.0 to 4.81 GHz frequency range. The second structure is designed using an array of H and I shaped resonators. The effective parameters show negative real values in the 4.0 to 5.045 GHz frequency range. The third structure consists of the compounded double split-ring shaped resonator. Negative real values of effective parameters are observed in the 4.0 to 8.31 GHz range. The real values of the refractive index are also negative in these frequency ranges. Thus, these structures demonstrate the characteristics of left-handed metamaterials.

In the second phase, the planar frequency reconfigurable antennas have been designed using novel metasurface structures. The designed antennas are constructed using two circularly shaped stacking layers. The lower layer constitutes the patch antenna whereas, an upper layer is formed using an array of regularly ordered unit cells constituting the metasurface. Metasurfaces are incorporated into these structures to enhance the bandwidth and fractional tuning range. A coaxial feed line is used that provides excitation to these antennas. Frequency reconfiguration is achieved by rotating the metasurface relative to the patch antenna. In the first design, an array of orthogonally placed dual split-ring shaped resonators is placed onto the rectangular-shaped patch antenna. In the second design, a periodical array of H and I shaped metallic inclusions are mounted on the rectangular-shaped patch antenna with a feedline. The third design consists of a repetitive arrangement of compounded double split-ring shaped resonators placed above the patch antenna. These designs are simulated using the above-said tool. Results show that all three low profile designs are compact, thereby providing a wide fractional tuning range.

In the third phase, the designed antenna structures have been fabricated and experimentally analyzed. Their performance is evaluated with or without applying metasurface. A reasonable agreement is observed between the measured outcomes and simulated ones. The dual split-ring shaped resonator based planar frequency reconfigurable antenna reconfigures from 4.40 to 5.34 GHz range with fractional tuning range and bandwidth of 19.3% and 940 MHz, respectively. The structure provides a gain of around 5 dB. The H and I shaped resonator based planar frequency reconfigurable antenna tunes from 4.86 to 5.89 GHz with a 19.3% tunable range. The compounded double split-ring shaped resonator based planar frequency reconfigurable antenna effectively tunes from 5.03 to 6.13 GHz, thereby providing a fractional tuning range of 19.7%. The artificial neural network tool is further deployed on all these antenna structures for estimating their performance parameters. All these designed structures are suitable for wireless applications.

All the antenna structures proposed in this work have been evaluated in the microwave laboratory to ensure that the standard characteristics belonging to antenna performance, such as return loss, radiation pattern, and gain, are accurate. Minor variations seen in the results are mainly due to fabrication tolerances, feed connector misalignments, copper loss, environmental conditions, etc. As a result, the desired goal of designing antenna solutions for wireless applications has been achieved. The findings of this study offer a new path for the development of future wireless communication systems.

6.2 Future Scope

Future research on high-speed wireless systems will necessitate antennas with greater capability than standard designs can offer. Reconfigurable antennas are critical and desirable in present-day radio frequency systems, microwave sensing, and imaging. This research work can be taken forward from several perspectives. Till date, researchers have been mainly focused on developing reconfigurable antennas for wireless applications but less interest is directed towards other applications. As a result, multiple additional antenna designs appropriate for other applications might be possible. The study is further carried out to determine how to expand the antenna's adaptability.

For further developments, following are some potential future directions of this research:

- Optimization techniques can be applied to estimate performance metrics.
- Frequency reconfigurable antennas can be designed and developed for optical, biomedical, 5G, and 6G applications.
- Fractal and defective ground structure approaches can also be embedded into the designed structure of the metasurface.
- This work can be further carried out for arrays and smart systems.

REFERENCES

[1] C. A. Balanis, "Antenna theory: Analysis and design" , 3rd Edition, John Wiley & Sons, New Jersey, 2005.

[2] R. L. Haupt, and M. Lanagan, "Reconfigurable Antennas" , *IEEE Antennas and Propagation Magazine*, vol. 55, no. 1, pp. 49-61, 2013.

[3] C. G. Christodoulou, Y. Tawk, S. A. Lane, and S. R. Erwin, "Reconfigurable Antennas for Wireless and Space Applications" , *Proceedings of the IEEE*, vol. 100, no.7, pp. 2250-2261, 2012.

[4] J. Constantine, Y. Tawk, S. E. Barbin, and C. G, Christodoulou, "Reconfigurable Antennas: Design and Applications" , *Proceedings of the IEEE*, vol. 103, no. 3, pp. 424-437, 2015.

[5] A. Bharathi, M. Lakshminarayana, and P. V. D. S. Rao, "A quad-polarization and frequency reconfigurable square ring slot loaded microstrip patch antenna for WLAN applications" , *International Journal of Electronics and Communications*, vol. 78, pp. 15-23, 2017.

[6] H. L. Zhu, X. H. Liu, S. W. Cheung, and T. I. Yuk, "Frequency Reconfigurable Antenna Using Metasurface" , *IEEE Transactions on Antennas and Propagation*, vol. 62, no.1, pp. 80-85, 2014.

[7] H. L. Zhu, S. W. Cheung, and T. I. Yuk, "Mechanically pattern reconfigurable antenna using metasurface" , *IET Microwaves, Antennas & Propagation*, vol. 9, issue 12, pp. 1331-1336, 2015.

[8] H. L. Zhu, S. W. Cheung, X. H. Liu, and T. I. Yuk, "Design of Polarization Reconfigurable Antenna Using Metasurface" , *IEEE Transactions on Antennas and Propagation*, vol. 62, no. 6, pp. 2891-2898, 2014.

[9] J. Constantine, Y. Tawk, and C. G. Christodoulou, "Reconfigurable Antennas and their Applications" , *Handbook of Antenna Technologies*, Springer Science + Busineess Media, Singapore, 2015.

[10] L. A. Bronckers, A. Roc'h, and A. B. Smolders, "A New Design Method for Frequency Reconfigurable Antennas Using Multiple Tuning Components" , *IEEE Transactions on Antennas and Propagation*, vol. 67, no. 12, pp. 7285-7295, 2019.

[11] G. Keiser, "Optical Fiber Communications" , 3rd Edition, McGraw Hill, Singapore, 2000.

[12] D. Costa, I. F, and D. H. Spadoti, "Optically controlled reconfigurable antenna for 5G future broadband cellular communication networks" , *Journal of Microwaves, Optoelectronics and Electromagnetic Applications*, vol. 16, no. 1, pp. 208-217, 2017.

[13] Y. Tawk, J. Constantine, F. Ayoub, C. Christodoulou, D. Doyle, and S. A. Lane, "Physically reconfigurable antennas: Concepts and automation" , in *Proceedings of the 2017 IEEE International Symposium on Antennas and Propagation & USNC/URSI National Radio Science Meeting*, pp. 419-420, San Diego, California, USA, 2017.

[14] M. Konca, and P. A. Warr, "A Frequency Reconfigurable Antenna Architecture using Dielectric Fluids" , *IEEE Transactions on Antennas and Propagation*, vol. 63, no. 12, pp. 5280-5286, 2015.

[15] C. L. Holloway, E. F. Kuester, J. A. Gordon, J. O. Hara, J. Booth, and D. R. Smith, "An Overview of the Theory and Applications of Metasurfaces: The Two-Dimensional Equivalents of Metamaterials" , *IEEE Antennas and Propagation Magazine*, vol. 54, no. 2, pp. 10-35, 2012.

[16] F. Costa, M. Borgese, M. Degiorgi, and A. Monorchio, "Electromagnetic Characterisation of Materials by Using Transmission/Reflection (T/R) Devices" , *Electronics*, vol. 6, no. 95, pp. 1-27, 2017.

[17] R. Liu, C. Ji, Z. Zhao, and T. Zhou, "Advanced Materials and Materials Gnome-Review Metamaterials: Reshape and Rethink" , *Engineering*, vol. 1, no. 2, pp. 179-184, 2015.

[18] S. S. Islam, M. R. I. Faruque, and M. T. Islam, "A New Double Negative Metamaterial for C-Band Microwave Applications" , *Advanced Materials research*, vol. 974, pp. 33-37, 2014.

[19] A. Sihvola, "Metamaterials in electromagnetic" , *Metamaterials*, vol. 1, pp. 2-11, 2007.

[20] C. Caloz, and T. Itoh, "Application of the Transmission Line Theory of Left-Handed Materials to the Realization of a Microstrip "LH Line" " , in *Proceedings of the IEEE Antennas and Propagation Society International Symposium*, vol. 2, pp. 412-415, San Antorio, Texas, USA, 2002.

[21] F. H. Bautista, C. A. Vargas, and J. M. V. Arcos, "Negative refractive index in split ring resonators" , *Materials*, vol. 59, no. 1, pp. 141-146, 2013.

[22] A. B. Numan, and M. S. Sharawi, "Extraction of Material Parameters for Metamaterials Using a Full-Wave Simulator" , *IEEE Antennas and Propagation Magazine*, vol. 55, no. 5, pp. 202-211, 2013.

[23] B. Anandhimeena, P. T. Selvan, and S. Raghavan, "Compact Metamaterial Antenna with High Directivity for Bio-Medical Systems" , *Circuits and Systems*, vol. 7, no. 12, pp. 4036-4045, 2016.

[24] A. Salim, and S. Lim, "Review of Recent Metamaterial Microfluidic Sensors" , *Sensors*, vol. 18, no. 1, pp. 232, 2018.

[25] B. A. Munk, "Metamaterials: Critics and Alternatives" , John Wiley & Sons, Hoboken, New Jersey, 2009.

[26] J. C. Bose, "On the rotation of plane of polarisation of electric waves by a twisted structure" , in *Proceedings of the Royal Society of London*, vol. 63, pp. 146-152, 1898.

[27] H. Lamb, "On Deep-Water Waves" , *Proceedings of the London Mathematical Society*, vol. s2-2, issue 1, pp. 371-400, 1905.

[28] H. C. Pocklington, "Growth of a wave-group when the group velocity is negative" , *Nature*, vol. 71, pp. 607-608, 1905.

[29] I. V. Lindell, A. H. Sihvola, and J. Kurkijarvi, "Karl F. Lindman: The last Hertzian, and a Harbinger of electromagnetic chirality" , *IEEE Antennas and Propagation Magazine*, vol. 34, no. 3, pp. 24-30, 1992.

[30] W.E. Kock, "Metallic delay lenses" , *The Bell System Technical Journal*, vol. 27, no. 1, pp. 58-82, 1948.

[31] A. D. Tadesse, O. P. Acharya, and S. Sahu, "Application of metamaterials for performance enhancement of planar antennas: A review" , *International Journal of RF and Microwave Computer-Aided Engineering*, vol. 30, no. 5, e22154, 2020.

[32] L. I. Mandel'shtam, "Group velocity in a crystal lattice" , *Zhurn. Eksp. Teor. Fiz.*, vol. 15, no. 9, pp. 475-478, 1945.

[33] V. G. Veselago, "The electrodynamics of substances with simultaneously negative values of ε and μ" , *Soviet Physics Uspekhi*, vol. 10, no. 4, pp. 509-514, 1968.

[34] J. B. Pendry, A. J. Holden, W. J. Stewart, and I. Youngs, "Extremely low frequency plasmons in metallic mesostructures" , *Physical Review Letters*, vol. 76, no. 25, pp. 4773-4776, 1996.

[35] J. B. Pendry, A. J. Holden, D. J. Robbins, and W. J. Stewart, "Magnetism from conductors and enhanced nonlinear phenomena" , *IEEE Transactions on Microwave Theory and Techniques*, vol. 47, no. 11, pp. 2075-2084, 1999.

[36] S. Schultz, D. R. Smith, W. J. Padilla, D. C. Vier, and S. C. N. Nasser, "Composite medium with simultaneously negative permeability and permittivity" , *Physical Review Letters*, vol. 84, no. 18, pp. 4184-4187, 2000.

[37] R. A. Shelby, D. R. Smith, and S. Schultz, "Experimental verification of a negative index of refraction" , *Science*, vol. 292, no. 5514, pp. 77-79, 2001.

[38] C. Sabah, "Tunable Metamaterial Design Composed of Triangular Split Ring Resonator and Wire Strip for S- and C- Microwave Bands" , *Progress in Electromagnetics Research B*, vol. 22, pp. 341-357, 2010.

[39] S. S. Bukhari, J. Vardaxglou, and W. Whittow, "A Metasurfaces Review: Definitions and Applications" , *Applied Sciences*, vol. 9, no. 13, pp. 1-14, 2019.

[40] H. Singh, B. S. Sohi, and A. Gupta, "Thickness invariant parameter retrieval techniques for permittivity and permeability measurement" , *Journal of Microwave Power and Electromagnetic Energy*, vol. 52, no. 3, pp. 215-239, 2018.

[41] M. Dhillon, and P Dimri, "Design of Metamaterials in HFSS and Extraction of Permittivity and Permeability using NRW Method" , *International Journal of Electronics, Electrical and Computational System*, vol. 4, pp. 28-43, 2015.

[42] S. Takeda, and T. Yoshinaga, "Left-Handed Metamaterial Technologies Significant for Information and Communication Devices" , *Science & Technology Trends*, no. 34, pp. 36-50, 2009.

[43] N. Engheta, and R. W. Ziolkowski, "Metamaterials Physics and Engineering Explorations" , Wiley-IEEE Press, Hoboken, 2006.

[44] B. Tutuncu, H. Torpi, and B. Urul, "A comparative study on different types of metamaterials for enhancement of microstrip patch antenna directivity at the Ku-band (12 GHz)" , *Turkish Journal of Electrical Engineering & Computer Sciences*, vol. 26, no. 3, pp. 1171-1179, 2018.

[45] A. Nemati, Q. Wang, M. Hong, and J. Teng, "Tunable and reconfigurable metasurfaces and metadevices" , *Opto-Electronic Advances*, vol. 1, no. 5, pp. 180009-1-180009-25, 2018.

[46] H. Jeong, D. H. Le, D. Lim, R. Phon, and S. Lim, "Reconfigurable Metasurfaces for Frequency Selective Absorption" , *Advanced Optical Materials*, vol. 8, no. 13, 1902182, 2020.

[47] Tsilipakos et al., "Toward Intelligent Metasurfaces: The Progress from Globally Tunable Metasurfaces to Software-Defined Metasurfaces with an Embedded Network of Controllers" , *Advanced Optical Materials*, vol. 8, no. 17, 2000783, 2020.

[48] A. G. Farizawani, M. Puteh, Y. Marina, and A. Rivaie, "A review of artificial neural network learning rule based on multiple variant of conjugate gradient approaches" , *Journal of Physics: Conference Series*, vol. 1529, issue 2, 022040, 2020.

[49] B. R. Archambeault, C. Brench, and O. M. Ramahi, "EMI/EMC Computatiional Modeling Handbook" , *The Springer International Series in Engineering and Computer Science*, vol. 630, 2nd Edition, Kluwer Academic Publishers, New York, 1998.

[50] C. Warren, S. Sesnic, A. Ventura, L. Pajewski, D. Poljak, and A. Giannopoulos, "Comparison of Time-Domain Finite-Difference, Finite-Integration, and Integral-Equation Methods for Dipole Radiation in Half Space Environments" , *Progress In Electromagnetics Research M*, vol. 57, pp. 175-183, 2017.

[51] W. J. R. Hoefer, "The Transmission-Line Matrix Method – Theory and Applications" , *IEEE Transactions on Microwave Theory and Techniques*, vol. MTT-33, no. 10, pp. 882-893, 1985.

[52] W. C. Gibson, "The Method of Moments in Electromagnetics" , Chapman & Hall/CRC, Taylor & Francis Group, Newyork, 2008.

[53] M. M. Ney, "Method of Moments as Applied to Electromagnetic Problems" , *IEEE Transactions on Microwave Theory and Techniqoes*, vol. 33, no. 10, pp. 972-980, 1985.

[54] L. M. Yang, "HFSS antenna design", 2nd Edition, Electronic Industry Press, China, 2014.

[55] L. M. Yang, "HFSS electromagnetic simulation design from entry to the master" , Peaple's Posts and Telecommunications Press, China, 2013.

[56] R. Pratap, "Getting Started with MATLAB: A Quick Introduction for Scientists and Engineers" , 7th Edition, Oxford University Press, 2019.

[57] S. J. Chapman, "MATLAB Programming for Engineers" , 5th Edition, Cengage Learning, USA, 2015.

[58] E. Werndl, "Antenna Tunable in Its Length" , U.S. Patent 2,278,601, 7 1942.

[59] D. Schaubert, "Frequency-agile polarization diversity microstrip antennas and frequency scanned array" , *US Patent*, vol. 4, pp. 367-474, 1983.

[60] J. K. Smith, "Reconfigurable aperture antenna (RECAP)", *DARPA*, 1999 [Online]. Available: www.darpa.mil.

[61] J. T. Bernhard, and G. Washington, "A Smart Mechanically Actuated Two-Layer Electromagnetically Coupled Microstrip Antenna with Variable Frequency, Bandwidth, and Antenna Gain" , *IEEE Transactions on Antennas and Propagation*, vol. 49, no. 4, pp. 597-601, 2001.

[62] J. C. Langer, J. Zou, C. Liu, and J. T. Bernhard, "Micromachined Reconfigurable Out-of-Plane Microstrip Patch Antenna Using Plastic Deformation Magnetic Acruation" , *IEEE Microwave and Wireless Components Letters*, vol. 13, no. 3, pp. 120-122, 2003.

[63] D. Peroulis, K. Sarabandi, and L. P. B. Katehi, "Design of Reconfigurable Slot Antennas" , *IEEE Transactions on Antennas and Propagation*, vol. 53, no. 2, pp. 645-654, 2005.

[64] C. J. Panagamuwa, A. Chauraya, and J. C. Vardaxoglou, "Frequency and Beam Reconfigurable Antenna Using Photoconducting Switches" , *IEEE transactions on Antennas and Propagation*, vol. 54, no. 2, pp. 645-65449-454, 2006.

[65] S. L. S. Yang, A. A. Kishk, and K. F. Lee, "Frequency Reconfigurable U-Slot Microstrip Patch Antenna" , *IEEE Antennas and Wireless Propagation Letters*, vol. 7, pp. 127-129, 2008.

[66] H. Li, J. Xiong, Y. Tu, and S. He, "A Simple Compact Reconfigurable Slot Antenna with a very Wide Tuning Range" , *IEEE Transactions on Antennas and Propagation*, vol. 58, no. 11, pp. 3725-3728, 2010.

[67] Y. Yu, J. Xiong, H. Li, and S. He, "An Electrically Small Frequency Reconfigurable Antenna With a Wide Tuning Range" , *IEEE Antennas and Wireless Propagation Letters*, vol. 10, pp. 103-106, 2011.

[68] E. Erfani, J. Nourinia, C. Ghobadi, M. N. Jazi, and T. A. Denidni, "Design and Implementation of an Integrated UWB/ Reconfigurable-Slot Antenna for Cognitive Radio Applications" , *IEEE Antennas and Wireless Propagation Letters*, vol. 11, pp. 77-80, 2012.

[69] H. A. Majid, M. K. A. Rahim, M. R. Hamid, and M. F. Ismail, "A Compact Frequency-Reconfihurable Narrowband Microstrip Slot Antenna" , *IEEE Antennas and Wireless Propagation Letters*, vol. 11, pp. 616-619, 2012.

[70] V. Sathi, N. Ehteshami, and J. Nourinia, "Optically Tuned Frequency-Reconfigurable Microstrip Antenna" , *IEEE Antennas and Wireless Propagation Letters*, vol. 11, pp. 1018-1020, 2012.

[71] H. A. Majid, M. K. A. Rahim, M. R. Hamid, N. A. Murad, and M. F. Ismail, "Frequency Reconfigurable Microstrip Patch-Slot Antenna" , *IEEE Antennas and Wireless Propagation* Letters, vol. 12, pp. 218-220, 2013.

[72] L. Ge, and K. M. Luk, "Frequency-Reconfigurable Low-Profile Circular Monopolar Patch Antenna" , *IEEE Transactions on Antennas and Propagation*, vol. 62, issue 7, pp. 3443-3449, 2014.

[73] H. A. Majid, M. K. A. Rahim, M. R. Hamid, and M. F. Ismail, "Frequency Reconfigurable Microstrip Patch-Slot Antenna with Directional Radiation Pattern" , *Progress In Electromagnetics Research*, vol. 144, pp. 319-328, 2014.

[74] H. Rajagopalan, J. M. Kovitz, and Y. R. Samii, "MEMS Reconfigurable Optimized E-Shaped Patch Antenna Design for Cognitive Radio" , *IEEE Transactions on Antennas and Propagation*, vol. 62, no. 3, pp. 1056-1064, 2014.

[75] Q. Liu, N. Wang, C. Wu, G. Wei, and A. B. Smolders, "Frequency Reconfigurable Antenna Controlled by Multi-Reed Switches" , *IEEE Antennas and Wireless Propagation Letters*, vol. 14, pp. 927-930, 2015.

[76] I. T. Nassar, H. Tsang, D. Bardroff, C. P. Lusk, and T. M. Weller, "Mechanically Reconfigurable, Dual-Band Slot Dipole Antennas" , *IEEE Transactions on Antennas and Propagation*, vol. 63, no. 7, pp. 3267-3271, 2015.

[77] R. Hussain, A. Ghalib, and M. S. Sharawi, "Annular Slot-based Miniaturized Frequency Agile MIMO Antenna System" , *IEEE Antennas and Wireless Propagation Letters*, vol. 16, pp. 2489-2492, 2017.

[78] A. Ali, K. Topalli, M. Ramzan, M. Alibakhshikenari, T. M. Khan, A. Altintas, and P. Colantonio, "Optically reconfigurable planar monopole antenna for cognitive radio application" , *Microwave and Optical Technology Letters*, vol. 61, no. 1, pp. 1-6, 2019.

[79] A. Boukarkar, X. Q. Lin, Y. Jiang, and X. F. Yang, "A Compact Frequency-Reconfigurable 36-States Patch Antenna for Wireless Applications" , *IEEE Antennas and Wireless Propagation Letters*, vol. 17, no. 7, pp. 1349-1353, 2018.

[80] Y. M. Cai, K. Li, Y. Yin, S. Gao, W. Hu, and L. Zhao, "A Low-Profile Frequency Reconfigurable Grid-Slotted Patch Antenna" , *IEEE Access*, vol. 6, pp. 36305-36312, 2018.

[81] Y. Yuan, X. Sun, Y. Zhang, L. Zhao, and Y. Wang, "Design of Frequency Reconfigurable Antenna Based on Metasurface" , in *2021 7th International Conference on Computer and Communications (ICCC),* pp. 2165-2169, Chengdu, China, 2021.

[82] H. Mirzaei, and G. V. Eleftheriades, "A Compact Frequency-Reconfigurable Metamaterial-Inspired Antenna" , *IEEE Antennas and Wireless Propagation Letters*, vol. 10, pp. 1154-1157, 2011.

[83] H. Cheribi, F. Ghanem, and H. Kimouche, "Metamaterial-based frequency reconfigurable antenna" , *Electronic Letters*, vol. 49, no. 5, pp. 315-316, 2013.

[84] V. Rajeshkumar, and S. Raghavan, "A compact metamaterial inspired triple band antenna for reconfigurable WLAN/WiMAX applications" , *International Journal of Electronics and Communications*, vol. 69, pp. 274-280, 2015.

[85] S. K. Patel, K. H. Shah, and Y. P. Kosta, "Frequency-reconfigurable and high-gain metamaterial microstrip-radiating structure" , *Waves in Random and Complex Media*, vol. 29, issue 3, pp. 1-17, 2018.

[86] G. Varamini, A. Keshtkar, and M. N. Moghadasi, "Miniaturization of microstrip loop antenna for wireless applications based on metamaterial metasurface" , *International Journal of Electronics and Communications*, vol. 83, pp. 32-39, 2018.

[87] D. Zhou, H. Wang, L. Deng, L-L Qiu, and S. Huang, "Metamaterial-based frequency reconfigurable microstrip antenna for wideband and improved gain performance" , *International Journal of RF and Microwave Computer-Aided Engineering*, vol. 32, no. 2, e22988, 2021.

[88] L. Abdelhadi, B. Khedidja, M. Bouzouad, and D. Herbadji, "Metamaterial-based reconfigurable antenna" , *International Journal of Systems, Control and Communications*, vol. 13, no. 4, pp. 327-339, 2022.

[89] H. L. Zhu, S. W. Cheung, X. H. Liu, Y. F. Cao, and T. I. Yuk, "Frequency Reconfigurable Slot Antenna Using Metasurface" , in *The 8th European Conference on Antennas and Propagation (EUCAP 2014)*, pp. 2575-2577, The Hague, Netherlands, 2014.

[90] M. N. Pawan, and N. Chattoraj, "Design and Analysis of a Frequency Reconfigurable Antenna Using Metasurface For Wireless Applications" , in *IEEE sponsored 2nd International Conference on Innovations in Information, Embedded and Communication Systems (ICIIECS 2015)*, pp. 1-5, Coimbatore, India, 2015.

[91] H. L. Zhu, S. W. Cheung, and T. I. Yuk, "Frequency-Reconfigurable Slot Antenna with Wide-Tuning Range using Metasurface" , *Microwave and Optical Technology Letters*, vol. 57, no. 6, pp. 1475-1481, June 2015.

[92] W. Ma, G. Wang, B. F. Zong, Y. Zhuang, and X. Zhang, "Mechanically Reconfigurable Antenna Based on Novel Metasurface for Frequency Tuning-range Improvement" , *IEEE International Conference on Microwave and Millimeter Wave Technology (ICMMT)*, pp. 629-631, Beijing, 2016.

[93] B. Majumder, K. Kandasamy, J. Mukherjee, and K. P. Ray, "Wideband compact directive metasurface enabled pair of slot antennas" , *Electronics Letters*, vol. 51, no. 17, pp. 1310-1312, 2015.

[94] P. P. Kumar, K. Sreelakshmi, B. Sangeeta, and S. Narayan, "Metasurface based Low Profile Reconfigurable Antenna" , in *2017 International Conference on Communication and Signal Processing (ICCSP)* pp. 2081-2085, Chennai, India, 2017.

[95] M. Zhu, and L. Sun, "Design of Frequency Reconfigurable Antenna Based on Metasurface" , in *IEEE 2nd Advanced Information Technology, Electronic and Automation Control Conference (IAEAC)*, pp. 1785-1788, Chongqing, China, 2017.

[96] X. F. Chen, and Y. J. Zhao, "Dual-band Polarization and Frequency Reconfigurable Antenna Using Double Layer Metasurface" , *International Journal of Electronics and Communications*, vol. 95, pp. 82-87, 2018.

[97] C. Ni, M. S. Chen, Z. X. Zhang, and X. L. Wu, "Design of Frequency-and Polarization-Reconfigurable Antenna Based on the Polarization Conversion Metasurface" , *IEEE Antennas and Wireless Propagation Letters*, vol. 17, no.1, pp. 78-81, 2018.

[98] H. Li, X. Man, and J. Qi, "Accurate and Robust Characterization of Metasurface-Enabled Frequency Reconfigurable Antennas by Radially Homogenous Model" , *IEEE Access*, vol. 7, pp. 122605-122612, 2019.

[99] G. S. Ulomi, and H. Kilavo, "A Dual Band Frequency Reconfigurable Metasurface Antenna" , *Handbook of Research on Nurturing Industrial Economy for Africa's Development*, pp. 246-254, Hershey, PA: IGI Global, 2021.

[100] B. K. Ledimo, P. Moaro, R. Ramogomana, M. Mosalaosi, and B. Basutli, "Design Procedure of a Frequency Reconfigurable Metasurface Antenna at mmWave Band", *Telecom,* vol. 3, no. 2, pp. 379-395, 2022.

[101] J. S. Sivia, A. P. S. Pharwaha, and T. S. Kamal, "Analysis and Design of Circular Fractal Antenna Using Artificial Neural Networks" , *Progress In Electromagnetics Research B*, vol.56, pp. 251-267, 2013.

[102] B. S. Dhaliwal, and S. S. Pattnaik, "BFO-ANN ensemble hybrid algorithm to design compact fractal antenna for rectenna system" , *Neural Computing and Applications*, vol. 28, pp. 917-928, 2017.

[103] M. Kaur, and J. S. Sivia, "Minkowski, Giuseppe Peano and Koch curves based design of compact hybrid fractal antenna for biomedical applications using ANN and PSO" , *International Journal of Electronics and Communications*, vol. 99, pp. 14-24, 2019.

[104] S. Rani, and J. S. Sivia, "Design and development of virtual instrument for fault diagnosis in fractal antenna array" , *International Journal of RF and Microwave Computer-Aided Engineering*, vol. 30, issue 1, e22026, 2019.

[105] M. Kaur, and J. S. Sivia, "ANN and FA Based Design of Hybrid Fractal Antenna for ISM Band Applications" , *Progress In Electromagnetics Research C, vol. 98,* pp. 127-140, 2020.

[106] S. S. Sran, and J. S. Sivia, "ANN and IFS based wearable hybrid fractal antenna with DGS for S, C and X band application" , *International Journal of Electronics and Communications*, vol. 127, 153425, 2020.

[107] K. Sharma, and G. P. Pandey, "Efficient modelling of compact microstrip antenna using machine learning" , *International Journal of Electronics and Communications*, vol. 135, e15373, 2021.

[108] J. Sun, Y. Hu, H. Fang, and Z. Wang, "Accurate S parameter prediction of L-shaped probe-fed patch antenna with an improved artificial bee colony algorithm based on artificial neural network" , *International Journal of RF and Microwave Computer-Aided Engineering*, vol. 31, no. 9, e22783, 2021.

[109] W. Y. Wei, Y. Shi, J. X. Yang, and H. X. Meng, "Artificial neural network and convex optimization enable antenna array design" , *International Journal of RF and Microwave Computer-Aided Engineering*, vol. 31, no. 5, e22593, 2021.

[110] T. D. J. Tanguy, M. Jacques, M. Yannick, and E. D. J. Francois, "Dimensioning of Fixed Frequency Patch Antennas Based on Neural Networks" , *International Journal of Scientific Research and Management,* vol. 10, no. 4, pp. 862-870, 2022.

[111] K. Umashankar, and A. Taflove, "Computational electromagnetic" , Artech House, Boston, London, 1993.

[112] A. U. Bhobe, C. L. Holloway, P. M. Melinda, "Meander delay line challenge problem: A comparison using FDTD, FEM, and MOM" , in *IEEE International Symposium on Eletcromagnetic Compatibility*, pp. 805-810, Montreal, Quebec, 2001.

[113] R. S. Sharma, "Analysis of electromagnetic field Using FEM: A Review", *International Journal of Advanced Electrical Engineering*, vol. 1, no. 1, pp. 1-10, 2012.

[114] P. P. Silvester, Ferrari, L. Ronald, "Finite elements for electrical engineers" , 1st edition, Cambridge University Press, 1983.

[115] P. P. Silvester, "A general high-order finite element wave-guide analysis program" , *IEEE transactions on Microwave Theory and Techniques*, vol. 4, pp. 204-210, 1969.

[116] J. Jin, "The finite element method in electromagnetic" , John Wiley and Sons Inc., New York, 1993.

[117] R. Coccioli, T. Itoh, G Pelosi, P. P. Silvester, "Finite-element methods in microwaves: a selected bibliography" , *IEEE Antennas and Propagation magazine,* vol. 38, no. 6, pp. 34-48, 1996.

[118] R. L. Ferrari, "The finite-element method, part 2: p. p. silvester, an innovator in electromagnetic numerical modeling" , *IEEE Antennas and Propagation Magazine*", vol. 49 no. 3, pp. 216-234, 2007.

[119] J. Moore, and R. Pizer, "Moment methods in electromagnetics: Techniques and applications" , Research Studies Press, New York, 1984.

[120] I. Babuska, and W. C. Rheinboldt, "A posteriori error estimates for the finite element method" , *International Journal for Numerical Methods in Engineering*, vol. 11, pp. 1597-1615, 1978.

[121] S. Y. Hahn, C. Calmels, G. Meunier, and J. L. Coulomb, "A posteriori error estimate for adaptive finite element mesh generation" , *IEEE Transactions on Magnetics,* vol. 24, no. 1, pp. 315-317, 1988.

[122] A. Darcherif, A. Raizer, G. Meunier, J. F. Imhoff, and J. C. Sabonnadikre, "New techniques in FEM field calculation applied to power cable characteristics computation" , *IEEE Transactions on Magnetics*, vol. 26, no. 5, pp. 2388-2390, 1990.

[123] J. Ackermann, B. Erdmann, and R. Roitzsch, "A self adaptive multilevel finite element method for the stationary schrodinger equation in three space dimensions" , *Journal of Chemical Physics*, vol. 101, no. 9, pp. 7643-7650, 1994.

[124] F. J. C. Meyer, and D. B. Davidson, "Adaptive-mesh refinement of finite element solutions for two dimensional electromagnetic problems" , *IEEE Antennas and propagation magazine*, vol. 38, no. 5, pp. 77-83, 1996.

[125] M. G. Vanti, and A. Raizer, "Optimal meshes and h-p adaptivity" , *IEEE Transactions on Magnetics*, vol. 33, no. 2, pp. 1752-1755, 1997.

[126] M. Dorica, and D. D. Giannacopoulos, "Toward optimal mesh quality improvements for adaptive finite element electromagnetics with tetrahedral" , *IEEE transactions on Magnetics*, vol. 40, no. 2, pp. 989-992, 2004.

[127] I. Babuska, and B. Q. Guo, "The h, p and h-p version of the finite element method: Basis theory and applications" , *Advance in Enggineering Software*, vol. 15, pp. 3-4, 1992.

[128] I. Bardi, G. Peng, and Z. J. Cendes, "Improvements in adaptive mesh refinement and multilevel methods in High-Frequency Electromagnetics by Ansoft Corporation", pp. 1-15, Pittsburgh, PA.

[129] N. Malhotra, A. Marwaha, and A. Kumar, "Reconfigurable tapered coaxial slot antenna for hepatic microwave ablation" , *Electromagnetic Biology and Medicine*, vol. 36, no. 3, pp. 214-221, 2016.

[130] E. J. Rottwell, J. L. Frasch, S. M. Ellison, P. Chahal, and R. O. Ouedraogo, "Analysis of the Nicolson-Ross-Weir Method for Characterizing the Electromagnetic Properties of Engineered Materials" , *Progress In Electromagnetics Research*, vol. 157, pp. 31-47, 2016.

[131] A. Sethi, and Rajni, "Determination of electromagnetic parameters of a new metasurface comprising of square loop" , *Journal of Engineering Science and Technology*, vol. 13, no. 1, pp. 48–57, 2018.

[132] R. Rajni, and A. Marwaha, "Electrically small microstrip patch antenna loaded with spiral resonator for wireless applications" , *Wireless Personal Communications*, vol. 96, no. 2, pp. 2621–2632, 2017.

[133] N. Sharma, and S. S. Bhatia, "Double split labyrinth resonator-based CPW-fed hybrid fractal antennas for PCS/UMTS/WLAN/Wi-Max applications" , *Journal of Electromagnetic Waves and Applications*, vol. 33, no. 18, pp. 2476–2498, 2019.

[134] Rajni, and A. Marwaha, "Resonance characteristics and effective parameters of new left hand metamaterial" , *Telkomnika Indonesian Journal of Electrical Engineering*, vol. 15, no. 3, pp. 497–503, 2015.

[135] R. Rajni, and A. Marwaha, "An accurate approach of mathematical modeling of SRR and SR for metamaterials" , *Journal of Engineering Science and Technology Review*, vol. 9, no. 6, pp. 82–86, 2016.

[136] Rajni and A. Marwaha, "CSC-SR structure loaded electrically small planar antenna" , Applied Computational Electromagnetics Society Journal, vol. 31, no. 5, pp. 591-598, 2016.

[137] S. J. M. Rao, R. Sarkar, G. Kumar, and D. B. Chowdhury, "Gradual cross polarization conversion of transmitted waves in near field coupled planar terahertz metamaterials," *OSA Continuum*, vol. 2, no. 3, pp. 603–614, 2019.

[138] J. Chatterjee, A. Mohan, and V. Dixit, "A novel frequency reconfigurable slot antenna using metasurface," *IEEE Indian Conference on Antennas and Propogation (InCAP)*, Hyderabad, India, 2018.

Received: 8 February 2021 | Revised: 28 April 2021 | Accepted: 14 June 2021

DOI: 10.1002/mmce.22793

RESEARCH ARTICLE

INTERNATIONAL JOURNAL OF RF AND MICROWAVE COMPUTER-AIDED ENGINEERING WILEY

Artificial neural network based metasurface inspired planar frequency reconfigurable antenna for wireless applications

Navneet Kaur[1] | **Jagtar Singh Sivia**[2] | **Rajni**[3]

[1]Department of Electronics and Communication Engineering, Punjabi University, Patiala, Punjab, India

[2]YCoE, Punjabi University Guru Kashi Campus Talwandi Sabo, Bathinda, Punjab, India

[3]Department of Electronics and Communication Engineering, Shaheed Bhagat Singh State Technical Campus, Ferozepur, Punjab, India

Correspondence
Navneet Kaur, Research Scholar, Department of Electronics and Communication Engineering, Punjabi University, Patiala, Punjab, India.
Email: navsandhu31696@gmail.com

Abstract

The growing interest in attaining various appealing features of wireless communication systems has motivated researchers to design innovative antennas. This paper analyzes the behavior of a low profile artificial neural network-based metasurface (MS) inspired two-layered frequency reconfigurable antenna (ANN-MSFRA) using planar technology. The designed two-layered structure is a combination of two substrates mounted one above the other, having no air gap between them. The prototype of the proposed antenna is fabricated on Rogers RO4350B material having permittivity (ε_r) = 3.48, and thickness (h) = 1.524 mm. The MS is represented as an artificially generated periodical array of H and I-shaped metallic inclusions. Numerically analyzed results validate the double negative properties of metamaterial. To verify the effectiveness of the projected two-layered approach, the performance of the reconfigurable antenna is analyzed through both simulations and measurements. The antenna successfully reconfigures the operating frequency from 4.86 to 5.89 GHz, covering the operating bandwidth of 1.03 GHz with a fractional tuning range of 19.1%. The presented simulated and measured outcome provides a positive correlation.The developed ANN model suggested for the estimation of specific output parameters shows minimum error during analysis and synthesis.

KEYWORDS

artificial neural network, frequency reconfigurable antenna, metamaterial, metasurface, reflection coefficient

1 | INTRODUCTION

The technology sector is developing very rapidly according to the growing demands of the users.[1] The technological advancements in wireless systems have stimulated the market demand for developing novel antennas with unique functionalities.[2,3] These antennas can modify dynamically the important characteristics in a controlled and reversible way.[4] The fundamental requirements such as multifunctionality, strong reliability, small volume, high data rate are accomplished by embedding the wireless devices with reconfigurable antennas. Therefore, reconfigurable antennas with their diverse attributes are deployed to cater all these functionalities.[5] These antennas have gained huge interest in the last decade as they have the strong ability to reduce the problems associated with single-band and multiband antennas.[6] Moreover, they have the potential to switch between different working frequencies, polarization, and radiation pattern modes to provide versatility depending upon the environmental needs.[7] Frequency reconfigurable antennas are primarily used as they can resonate dynamically at multiple tuning frequencies.[8] The desirable characteristics are a wide tunable range, better frequency selectivity, and stable patterns. A reconfigurable antenna changes its state of conduct by changing the distribution of current on the surface of the antenna.[9] Tremendous attempts have been made during the previous years to investigate the frequency reconfigurable antennas. Various strategies are employed to achieve the reconfigurability operation. The widely used approaches for frequency reconfigurability are electrical and/or mechanical. Electrical switching employs micro-electro-mechanical switches (MEMS), positive intrinsic negative (PIN) diodes, varactors, etc for performing its switchable operations,[10] whereas the mechanically reconfigurable antenna uses actuators, counterweights, motor, pulley, etc. These devices occupy more space and thus increase the size of an antenna. Thus, the selection of proper size and shape becomes a great difficulty in designing mechanically reconfigurable antennas.[11] Electrically reconfigurable antennas are popular as they can easily integrate with other planar antennas. But, they possess few limitations like negative biasing effects, slow tuning, nonlinearities, etc.[12]

To solve all such difficulties, metamaterial (MM) based reconfigurable antennas have developed in recent years. Several researchers have developed numerous metamaterial structures such as triangular, elliptical, S, L, phi-shaped to enhance the operational characteristics of the antenna.[13-17] Though the three-dimensional (3D) metamaterials are in high demand for various electromagnetic applications, yet their design and fabrication is still a challenging task. Therefore, an immense interest has been emerged out in the area of two-dimensional (2D) patterns. The peculiar properties of 3D metamaterials are retained by extending them to their 2D equivalents known as "Metasurface (MS)". MS is an artificially generated periodical array that can efficiently manage the propagation behavior of EM waves.[12] By adjusting the design parameters of the unit cells, the electromagnetic response of the MS can be changed. These variations in the configuration of unit cells could derive dramatic alternations in the component values, thus generating the new resonant frequencies.[18] Moreover, they occupy less space and can reduce the path required for transmission. Hence they offer the facility of less-loss in structures. Due to all these merits, MS provides a lot of inherent applications viz. controllable smart surfaces, miniaturized cavity resonators, biomedical devices, novel waveguiding structures, terahertz switches, etc.[19] It was demonstrated,[20] that by mounting MS on the simple patch antenna, the overall performance remarkably builds up. In this design, an air gap exists between both the substrates, which in turn increases the volume of the antenna. Zhu et. al[11] designed a compact and low profile frequency reconfigurable MS antenna using patch antenna by eliminating the air gap. This antenna provides a tuning range of 4.76-5.51 GHz. Zhu et al.[21] extended his work by placing MS above a slot antenna thereby provided a fractional tuning range of 28%. Pavan et al.[22] elucidated Rogers RO4350B based frequency reconfigurable patch antenna using MS. This low profile antenna showed resonance from 5.2 to 5.9 GHz with applications in wireless local area network (WLAN) and industrial scientific and medical (ISM) band. Majumder et al.[23] described the behavior of double-layered anisotropic MS structure using slot antenna. Dual-band frequency and polarization reconfigurable antenna using double-layer MS were demonstrated.[24] It was illustrated that this antenna could function in both linear and circular polarization modes. Radially homogenous model-based antenna to estimate the operating frequency using ellipse and wire type MSs was reported.[25] This antenna provides better accuracy and robustness. Implementation of an artificial neural network for analysis and synthesis of the designed circular fractal antenna was proposed.[26]

In this research paper, an ANN-based two-layered frequency reconfigurable MS antenna is demonstrated for wireless applications. The antenna provides wide operational bandwidth and tuning range. After describing the introduction and brief literature review, the manuscript is organized as: Section 2 demonstrates the design configuration of frequency reconfigurable MS antenna. The electromagnetic properties of the metamaterial are justified in Section 3. Section 4 elucidates the framework of the simplified ANN model. Section 5 elaborates the simulated, estimated, and measured results. Finally, the whole paper is summarized and concluded in Section 6.

2 | DESIGN EVOLUTION

The proposed antenna structure consists of two layers: patch antenna and MS mounted one above the other with no air gap between them as described in Figure 1A. The substrate used for both the layers is Rogers RO4350B ($\varepsilon_r = 3.48$, $\tan\delta = 0.0037$) with a thickness of 1.524 mm. A Rectangular shaped patch is printed on the upper side of the first layer and circular shaped ground on its lower side. The designed 50 Ω impedance matching is achieved by tuning the dimensions ("L_f" and "W_f") of the feedline. The MS is specified as a periodical array of H and I-shaped metallic inclusions, which is printed on the upper

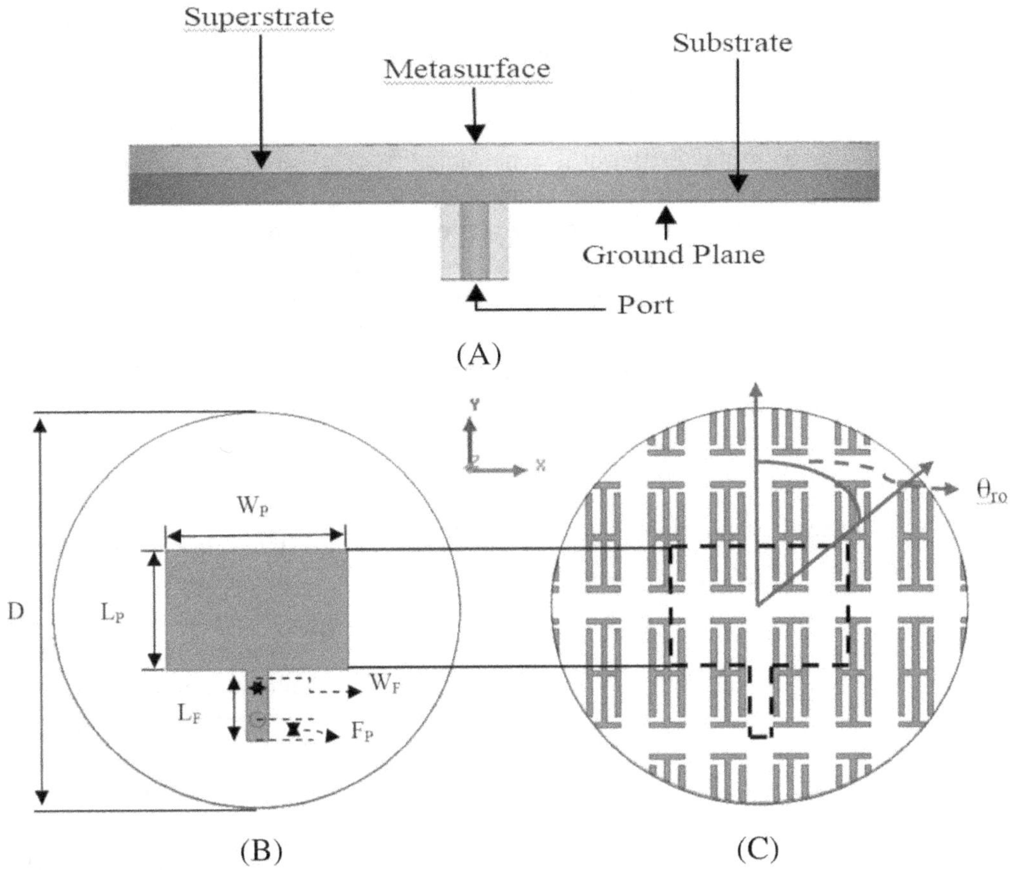

FIGURE 1 Description of designed antenna A, side view, B, patch, and C, metasurface

TABLE 1 Optimized parameters of the proposed antenna

Parameter	Description	Value (mm)
D	Diameter	36
L_P	Length of patch	11
W_p	Width of patch	16
L_F	Length of feedline	6.5
W_F	Width of feedline	2
F_P	Feed position from edge	2

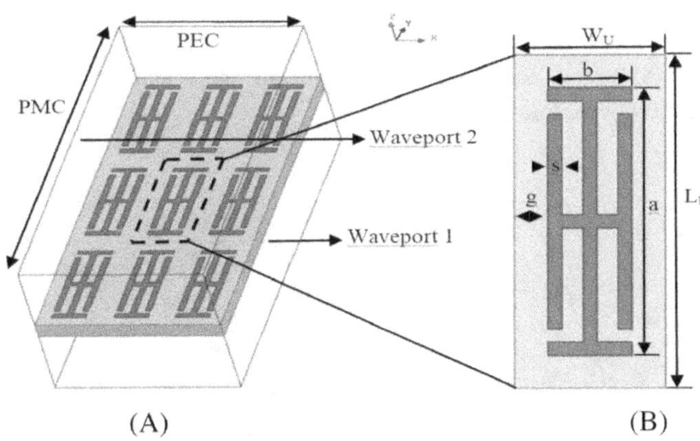

FIGURE 2 Geometrical framework of A, Waveguide set up and B, Zoomed unit cell

side of the second layer. For simplicity in the design process, both the layers are circular with a diameter of 36 mm. The schematic model of patch and MS is shown in Figure 1B,C respectively. To achieve the frequency reconfigurability of the proposed antenna, the MS is mechanically rotated with reference to the center of the rectangular-shaped patch antenna. During measurements, the angle of rotation (θ_{ro}) is varied along the y-axis. Due to equal symmetries (horizontal and vertical) of the MS, it is assumed that $\theta_{ro} = -\theta_{ro}$, and for performance evaluation, the maximum rotation angle considered is $90^{0.11}$ The optimized values of the proposed antenna are illustrated in Table 1.

3 | BEHAVIORAL ANALYSIS OF METAMATERIAL

The origin of metamaterials in the field of research reveals an outstanding achievement in comparison to conventional materials. The idea of metamaterial was first suggested by V. Veselago in 1967. This special class of artificially designed engineered materials exhibits eccentric and anomalous electromagnetic properties that are not observed in nature. Such materials exhibit negative permittivity and negative permeability properties.[27] Due to these attractive features metamaterial has several useful applications in the field of science, medicine, and engineering. The word metamaterial is constructed from the Greek word 'meta' that means something apart from natural things.[28] The symbolic representation of the H and I-shaped resonator (HI-SR) array and its zoomed version of the unit cell are illustrated in Figure 2A,B, respectively. This structure comprises of 3x3 array of HI-shaped unit cells arranged repetitively is placed on Rogers RO4350B substrate (ε_r = 3.48) with a thickness of 1.524 mm. The geometrical specifications of a single unit cell are elucidated in Table 2. The perfect electric conductor (PEC) and perfect magnetic conductor (PMC) boundary conditions are applied on the z-faces and y-faces of the 3 × 3 array, respectively.[29] The waveports are applied along the x-faces. For proper excitation of the electromagnetic wave, suitable waveports and boundary conditions are applied.[30] The whole structure is modeled and analyzed with a full-wave high-performance 3D simulator that is, high frequency structure simulator (HFSS) v.15 software. Simulations are carried out in the frequency range of 4–6 GHz to extract the transmission and reflection spectra of scattering parameters.

TABLE 2 Dimensional parameters of the unit cell (mm)

L_U	L_U	a	b	g	s
12.4	5.4	10	3	1.2	0.5

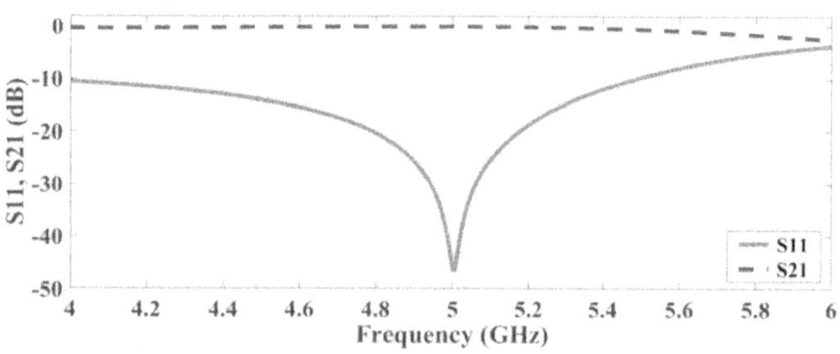

FIGURE 3 Reflection and transmission coefficients of scattering parameters

Scattering parameters (S_{11} and S_{21}) vs frequency are examined in Figure 3. It is observed that at 5 GHz frequency, the observed S_{11} value is - 46.47 dB. Hence, it is stated that the HI-SR structural array shows a resonance at the fundamental frequency of 5 GHz. The magnitude and phase of S_{11} and S_{21} are displayed in Figure 4A,B, respectively. From these figures, it is depicted that metamaterial behavior is confirmed from phase reversal characteristics of S_{11} and S_{21}.

The real and imaginary parts of S_{11} and S_{21} are described in Figure 5A,B, respectively. From these values, the negative characteristics of both permittivity and permeability are determined. The values of effective parameters are retrieved by applying four equations of Nicolson Ross Weir approach through Matrix Laboratory.[31,32]

$$V_1 = S_{21} + S_{11}, \tag{1}$$

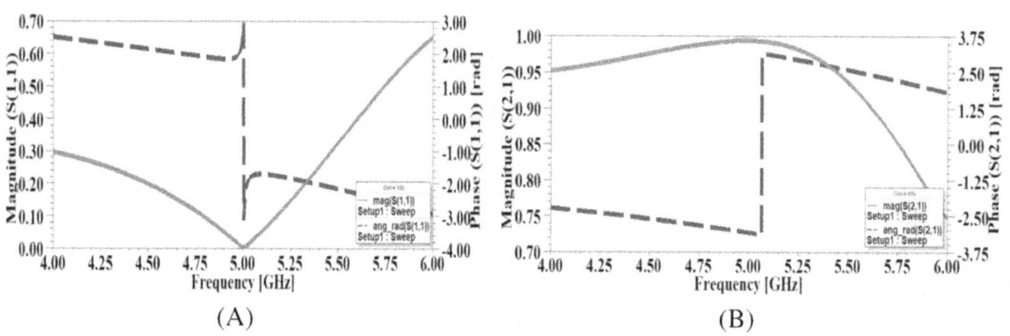

FIGURE 4 Magnitude and Phase of A, S_{11} and B, S_{21}

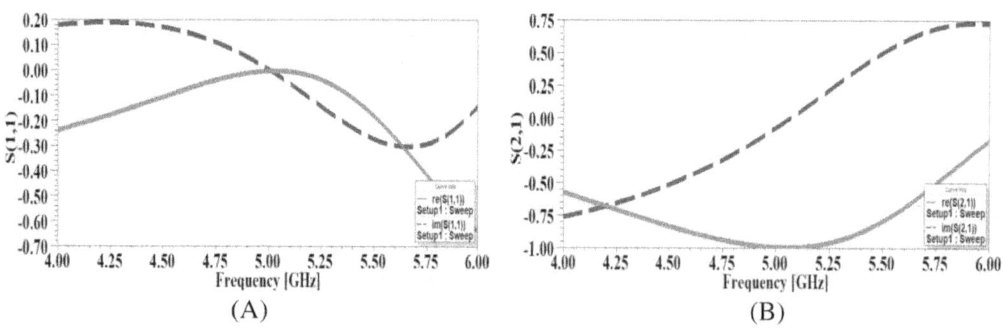

FIGURE 5 Real and Imaginary parts of A, S_{11}, and B) S_{21}

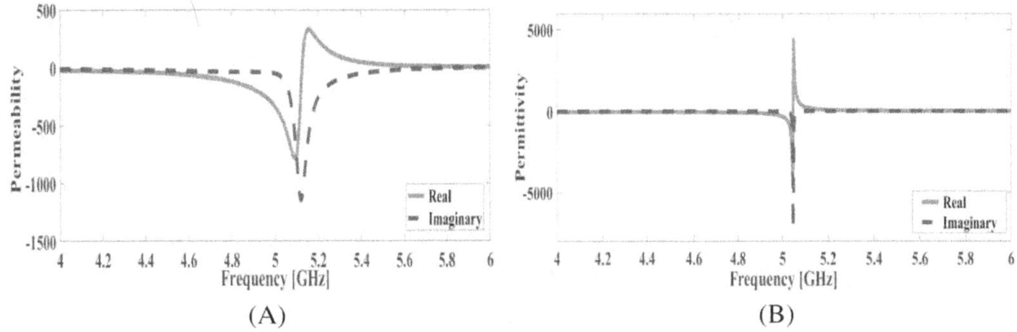

FIGURE 6 Extracted real and imaginary parts of A, permeability and B, permittivity

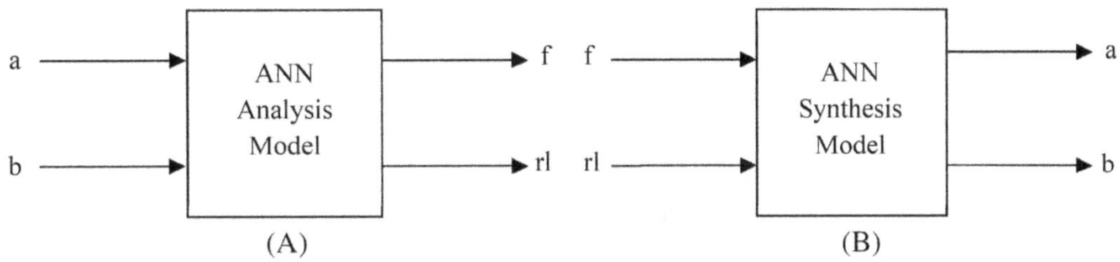

FIGURE 7 ANN model for A, analysis and B, synthesis

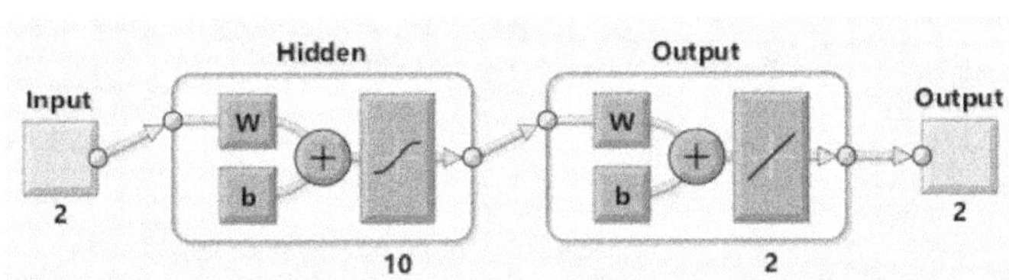

FIGURE 8 Proposed FFBP-NN model

$$V_2 = S_{21} - S_{11}, \tag{2}$$

$$\mu_r = \frac{2}{jk_o d} \frac{1 - V_2}{1 + V_2}, \tag{3}$$

$$\varepsilon_r = \frac{2}{jk_o d} \frac{1 - V_1}{1 + V_1}, \tag{4}$$

In these equations, V_1 and V_2 are the composite terms that express the sum and difference of S_{11} and S_{21} of scattering parameters, k_o represents the free space wavenumber, d is the thickness of the substrate, μ_r is the effective permeability and ε_r is the effective permittivity of the metamaterial.

Figure 6A,B displays the corresponding real and imaginary parts of effective permittivity and permeability. Here the bold line indicates the real value and the specked line indicates the imaginary value of the respective parameter. The negative range of effective permittivity and permeability lies in between 4 and 5.04 GHz respectively. Therefore, in this frequency range, the HI-SR array behaves like double negative (DNG) metamaterial. From the simulated results, it is demonstrated that the aforementioned structure exhibits left-handed metamaterial characteristics.

4 | ARTIFICIAL NEURAL NETWORK APPROACH

Artificial Neural Network is a computational framework that behaves like a human brain and is widely employed in several fields of science and engineering for efficient modeling and prediction.[33] These networks are preferred for antenna designing as they can acquire, process, and store the information. The feed-forward back propagation neural network (FFBP-NN) model consists of many interconnected units that are structured systematically in the form of three layers: an input layer, hidden layer, and output layer.[34] The signal from the input layer travel to the output layer, after traversing through one or more hidden layers. The neurons of the succeeding layers are joined together by connection links. A weight value is associated with each connection link.[35] The overall output of ANN is calculated and then the error signal is computed by taking the difference between the desired output and network output. The computed error is fed back and synaptic weights are adjusted accordingly.[36]

The ANN model for analysis and synthesis of the designed antenna is shown in Figure 7. The model holds two input layer neurons, 10 hidden layer neurons, and two output layer neurons. The proposed FFBP-NN model is illustrated in Figure 8. The dimensions of the unit cell are applied as input to the analysis model and corresponding resonant frequency and return loss values

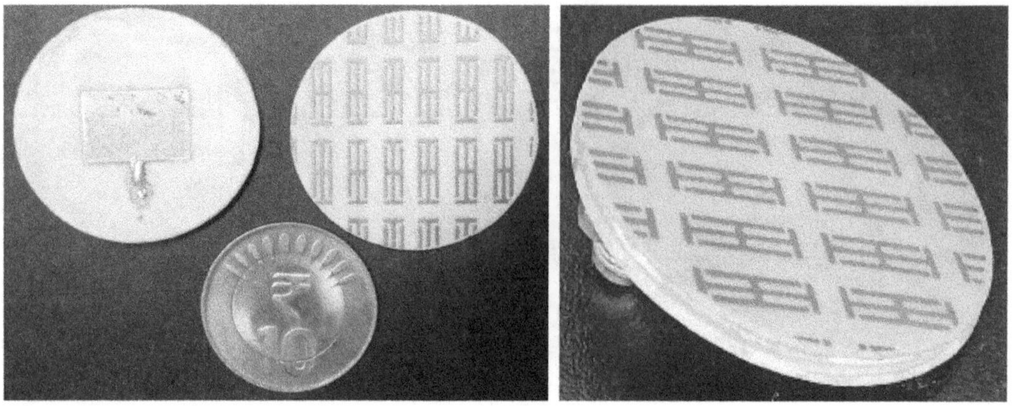

(A) (B)

FIGURE 9 Pictorial view of fabricated ANN-MSFRA using Rogers RO4350B substrate

TABLE 3 Simulated and measured S_{11} characteristics for $0^0 < \theta_{ro} < 90^0$

	Simulated		Measured	
Rotation angle 'θ_{ro}'	Resonant frequency 'f_r' (GHz)	S_{11} (dB)	Resonant frequency 'f_r' (GHz)	S_{11} (dB)
0°	4.86	−22.95	4.86	−26.53
30°	5.19	−17.58	5.18	−19.72
60°	5.74	−52.36	5.72	−27.72
90°	5.90	−11.91	5.89	−11.93

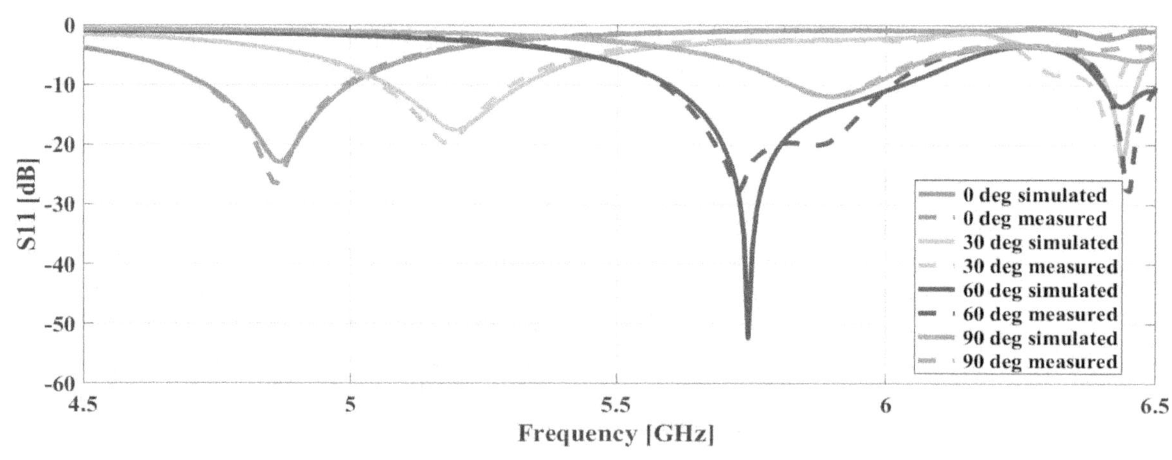

FIGURE 10 Simulated and measured S_{11} characteristics at different rotation angles

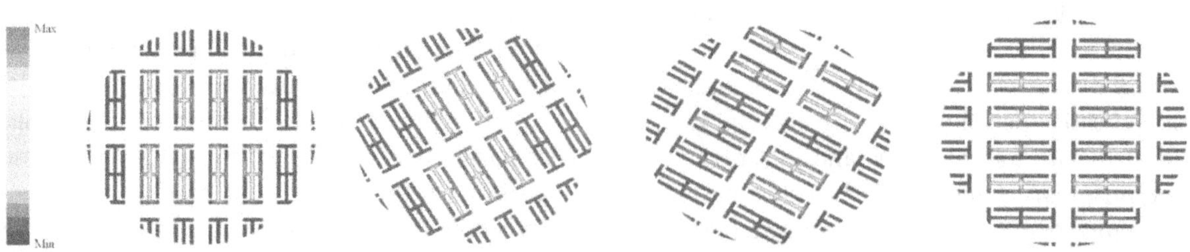

(A) (B) (C) (D)

FIGURE 11 Surface current distribution at A, 0°, B, 30°, C, 60°, and D, 90°

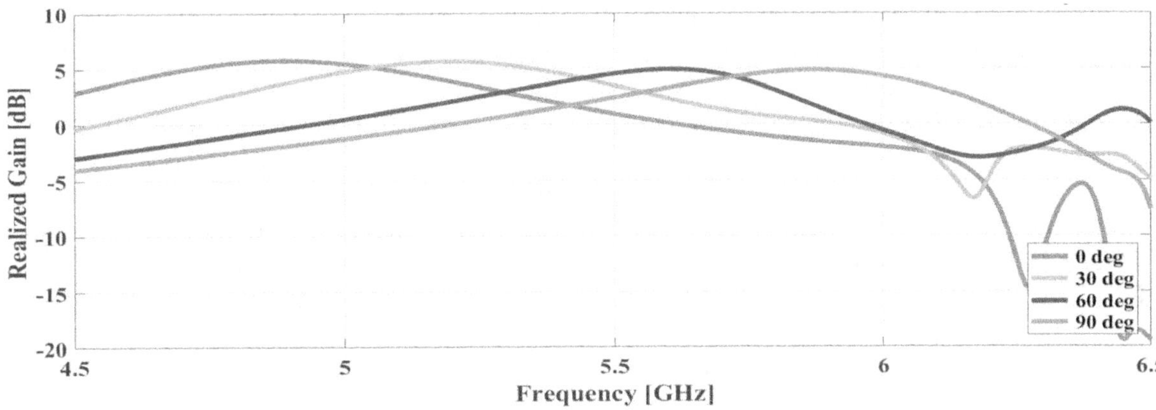

FIGURE 12 Realized Gain Plot at different rotation angles

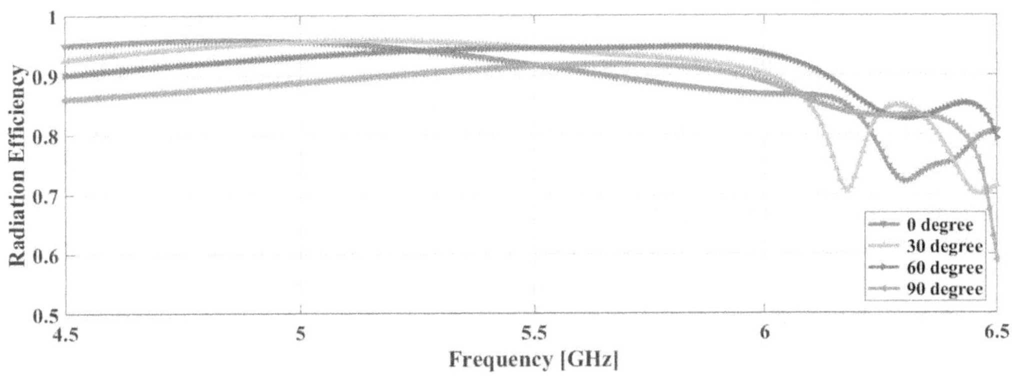

FIGURE 13 Radiation efficiency vs frequency plot at different rotation angles

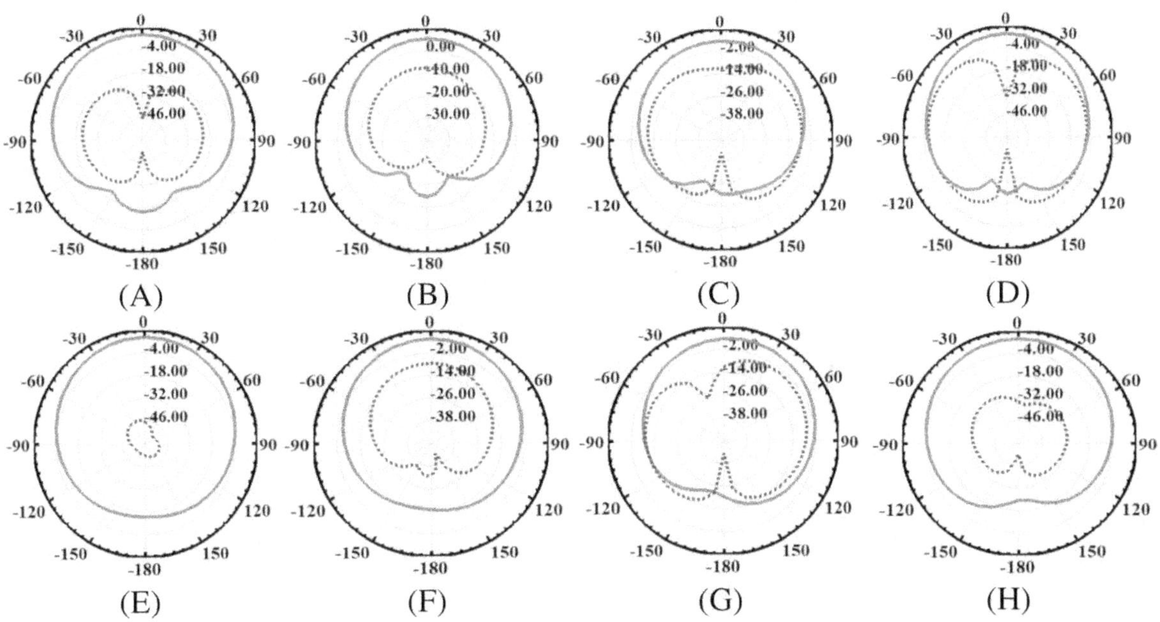

FIGURE 14 Radiation pattern of H-I SR FRMA corresponding to resonating frequencies 4.86 GHz, 5.19 GHz, 5.74 GHz, and 5.90 GHz in x-z plane A, 0°, B, 30°, C, 60°, D, 90° and in y-z plane D, 0°, E, 30°, F, 60°, and G, 90° (solid line indicates the co-polarization and the dotted line indicates the cross-polarization)

are estimated. Similarly, for the synthesis model, a reverse process is followed. A data pool of 40 samples is created to evaluate the process. Out of the total, 28 samples are present in the training set, six in the validation set, and the rest six in the testing set.

5 | EXPERIMENTAL RESULTS AND DISCUSSION

To validate the performance, the prototype is fabricated and experimentally verified. The pictorial view of the fabricated prototype is shown in Figure 9. The designed prototype is tested with vector network analyzer MS46322A manufactured by Anritsu company.

5.1 | Antenna results

Reflection coefficient (S_{11}) is an essential antenna performance parameter that demonstrates the input-output relationship between the terminals of an electrical system. In this work, this parameter is computed to illustrate the frequency reconfigurable operation. The value of S_{11} is calculated at four different rotation angles (0°, 30°, 60°, and 90°). Simulations and measurements related to resonant frequencies are taken with the rotation angle $0^0 < \theta_{ro} < 90^0$. During the analysis process, the step size chosen is 30°. An extensive parametric analysis is carried out in the range of 4.5–6.5 GHz. The results obtained from different rotation angles are revealed in Table 3. S_{11} characteristics at different rotation angles are plotted in Figure 10. It is observed that as the value of θ is increased, the resonant frequency gets shifted towards the higher side. The best matching condition is obtained at $\theta_{ro} = 60^0$. With further increase in rotation angle, the matching condition degrades. Thus, resonant frequency progressively advances from 4.86 to 5.90 GHz providing a fractional tuning of 19.3% with the bandwidth of 1.04 GHz in simulation results.

The surface current distribution on the MS is plotted in Figure 11. This distribution is evaluated at different rotation angles. Gain is another crucial parameter that illustrates the behavior of the antenna. It is related to efficiency and directivity. The realized gain plot at different rotation angles is portrayed in Figure 12. It is found that the antenna provides a gain of 5.75 dB at 0°, 5.67 dB at 30°, 4.71 dB at 60°, and 4.80 dB at 90° rotation angles.

TABLE 4 Evaluated performance during the analysis

	Samples	MSE	Regression
Training	28	7.43209e-2	9.99810e-1
Validation	6	6.50986e-2	9.99853e-1
Testing	6	3.75510e-2	9.99923e-1

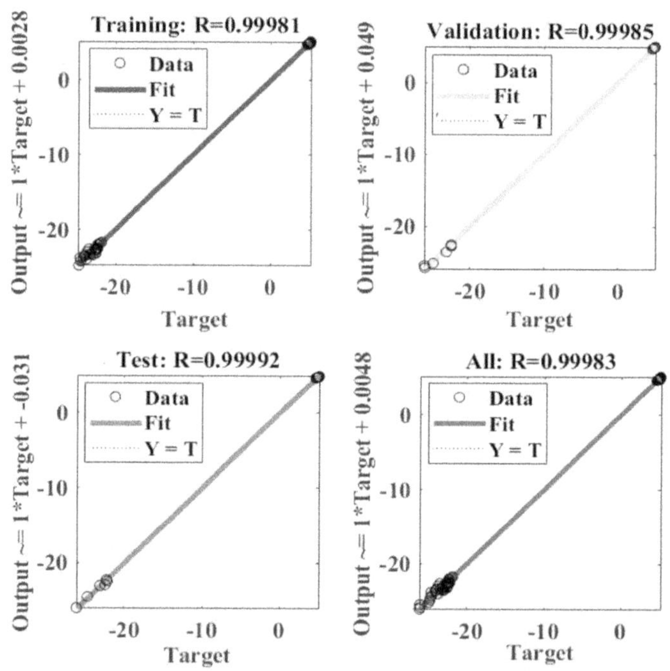

FIGURE 16 Scatter plot comparing the target value and ANN output for training, validation, testing, and overall output during the analysis

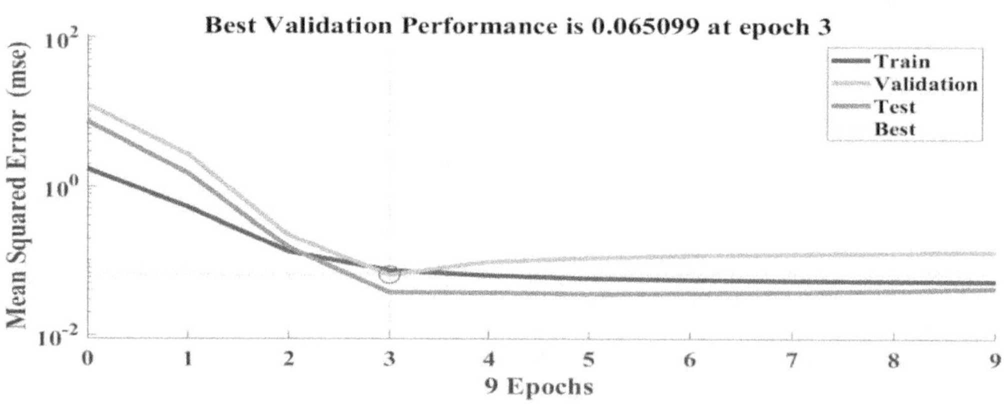

FIGURE 15 Performance plot during the analysis of designed antenna

TABLE 5 Absolute error estimation during the analysis of designed antenna

	Inputs		HFSS outputs		ANN outputs		Absolute error	
S. No.	a	b	f	rl	f	rl	f	rl
1	10	3	4.8695	−22.9529	4.849	−23.460	0.020	0.508
2	10	3.5	4.8213	−22.6574	4.839	−22.812	−0.018	0.155
3	10	4	4.7972	−22.4594	4.793	−22.586	0.003	0.127
4	10	2.7	4.9096	−23.1008	4.855	−23.116	0.053	0.015
5	10	2	5.0141	−22.4235	5.012	−22.433	0.002	0.009
6	11	3	4.6044	−26.1078	4.726	−26.045	−0.122	−0.062
7	9.6	3	4.9739	−22.4958	4.888	−22.769	0.085	0.273
8	9.2	3	5.1024	−22.2778	5.065	−21.978	0.037	−0.298
9	10.3	3	4.7972	−23.8064	4.831	−24.026	−0.034	0.219
10	9.7	3	4.9578	−22.4388	4.872	−22.976	0.085	0.537
Average absolute error							0.011	0.148

Abbreviation: HFSS, high frequency structure simulator.

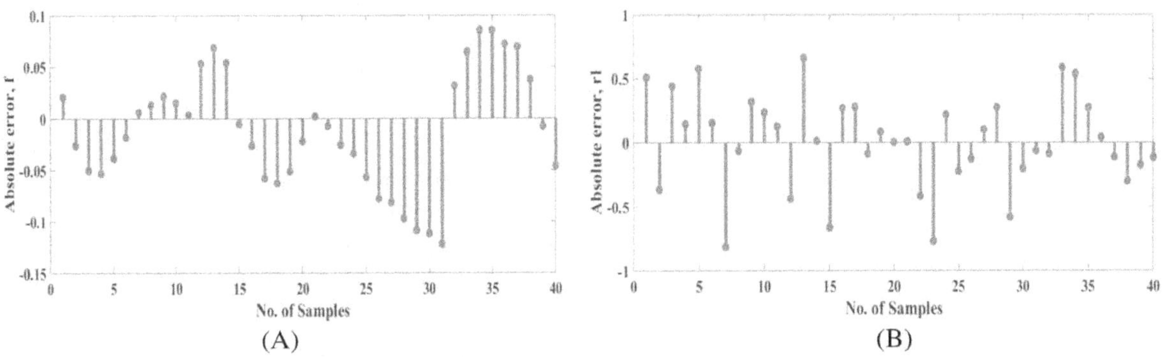

FIGURE 17 Absolute error during analysis for estimating A, f and B, rl

TABLE 6 Evaluated performance during synthesis

	Samples	MSE	Regression
Training	28	2.61627e-2	9.98934e-1
Validation	6	2.30280e-2	9.99578e-1
Testing	6	2.88933e-2	9.98886e-1

Radiation efficiency describes the ability of the device to transmit and efficiently receive the signals. The radiation efficiencies against frequency at rotation angles corresponding to 0°, 30°, 60°, and 90° are displayed in Figure 13. It is observed that radiation efficiency is above 90% at all resonating frequencies.

FIGURE 18 Performance plot during the synthesis of the designed antenna

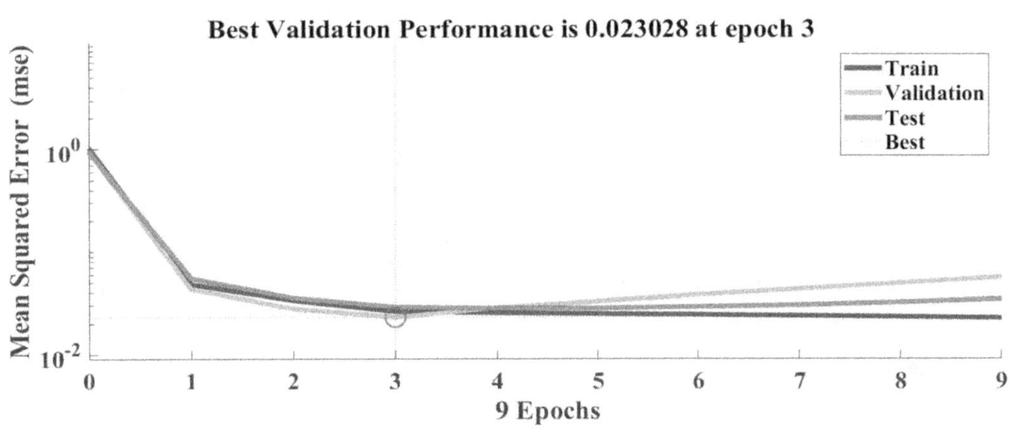

The radiation pattern is plotted to determine the far-field radiation properties of an antenna. The 2D radiation pattern of the designed antenna at θ = 0°, 30°, 60°, and 90° are shown in Figure 14. These patterns also demonstrate the co and cross-polar components in x-z and y-z planes. The observed front to back ratio at all the four rotation angles is greater than 19 dB. From the figure, it is noticed that patterns are almost similar. Thus, the designed MS based antenna successfully reconfigures the resonant frequency while maintaining the polarization and radiation pattern characteristics constant.

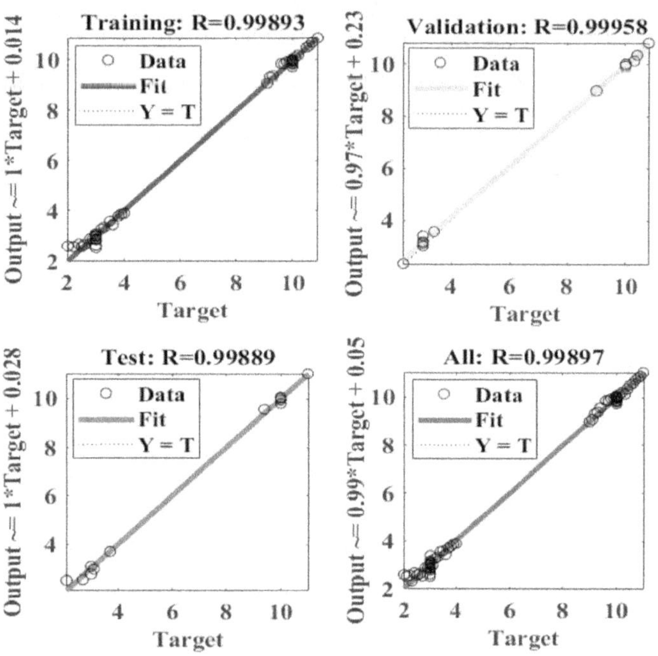

FIGURE 19 Scatter plot comparing the target value and ANN output for training, validation, testing, and overall output during synthesis

5.2 | ANN results

For the training of the ANN model, 40 samples are created by varying the dimensions of the unit cell employed in the MS. For analysis purpose, the input parameters are 'a' and 'b', and the output parameters are 'f' and "rl". For synthesis purpose, the input parameters are 'f' and 'rl', and the output parameters are 'a' and 'b'. The Levenberg-Marquardt based ANN model is used for achieving the desired degree of accuracy and to estimate the output parameters. The transfer function employed in the hidden layer and output layer is tansig and purelin, respectively. The performance of the model is analyzed in terms of three important statistical parameters such as mean squared error (MSE), number of epochs taken, and maximum absolute error. The evaluated performance characteristics during the analysis of the designed antenna are described in Table 4. The average of squared differences between the ANN outputs and the HFSS outputs is called a mean squared error (MSE). The smaller the value of MSE, the better are the results. Performance plot LM based ANN model is shown in Figure 15. From the graph, it is examined that the best validation performance occurs at 0.065099 at epoch 3.

Regression (R) is a statistical measure that evaluates the degree of correlation between the target value and network outputs. Its value should be close to 1, which specifies good modal performance. The R plot for training, validation, and testing during the analysis phase is shown below in Figure 16. It is analyzed from the plot that the total R value obtained during analysis is 0.999.

TABLE 7 Absolute error estimation during the synthesis of the designed antenna

	Outputs		HFSS outputs		ANN outputs		Absolute error	
S. No.	f	rl	a	b	a	b	a	b
1	4.8695	−22.9529	10	3	9.972	3.029	0.027	−0.029
2	4.8133	−24.5694	10.2	3	10.197	2.983	0.002	0.016
3	4.8133	−22.1812	10	3.8	9.961	3.792	0.038	0.007
4	4.8775	−23.7685	10	2.9	9.998	2.878	0.001	0.021
5	4.9096	−23.1008	10	2.7	9.950	2.555	0.049	0.144
6	5.0141	−22.4235	10	2	9.730	2.603	0.269	0.603
7	4.6847	−24.8617	10.7	3	10.717	2.980	−0.017	0.019
8	4.8855	−23.402	9.9	3	9.954	2.894	−0.054	0.105
9	5.0221	−22.2771	9.4	3	9.569	2.788	−0.169	0.211
10	5.1506	−21.8183	9	3	8.987	3.175	0.012	−0.175
Average absolute error							0.015	0.092

Abbreviation: HFSS, high frequency structure simulator.

Table 5 shows the results of absolute error estimation during the analysis of the designed antenna. In this table, a random set of 10 samples is presented. Based on these input samples, outputs are taken and the absolute error value is evaluated. The average absolute error estimated corresponding to resonant frequency is 0.011 and return loss is 0.148. Absolute error estimations corresponding to the output parameters are plotted in Figure 17.

The evaluated performance characteristics of the network model during the synthesis are described in Table 6. The performance plot for LM based ANN model during synthesis is shown in Figure 18. In this plot, the best validation performance is examined at 0.023028 at epoch 3.

The R plot for training, validation, and testing during the synthesis phase is shown below in Figure 19. It is analyzed from the plot that the total R value obtained during synthesis is 0.998. Table 7 shows the results of absolute error estimation during the synthesis of the designed antenna. The average estimated absolute error corresponding to 'a' is 0.015 and 'b' is 0.092. For synthesis, the absolute error estimations vs number of samples are plotted in Figure 20.

The overall performance of the designed frequency reconfigurable antenna in comparison to other existing antennas is summarized in Table 8. From the comparison results, it is examined that the proposed design shows significant improvements in terms of area, tunable range, bandwidth, efficiency, and front to back ratio. The outputs parameters are estimated through the artificial neural network approach. Hence, it is confirmed that the antenna is well suited for wireless applications.

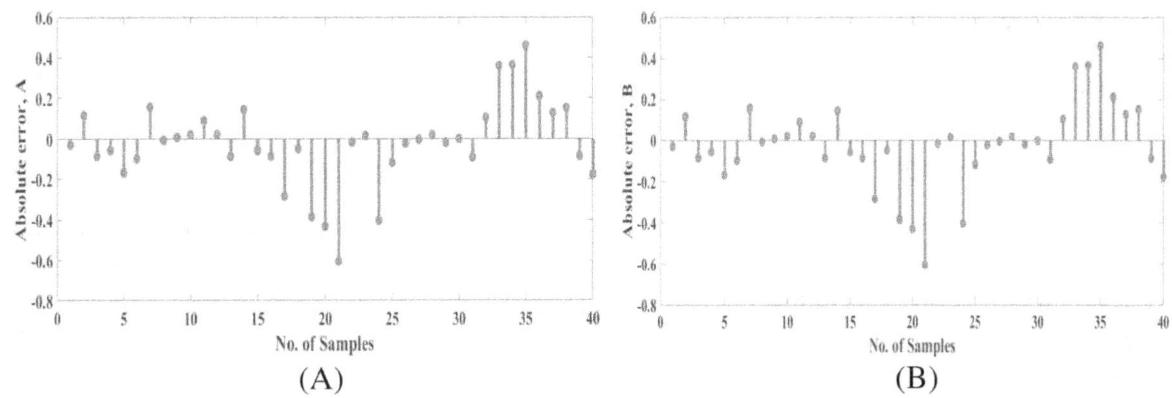

FIGURE 20 Absolute error during synthesis for estimating A, dimension 'a', B, dimension 'b'

TABLE 8 Comparison of proposed work with existing designs

	11	21	24	25	**Proposed work**
Diameter	40 mm	50 mm	—	50 mm	36 mm
Operating freq	5 GHz	3 GHz	—	—	5.4 GHz
Antenna	patch	slot	patch	slot	patch
Metasurface	Rectangular loop unit cells	Rectangular loop unit cells	Rectangular loop unit cells	Ellipse type and wire type unit cells	HI-SR unit cells
Tuning range	4.76-5.51 GHz	2.64-3.5 GHz	4-4.35	3.97-4.74 GHz and 3.84-4.55 GHz (ellipse) and 3.82-4.87 GHz (wire)	4.86-5.89 GHz
Bandwidth	750 MHz	860 MHz	350 MHz	—	1.03 GHz
Fractional Tuning range	14%	28%	8.4%	21.1%, 18.9% (ellipse) and 24.2% (wire)	19.1%
Efficiency	> 80%	> 85%	—	—	> 90%
Front to back ratio	> 15 dB	—	—	—	> 19 dB
Gain	5 dBi	—	5 dBi	—	Around 5 dB
Technique used	—	—	—	Radially homogenous model	ANN approach

6 | CONCLUSION

In this paper, ANN based MS inspired two-layered frequency reconfigurable antenna using planar technology is developed and experimentally analyzed. The periodical array of H-I shaped resonator unit cells representing MS is loaded on the top of the superstrate that helps in achieving the desired tuning range. The numerically analyzed results demonstrate the DNG properties of metamaterial in the 4.0-5.04 GHz frequency range. Measured results verify that by mechanically changing the position of MS with reference to the stationary patch antenna, a wide tuning range of 19.1% and bandwidth around 1.03 GHz is achieved. The developed ANN model effectively proves its suitability for the estimation of desired output parameters.

ACKNOWLEDGEMENT

The authors would like to thank Rogers Corporation for providing support material for fabricating the antenna prototype and the National Institute of Technical Teachers Training and Research (NITTTR), Chandigarh and IIT Delhi for providing the facility to test the fabricated prototype.

DATA AVAILABILITY STATEMENT

Data sharing is not applicable to this article as no new data were created or analyzed in this study.

ORCID

Navneet Kaur https://orcid.org/0000-0001-6192-2306

REFERENCES

1. Ullah S, Hayat S, Umar A, Ali U, Tahir FA, Flint JA. Design, fabrication and measurement of triple band frequency reconfigurable antennas for portable wireless applications. *Int J Electron Commun*. 2017;81:236-242.
2. Madi MA, Husseini MA, Ramadan AH, Kabalan KY, Hajj AE. A reconfigurable cedar-shaped microstrip antenna for wireless applications. *Progress Electromag Res*. 2012;25:209-221.
3. Li PK, Shao ZH, Wang Q, Cheng YJ. Frequency and pattern reconfigurable antenna for multistandard wireless applications. *IEEE Antennas Wireless Propag Lett*. 2015;14:333-336.
4. Nazir I, Rana IE, Mir NA, Afreen K. Design and analysis of a frequency reconfigurable microstrip patch antenna switching between four frequency bands. *Progress Electromag Res C*. 2016;68:179-191.
5. Dwivedy B, Behera SK, Singh V. A versatile triangular patch Array for wideband frequency alteration with concurrent circular polarization and pattern Reconfigurability. *IEEE Transac Antennas Propag*. 2018;67(3).
6. Ahmad A, Arshad F, Naqvi SI, Amin Y, Tenhunen H, Loo J. Flexible and compact spiral-shaped frequency reconfigurable antenna for wireless applications. *IETE J Res*. 2018;66(1):22-29.
7. Selvam YP, Alsath MGN, Kanagasabai M, et al. A patch-slot antenna Array with compound reconfiguration. *IEEE Antennas Wireless Propag Lett*. 2018;17(3):525-528.
8. Bernhard JT. *Reconfigurable Antennas*. San Rafael: Morgan & Claypool Publishers; 2007.
9. Haupt RL, Lanagan M. Reconfigurable Antennas. *IEEE Antennas Propag Mag*. 2013;55(1):49-61.
10. Ramli N, Ali MT, Yusof AL, Kayat M, Alias H. Aperture-coupled frequency-reconfigurable stacked patch microstrip antenna (FRSPMA) integrated with PIN diode switch. *Progress Electromag Res C*. 2013;39:237-254.
11. Zhu HL, Liu XH, Cheung SW, Yuk TI. Frequency-reconfigurable antenna using metasurface. *IEEE Transac Antennas Propag*. 2014;62(1):80-85.
12. Zhu HL, Cheung SW, Liu XH, Yuk TI. Design of Polarization Reconfigurable Antenna Using Metasurface. *IEEE Transac Antennas Propag*. 2014;62(6):2891-2898.
13. Sabah C. Tunable metamaterial design composed of triangular Split ring resonator and wire strip for S and C microwave bands. *Prog Electromag Res B*. 2010;22:341-357.
14. Sharma V, Patnaik SS, Garg T, Devi S. A microstrip metamaterial split ring resonator. *Int J Phys Sci*. 2011;6(4):660-663.
15. Benosman H, Hacene NB. Design and simulation of double "S" shaped metamaterial. *Int J Comput Sci Issue (IJCSI)*. 2012;9(2):534-537.
16. Lv JH, Hu XW, Liu MH, Yan BR, Kong LH. Negative refraction of a double L-shaped metamaterial. *J Opt A: Pure Appl Opt*. 2009;11(8).
17. Sharma V, Patnaik SS, Nitin TG, Devi S. A metamaterials inspired miniaturized phi-shaped antenna. *Int J Phys Sci*. 2011;6(18):4378-4381.
18. Chen X, Gao J, Kang B. Achieving a tunable metasurface based on a structurally reconfigurable array using SMA. *Opt Express*. 2018;26(4):4300-4308.
19. Holloway CL, Kuester EF, Gordon JA, Hara JO, Booth J, Smith DR. An overview of theory and applications of metasurfaces: the two dimensional equivalents of metamaterials. *IEEE Antennas Propag Mag*. 2012;54(2):10-35.
20. Chung KL, Chaimool S. Diamagnetic metasurfaces for performance enhancement of microstrip patch antennas. *Proc 5th Eur Conf Antennas Propag (EUCAP)*. 2011;48-52.
21. Zhu HL, Cheung SW, Yuk TI. Frequency reconfigurable slot antenna with wide-tuning range using metasurface. *Microwave Opt Technol Lett*. 2015;57(6):1475-1481.
22. Pavan MN, Chattoraj N. Design and analysis of a frequency reconfigurable antenna using metasurface for wireless applications. *IEEE Sponsored 2nd Int Conf Innov Info Embedded Commun sys (ICIIECS)*. 2015.
23. Majumder B, Krishnamoorthy K, Mukherjee J, Ray KP. Frequency reconfigurable slot antenna enabled by thin anisotropic double layer metasurface. *IEEE Transac Antennas Propag*. 2016;64(4):1218-1225.
24. Chen XF, Zhao YJ. Dual-band polarization and frequency reconfigurable antenna using double layer Metasurface. *Int J Electron Commun*. 2018;95:82-87.
25. Li H, Man X, Qi J. Accurate and robust characterization of Metasurface-enabled frequency reconfigurable antennas by radially homogeneous model. *IEEE Access*. 2019;7:122605-122612.

26. Sivia JS, Pharwaha APS, Kamal TS. Analysis and design of circular fractal antenna using artificial neural networks. *Prog Electromag Res B*. 2013;56:251-267.
27. Veselago VG. The electrodynamics of substances with simultaneously negative values of ε and μ. *Soviet Physics Uspekhi*. 1968;10(4).
28. Bilotti F, Sevgi L. Metamaterials: definitions, properties, applications, and FDTD-based modeling and simulation. *Int J RF Microwave Comput-Aid Eng*. 2012;22(4):422-438.
29. Rajni R, Marwaha A. Electrically small microstrip patch antenna loaded with spiral resonator for wireless applications. *Wireless Person Commun*. 2017;96(2):2621-2632.
30. Sethi A, Rajni. Determination of electromagnetic parameters of a new Metasurface comprising of square loop. *J Eng Sci Technol*. 2018;13(1):48-57.
31. Rajni, Marwaha A. CSC-SR structure loaded electrically small planar antenna. *Appl Comput Electromag Soc J*. 2016;31(5):591-598.
32. Rajni, Marwaha A. Resonance characteristics and effective parameters of new left hand metamaterial. *TELKOMNIKA Indonesian J Electric Eng*. 2015;15(3):497-503.
33. Kaur M, Sivia JS. ANN and FA based Design of Hybrid Fractal Antenna for ISM band applications. *Prog Electromag Res C*. 2020;98:127-140.
34. Kaur M, Sivia JS. ANN-based Design of Hybrid Fractal Antenna for biomedical applications. *Int J Electron*. 2019;106(8):1184-1199.
35. Kaur M, Sivia JS. Minkowski, Giuseppe Peano and Koch curves based Design of Compact Hybrid Fractal Antenna for biomedical applications using ANN and PSO. *Int J Electron Commun*. 2019;99:14-24.
36. Kaur M, Sivia JS. Giuseppe Peano and cantor set fractals based miniaturized hybrid fractal antenna for biomedical applications using artificial neural network and firefly algorithm. *Int J RF Microwave Comput-Aid Eng*. 2019;30(1):1-11.

AUTHOR BIOGRAPHIES

Ms. Navneet Kaur, received his Bachelor's Degree (B. Tech.) in Electronics and Instrumentation Engineering from Punjab Technical University, Jalandhar and Master's Degree (M. Tech.) in Electronics and Communication Engineering from Punjabi University Patiala, Punjab, India in 2005 and 2007, respectively. She is currently working towards the Ph.D. degree in Electronics and Communication Engineering (ECED) from Punjabi University Patiala, Punjab, India. She has published more than 10 research papers in several International Journals, International and National conferences. Her current research interests include microstrip antennas, artificial neural networks, and reconfigurable antennas in wireless communication systems.

Dr. Jagtar Singh Sivia born in Bathinda, Punjab in 1976. He has received his B. Tech degree from Punjab Technical University, Jalandhar, Punjab in Electrical and Electronics Communication Engineering in 1999 and he had obtained his master degree from Punjab Technical University, Jalandher in 2005. He had received his PhD degree from Sant Longowal Institute of Engineering and Technology, Longowal, Punjab. Currently, He is a professor in Electronics and Communication Section at Yadavindra College of Engineering, Off-Campus of Punjabi University, Patiala, Punjab, India. He has published more than 60 papers in several International Journals and International and National Conferences. His main interests are in Neural Networks, Electromagnetic Waves, Genetic Algorithms, Antenna System Engineering. Mr. Sivia is a member of Institution Engineers in India, Indian Society of Technical Education and International Association of Engineers.

Dr. Rajni is currently Professor at Shaheed Bhagat Singh State University (formerly known as Shaheed Bhagat Singh State Technical Campus) Ferozepur, India. She has done her B. Tech. from National Institute of Technology (formerly known as Regional Engineering College) Kurukshetra and M.E. from National Institute of Technical Teacher Training and Research (NITTTR), Chandigarh. She did her Ph.D. in Metamaterial Antennas from Sant Longowal Institute of Engineering and Technology, Longowal (SLIET), Sangrur, Punjab. She has approximately 23 years of academic experience. She has authored a number of research papers in International journals, National and International conferences. Her research interests include wireless communications and antenna design.

How to cite this article: Kaur N, Sivia JS, Rajni. Artificial neural network based metasurface inspired planar frequency reconfigurable antenna for wireless applications. *Int J RF Microw Comput Aided Eng*. 2021;31:e22793. https://doi.org/10.1002/mmce.22793

International Journal of Microwave and Wireless Technologies

cambridge.org/mrf

Research Paper

Cite this article: Kaur N, Sivia JS, Rajni (2022). Design of frequency reconfigurable planar antenna using artificial neural network. *International Journal of Microwave and Wireless Technologies* **14**, 1107–1118. https://doi.org/10.1017/S1759078721001434

Received: 15 May 2021
Revised: 11 September 2021
Accepted: 18 September 2021
First published online: 14 October 2021

Keywords:
Artificial electromagnetic materials; artificial neural network; metamaterial; metasurface superstrate; reconfigurable antenna; *S*-parameters; wireless communications

Author for correspondence:
Navneet Kaur,
E-mail: navsandhu31696@gmail.com

Design of frequency reconfigurable planar antenna using artificial neural network

Navneet Kaur[1], Jagtar Singh Sivia[2] and Rajni[3]

[1]Department of Electronics and Communication Engineering, Punjabi University, Patiala, Punjab, India; [2]YCoE, Punjabi University Guru Kashi Campus, Talwandi Sabo, Bathinda, Punjab, India and [3]Shaheed Bhagat Singh State Technical Campus, Ferozepur, Punjab, India

Abstract

In this paper, the design of frequency reconfigurable planar antenna by incorporation of metasurface superstrate (FRPA-MSS) is presented using an artificial neural network. The dual-layer radiating structure is created on a 1.524 mm thick Rogers RO4350B substrate board ($\epsilon_r = 3.48$, tan $\delta = 0.0037$). The candidate antenna is designed and analyzed using a high-frequency structure simulator (HFSS) tool. The transfer matrix method is employed for the successful retrieval of electromagnetic properties of the metamaterial. Frequency reconfiguration is achieved by placing the metasurface superstrate onto the rectangular patch antenna. A simplified ANN approach has been employed for the design of metasurface incorporated proposed antenna. Presented prototypes are characterized through experimental measurements. It is found from the practical observations that the proposed antenna effectively reconfigures the tuning range from 5.03 to 6.13 GHz. Moreover, the presented antenna operates efficiently with agreeable gain, good impedance matching, and stable pattern characteristics across the entire operational bandwidth. The experimental results obtained validate the simulated performance.

Introduction

In the present scenario, reconfigurable antennas have grabbed huge attention from the research community due to their ability to integrate multiple standards into a single platform [1]. Therefore, the wireless systems are empowered with reconfigurable antennas to enhance the overall performance and providing cost-effective solutions [2]. The important characteristics that are to be considered while designing these antennas are operating frequency, polarization, and radiation pattern [3]. Modern-day wireless communication systems such as mobile phones, laptops, watches, tablets, etc. support several wireless standards. To fulfill such requirements, multiband, wideband and frequency reconfigurable antennas are the probable choices. Frequency reconfigurable or tunable antennas act as the best alternative by opening up new horizons, thereby providing additional functionality levels [4]. These antennas can change their operating frequency while maintaining stable polarization and radiation pattern modes over the entire frequency range [5]. This feature is accomplished by redistributing the surface current within the radiating element by employing positive intrinsic negative (PIN) diode [6], varactor diode [7], radio frequency micro-electro-mechanical system (RF-MEMS) switches [8], multi-reed switches [9], and optical element [10]. Numerous reconfigurable antennas have been demonstrated based on different switching techniques. In [11], the spiral-shaped flexible and compact frequency reconfigurable antenna is implemented for wireless applications. Ouyang *et al.* [12] proposed a microstrip patch antenna with an electronically steerable parasitic array radiator. With the employment of switches and biasing networks, the non-linear effects and insertion loss increase, that in turn, degrades the performance of an antenna.

Over the previous decades, artificial materials have garnered prodigious attention in designing smart antenna structures with improved performance parameters [13]. The origination of metamaterial reveals an outstanding achievement in comparison to conventional materials. This idea first came into existence in 1967 [14]. After that, the concept of metamaterial has been explored widely to provide a wide tuning range, thus offering a promising solution to various research-oriented problems. The remarkable electromagnetic properties of metamaterial such as negative refractive index, permittivity, and permeability values, anti-parallel phase and group velocities, etc. are responsible for designing fascinating antenna structures with superior characteristics [15]. Ramachandran *et al.* [16] proposed a left-handed metamaterial design for satellite applications constructed using a combination of circular and square ring structures. Though the three-dimensional metamaterial is a young field and has achieved blooming technological advancements in several research areas such as microwaves and infrared regions yet they lack paucity in realizing lossless optical metamaterials. Thus to provide easy fabrication, two-dimensional metasurfaces have emerged out as a multifaceted branch

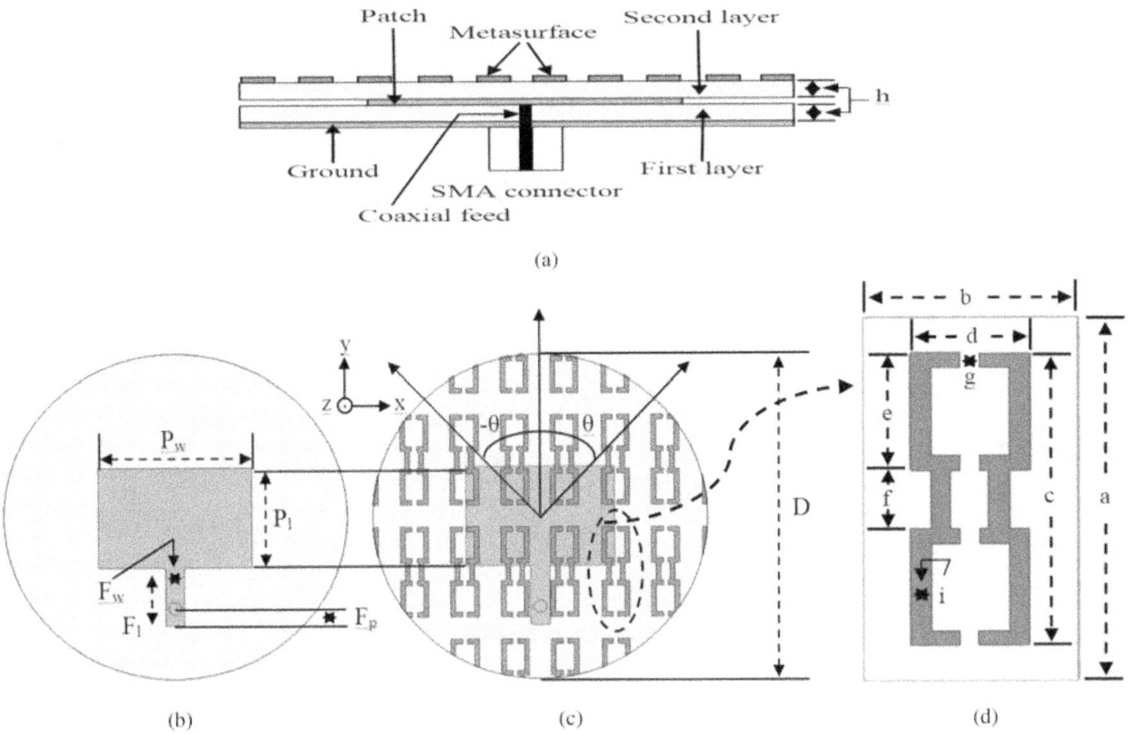

Fig. 1. Design schematic of FRPA-MSS (a) dual-layer module (b) patch antenna (c) metasurface, and (d) zoomed version of a unit cell.

Table 1. FRPA-MSS design specifications.

Parameters	D	h	P_l	P_w	F_l	F_w	F_p	a	b	c	d	e	f	g	i
Values (mm)	36	1.524	11	16	6.5	2	2	12.4	5.4	10	3	4	2	0.5	0.5

of engineering science in the last decade [17]. The surface variant of metamaterial is portrayed as metasurface which means a surface distribution of small apertures or holes [18]. Metasurfaces (MS) are uniformly arranged, two-dimensional planar periodic structure that is analogous to three-dimensional metamaterials [19]. A metasurface-based planar frequency reconfigurable antenna is designed with a fractional tuning range of 14.6% [20]. The frequency reconfigurable slot antenna is demonstrated using a single-layer metasurface [21]. Majumder *et al.* [22] proposed a frequency reconfigurable antenna by loading two metasurface layers onto the slot antenna. Frequency and polarization reconfigurable antenna is designed using polarization conversion metasurface [23]. Metasurface enabled mechanically frequency reconfigurable antenna by an equivalent radially homogenous model is demonstrated by Li *et al.* [24]. Singh *et al.* demonstrated the designing and analysis of circular fractal antenna using artificial neural networks (ANNs) [25]. Kaur *et al.* presented metasurface incorporated frequency reconfigurable antenna and used ANN approach to develop antenna [26, 27].

By thoroughly reviewing the aforementioned literature, the design of frequency reconfigurable planar antenna is presented using an ANN with enhanced performance characteristics. First, the designing process of a metasurface incorporated dual-layer frequency reconfigurable antenna is illustrated. Then the specific characteristics of metamaterial are analyzed. Afterwards, the ANN framework is illustrated. Followed by this, the results are discussed. In the end, the conclusion is presented.

Designing process of frequency reconfigurable antenna

The proposed work utilizes a dual-layer approach for implementing the frequency reconfigurable antenna. The schematic of the design is illustrated in Fig. 1. The dual-layer module is composed of two substrate layers as shown in Fig. 1(a). The rectangular-shaped patch antenna and circular ground plane are imprinted on the upper and lower side of the first layer, respectively. The periodical array of compounded double split-ring resonator (CDSRR) shaped unit cells forming the metasurface is printed on the upper side of the second layer. This module uses a flexible Rogers RO4350B substrate with a dielectric constant (ε_r) of 3.48 and loss tangent ($\tan \delta$) of 0.0037. A fixed thickness of 1.524 mm has opted for both layers, thus the total thickness is 3.048 mm. For the excitation purpose, a 2 mm wide feedline is used that provides a characteristic impedance of 50 Ω. The antenna is fed directly using coaxial feed and the SubMiniaturized version A (SMA) connector is used for connecting purposes. The overall dimensions of the structure are $D \times 2(h)$ mm^2. For proper matching conditions, both the layers are taken in circular form. The angle θ, the orientation angle of the metasurface, is measured with respect to the y-axis in a clockwise and anticlockwise direction and the maximum orientation angle is 90°. The schematic of the patch antenna and metasurface is demonstrated in Figs 1(b) and 1(c), respectively. The zoomed version of the unit cell is represented in Fig. 1(d). The optimized parametric design specifications of the proposed antenna are listed in Table 1.

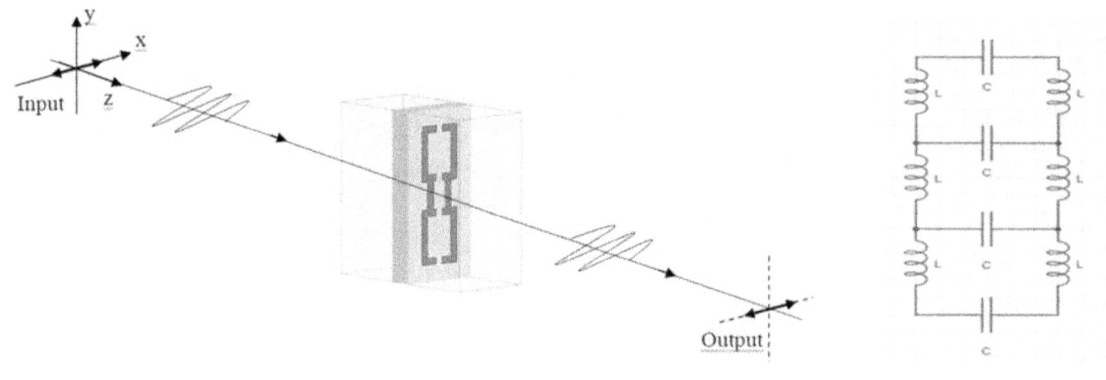

Fig. 2. Analysis of CDSRR (a) waveguide medium for extracting the *S*-parameters and (b) equivalent circuit of the unit cell.

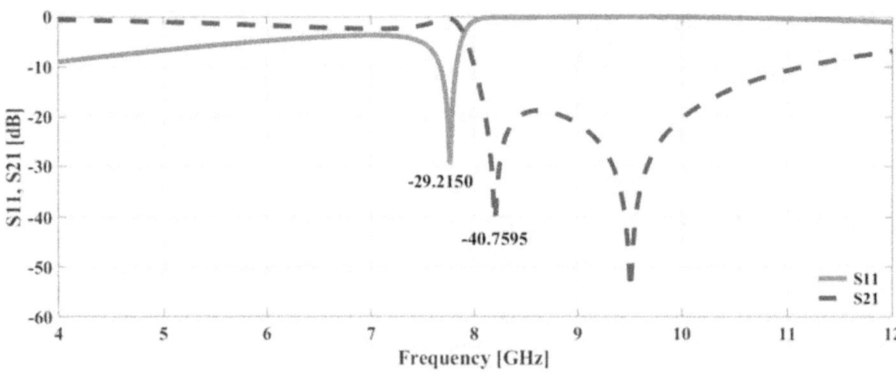

Fig. 3. Extracted *S*11 and *S*21 of the proposed unit cell structure.

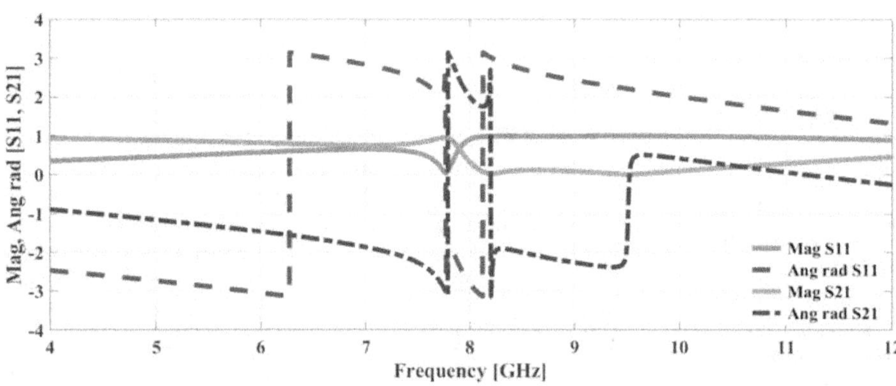

Fig. 4. Magnitude and phase characteristics of *S*11 and *S*21.

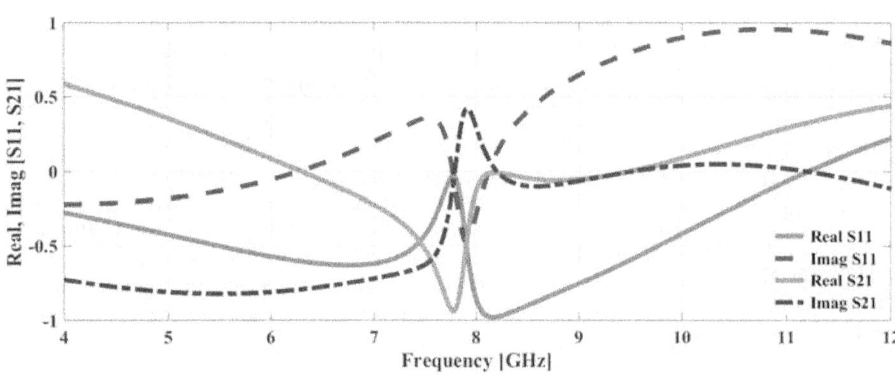

Fig. 5. Real and imaginary parts of *S*11 and *S*21.

https://doi.org/10.1017/S1759078721001434 Published online by Cambridge University Press

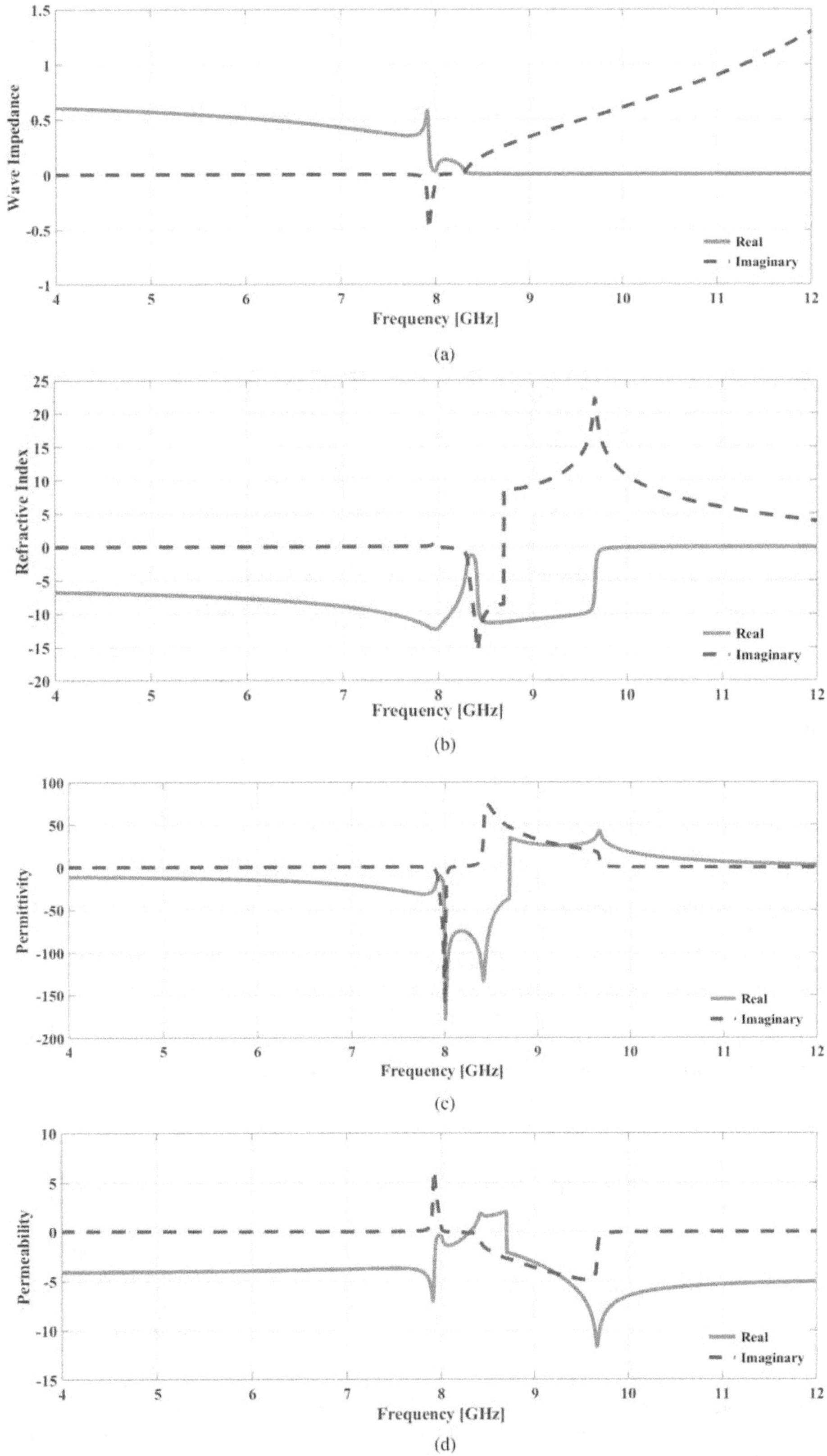

Fig. 6. Effective values of homogenous parameters (a) wave impedance (b) refractive index (c) permittivity, and (d) permeability.

Analysis of metamaterial

The effective electromagnetic parameters (permittivity ε_{eff}/permeability μ_{eff}/refractive index n_{eff}) of the unit cell structure are extracted by utilizing the scattering parameters. For this, the whole setup is placed inside the waveguide environment with ports, electric field, and magnetic field applied along the respective axis [28–31]. This waveguide medium is shown in Fig. 2(a). The structure functions like an LC resonator with a gap and

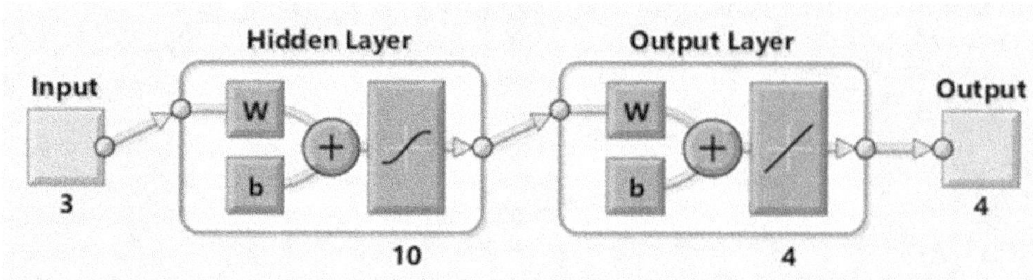

Fig. 7. Proposed FFBPN model.

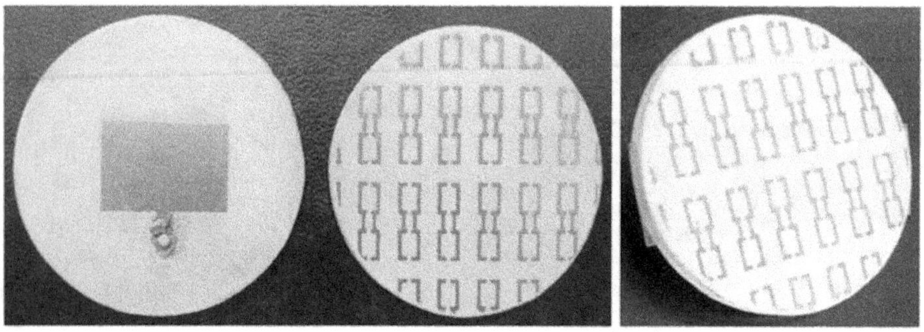

(a) (b)

Fig. 8. Photographic view of the fabricated antenna using RO4350B substrate (a) patch antenna and metasurface and (b) FRPA-MSS.

metal strip corresponds to capacitive and inductive elements, respectively. The LC equivalent circuit of the unit cell is depicted in Fig. 2(b).

Figure 3 shows the extracted reflection ($S11$) and transmission ($S21$) coefficient of the unit cell structure. It is evaluated that a strong reflection of −29.2 dB is observed at 7.7 GHz. This frequency points to the coexistence of electric and magnetic resonances [32]. The first transmission minimum is −40.7 dB at 8.2 GHz. The magnitude and phase characteristics of the reflection and transmission coefficient are delineated in Fig. 4. From these results, the phase reversal property of metamaterial is demonstrated. The real and imaginary parts of the reflection and transmission coefficient are described in Fig. 5. Further, results are imported to Matrix Laboratory (MATLAB) for determining the electromagnetic properties of metamaterial.

$$z = \sqrt{\frac{(1 + S11)^2 - S21^2}{(1 - S11)^2 - S21^2}} \tag{1}$$

$$n = \frac{1}{kd} \cos^{-1}\left[\frac{1}{2S21}(1 - S11^2 + S21^2)\right] \tag{2}$$

Different techniques have been employed so far for extracting the notable properties of metamaterial. Nicolson Ross Weir (NRW) and the transfer matrix method are popular as they are based on two-port analysis [33]. In this work, the transfer matrix method is employed as this is a direct method for determining the wave impedance. The wave impedance and refractive index are determined using (1) and (2), respectively. Here, z and n symbolize the wave impedance and refractive index, respectively. The literal k and d represent the wave number of the incident wave and thickness of the dielectric slab, respectively. The permittivity and permeability values can be attained using (3) and (4).

Table 2. Performance evaluation of ANN analysis.

	Samples	MSE	Regression
Training	26	2.76710×10^{-4}	9.99979×10^{-1}
Validation	5	6.27304×10^{-4}	9.99952×10^{-1}
Testing	5	1.95663×10^{-4}	$9.99984e \times 10^{-1}$

$$\varepsilon = \frac{n}{z} \tag{3}$$

$$\mu = nz \tag{4}$$

The material characteristics of the metamaterial are determined from the negative parts of permeability and permittivity. Thus, reflection and transmission are the integral parts of the said method. Figure 6 illustrates the effective values of homogenous parameters in the desired frequency range. The bold red line represents the real part and the dashed blue line indicates the imaginary part of the associated parameter. The positive real value of wave impedance exists from 4 to 8.5 GHz range. Similarly, the negative real value exhibited by permittivity exists in 4−8.47 GHz and permeability in 4−8.2 GHz and 8.46−12 GHz. The permittivity and permeability values show electric and magnetic plasma frequencies. The refractive index shows its negative real value in between the electric and magnetic plasma frequencies. The successful retrieval of results in the 4–8.2 GHz frequency range confirms that the aforementioned structure exhibits left-handed properties of metamaterial. This in turn shows the effectiveness of the designed approach.

The analysis of the mathematical model of an equivalent circuit of CDSRR [34] is determined using (5)–(9). The equations

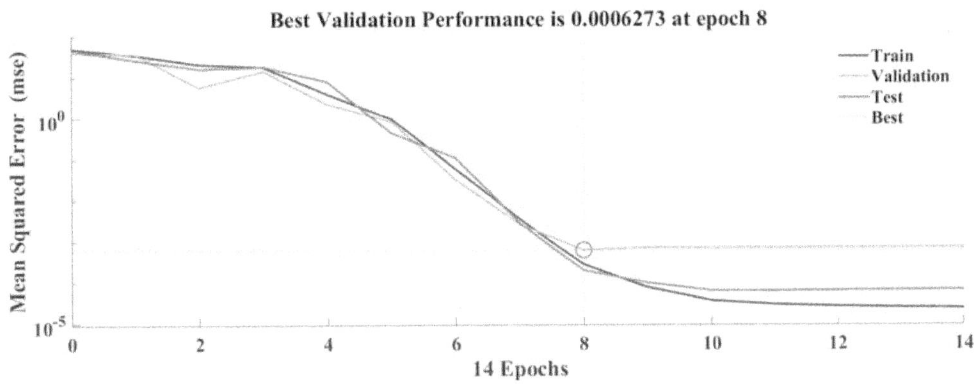

Fig. 9. Performance plot for analyzing the designed antenna.

have been modified as a single ring has been considered in the proposed design.

$$L^{CDSRR} = \frac{\mu_0}{2}\frac{l_{avg}^{CDSRR}}{4}\left[\ln\left(\frac{l_{avg}^{CDSRR}}{i}\right) - 2\right] \quad (5)$$

$$l_{avg}^{CDSRR} = 4l - 4g \quad (6)$$

$$C^{CDSRR} = 2\varepsilon_0\varepsilon_r^{sub}\frac{2i + g\sqrt{2}}{\pi}\operatorname{arccosh}\left[\frac{2i + g}{g}\right] \quad (7)$$

$$\varepsilon_r^{sub} = 1 + \frac{2}{\pi}\operatorname{arctg}\left[\frac{h}{2\pi i}\right](\varepsilon_r - 1) \quad (8)$$

$$f = \frac{1}{2\pi\sqrt{L^{CDSRR}C^{CDSRR}}} \quad (9)$$

where, L^{CDSRR} and C^{CDSRR} are the inductance and capacitance of the equivalent circuit, respectively. μ_0 and ε_0 are the absolute permeability and permittivity, respectively. l_{avg}^{CDSRR} and ε_r^{sub} are the average length of the unit cell and relative permittivity of the substrate. ϵ_r, and f represent the relative permittivity of material, and the analytical frequency, respectively. From the equations, it is evaluated that the analytical results show a frequency of 7.9 GHz that matches nearly its full wave simulated results.

Artificial neural network

It is imperative to design the metasurface unit cell precisely as the metallic loop represents inductance L, and the gap between them represents capacitance C, which in turn decides the resonating frequency of the unit cell. Thus the resonance can be controlled by changing the geometry of the structure. Therefore, an ANN has been developed for the analysis of metasurface and incorporated in antenna for reconfiguration.

ANN is a powerful data computational tool that analyzes and processes information in a similar way the human brain does. It also plays a crucial role in the designing and analysis of an antenna [35, 36]. The basic unit that acts as the building block of the neural network is an artificial neuron. The feed-forward back propagation network (FFBPN) is made up of many interconnected neurons that are organized in three layers: input, hidden, and output layer [37]. The information flows from the input layer to the output layer after progressing through one or more hidden layers. Each neuron is connected to other neurons via direct communication links with an individual weight connected to each link. The difference between the desired output and network output generates an error signal. Thus, ANN can adapt, learn and recollect the information just like a biological neural network [38]. The proposed FFBPN model is elucidated in Fig. 7. This model is constructed using three input layer neurons, four output layer neurons, and 10 hidden layer neurons. The unit cell dimensions and orientation angle of a frequency reconfigurable planar antenna by incorporation of metasurface superstrate (FRPA-MSS) are considered as inputs and their resonant frequencies are considered as output. To evaluate this process, a data set consisting of 36 samples is created through parametric analysis. From this total, the training set contains 26 samples, five samples in the validation set, and five samples in the testing set.

Results and discussion

The finite element method (FEM)-based 3D full-wave HFSS support tool is deployed for simulating the antenna prototype. The photographic view of the fabricated prototype is shown in Fig. 8. Anritsu MS2028C vector network analyzer (VNA) is used for evaluating the experimental results.

ANN results

A data set containing 36 samples is created by changing the basic dimensions of unit cell and the value of rotation angle for training the ANN model. For this purpose, the input parameters considered are "c", "d", and "θ", and output parameters are "f_{r1}", "f_{r2}", "f_{r3}", and "f_{r4}". The desired degree of accuracy is achieved using the Levenberg–Marquardt algorithm. The training function employed is trainlm. Tansig and purelin are the transfer functions used in the hidden and output layers, respectively. The output of the model is evaluated using three main statistical parameters mean squared error (MSE), number of epochs used, and maximum absolute error. The performance evaluation for analyzing the designed antenna is described in Table 2. The performance plot for analyzing the designed antenna is illustrated in Fig. 9. It is noticed in plot that best validation performance takes place at 0.0006273 at epoch 8.

doi.org/10.1017/S1759078721001434 Published online by Cambridge University Press

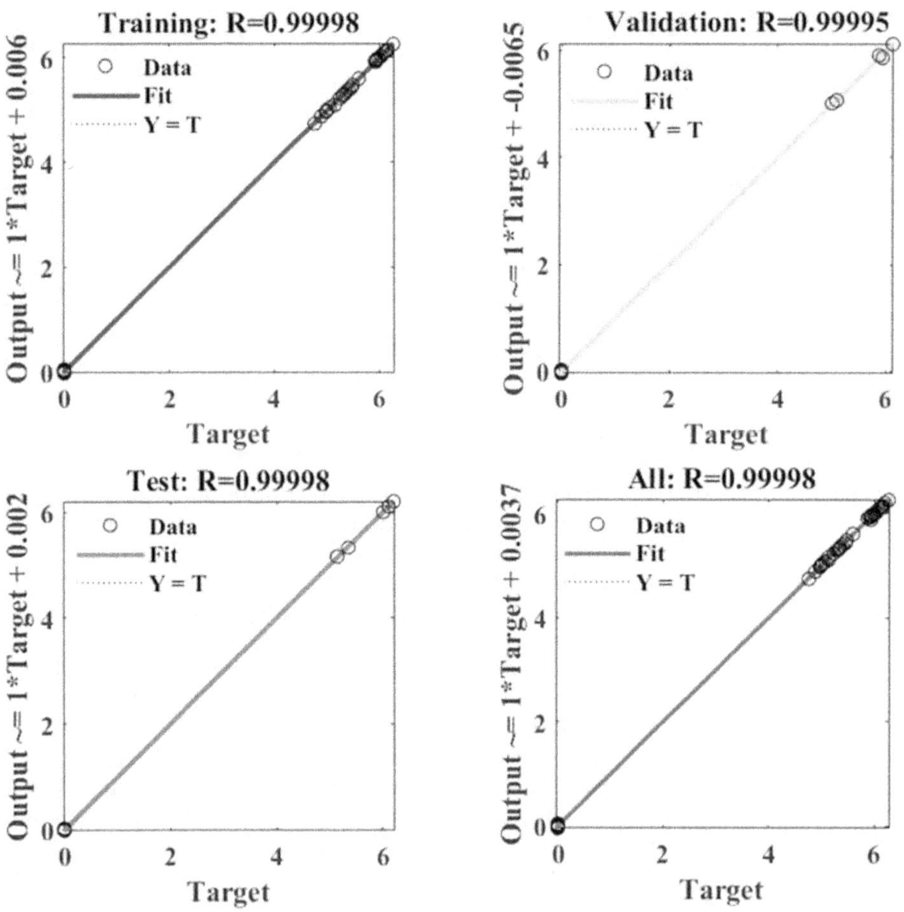

Fig. 10. Regression plot for analyzing the performance of the designed antenna.

Table 3. Absolute error estimation for the analysis of the designed antenna.

Inputs			HFSS outputs				ANN outputs				Absolute error			
c	d	θ	f_{r1}	f_{r2}	f_{r3}	f_{r4}	f_{r1}	f_{r2}	f_{r3}	f_{r4}	f_{r1}	f_{r2}	f_{r3}	f_{r4}
10	2	0	5.086	0	0	0	5.072	−0.003	0.025	−0.014	0.013	0.003	−0.025	0.014
10	3.5	0	4.990	0	0	0	4.991	−0.008	0.008	0.011	−0.001	0.008	−0.008	−0.011
9.5	3	0	5.134	0	0	0	5.152	−0.005	0.008	−0.010	−0.017	0.005	−0.008	0.010
10.5	3	0	4.885	0	0	0	4.882	−0.009	0.017	0.020	0.003	0.009	−0.017	−0.020
10	2.5	30	0	5.399	0	0	−0.009	5.383	−0.019	−0.021	0.009	0.016	0.019	0.021
10	3.5	30	0	5.343	0	0	−0.006	5.323	−0.023	−0.016	0.006	0.019	0.023	0.016
9	3	30	0	5.600	0	0	0.012	5.598	−0.005	0.0006	−0.012	0.001	0.005	−0.000
11	3	30	0	5.142	0	0	0.012	5.101	−0.034	−0.009	−0.012	0.041	0.034	0.009
10	2	60	0	0	6.002	0	−0.001	−0.003	6.002	−0.0001	0.001	0.003	−0.000	0.000
10	3	60	0	0	5.945	0	−0.005	−0.022	5.972	0.008	0.005	0.022	−0.026	−0.008
9	3	60	0	0	6.106	0	0.007	−0.006	6.114	0.014	−0.007	0.006	−0.007	−0.014
10.5	3	60	0	0	5.873	0	−0.017	−0.025	5.909	0.009	0.017	0.025	−0.036	−0.009
10	3.5	90	0	0	0	6.106	−0.017	−0.010	−0.026	6.105	0.017	0.010	0.026	0.000
10	4	90	0	0	0	6.074	−0.012	−0.004	−0.026	6.079	0.012	0.004	0.026	−0.005
9.5	3	90	0	0	0	6.202	−0.008	−0.009	−0.028	6.202	0.008	0.009	0.028	0.000
11	3	90	0	0	0	5.929	−0.003	−0.010	−0.050	5.920	0.003	0.010	0.050	0.009
Average absolute error											0.045	0.191	0.084	0.012

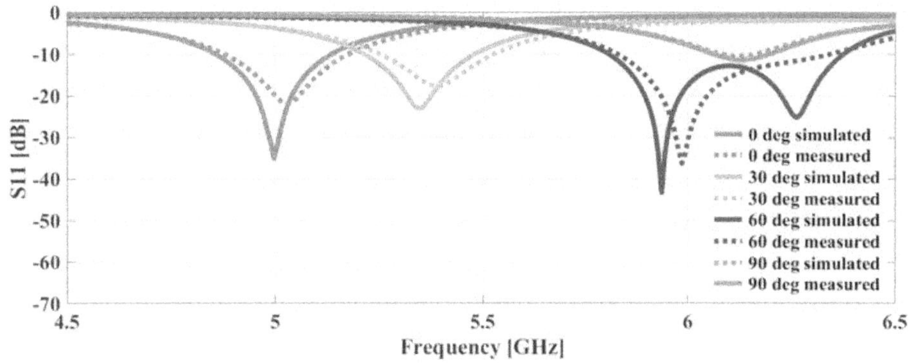

Fig. 11. Simulated (solid line) and measured (dotted line) *S*11 of the designed antenna.

Table 4. Summarized results of the designed antenna.

	Simulated		Measured	
Orientation angle	Resonant frequency (GHz)	Return loss	Resonant frequency (GHz)	Return loss
0°	4.99	−35.1748	5.03	−21.9950
30°	5.35	−23.0528	5.39	−17.7132
60°	5.93	−43.3927	5.98	−36.3314
90°	6.12	−10.5187	6.13	−11.4674

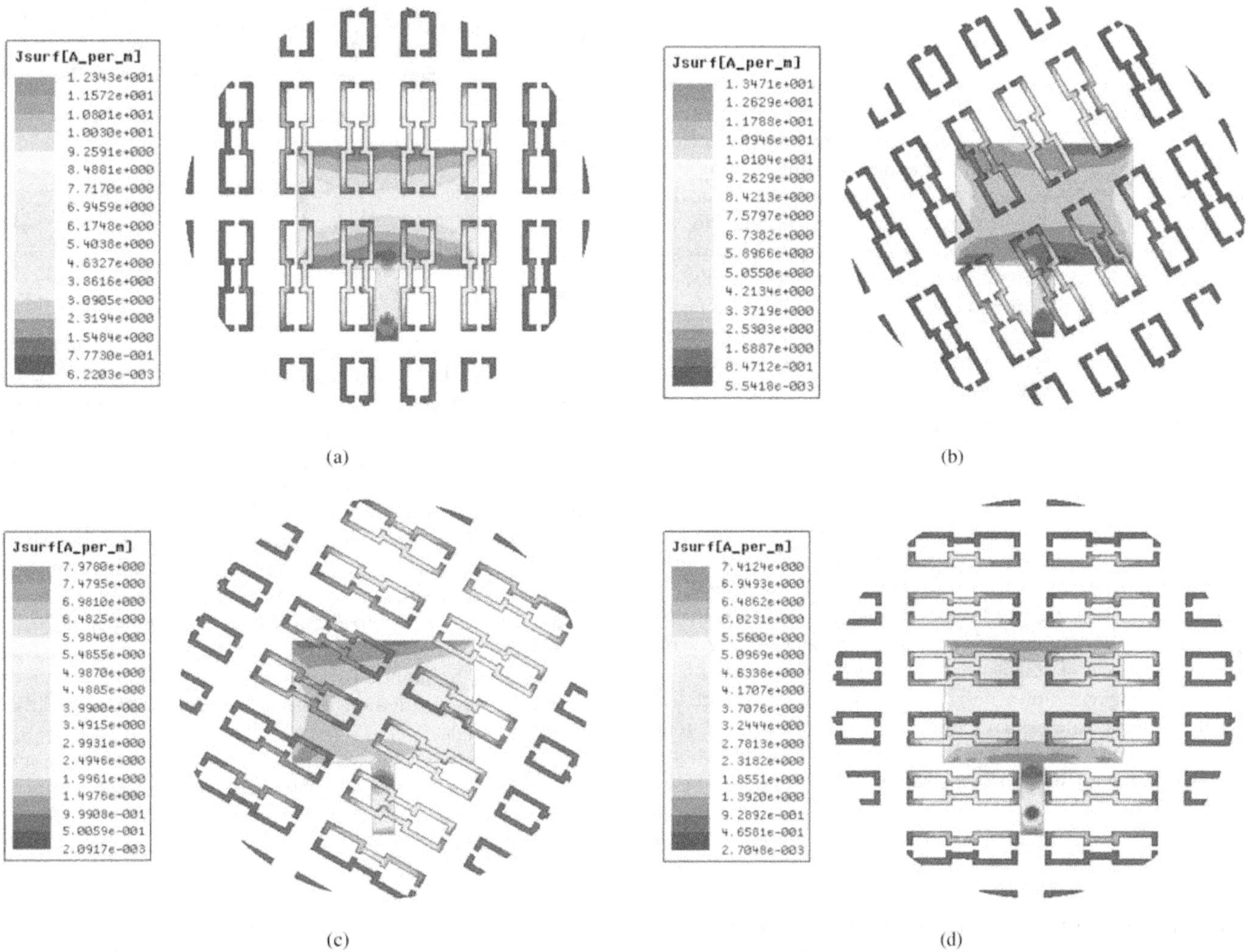

Fig. 12. Surface current distribution obtained at orientation angles (a) 0° (b) 30° (c) 60°, and (d) 90°.

/doi.org/10.1017/S1759078721001434 Published online by Cambridge University Press

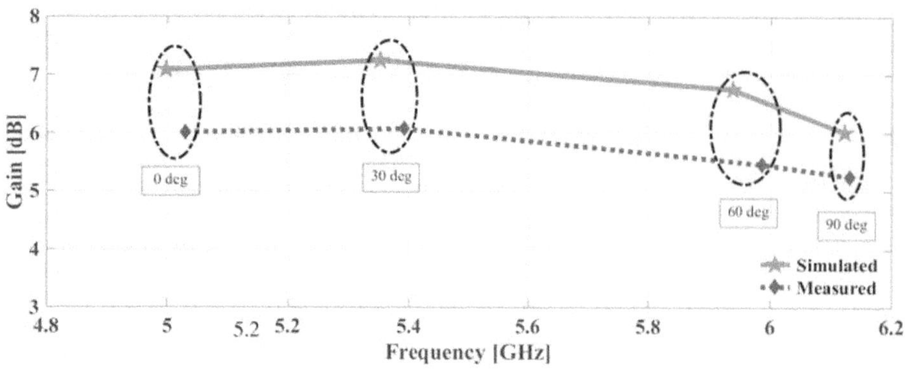

Fig. 13. Simulated and measured gain at different orientation angles.

Regression analysis is a statistical measure for examining and comprehending the relationship between target and output values. Its value should be close to 1 for getting a good performance results. The regression plot showing the performance analysis during training, validation, and testing is shown in Fig. 10. The total regression value of 0.99998 is obtained. The absolute error estimation for analyzing the designed antenna is shown in Table 3. It contains 16 samples that are randomly selected from the generated data set. The average absolute error estimated for f_{r1}, f_{r2}, f_{r3}, and f_{r4} are 0.045, 0.191, 0.084, and 0.012, respectively.

Reflection coefficient

The simulated and measured values of S11 of the designed antenna are illustrated in Fig. 11. Both the results are in good accord. It is anticipated from Fig. 11 that by rotating the metasurface from 0° toward 30°, 60°, and 90° with reference to the stationary patch antenna, the resonant frequency continuously shifts up from 4.99 to 5.35, 5.93, and 6.12 GHz, respectively. The best match occurs at an orientation angle corresponding to 60°. After further rotation of the metasurface, the matching decays. Thus, the metasurface plays an integral role in achieving the frequency reconfiguration property. Table 4 shows the summarized results of the proposed antenna with respect to different orientation angles. Slight disagreement is there between the simulated and measured results. This dissimilarity is basically due to the soldering bumps, fabrication, and measurement tolerances.

Current distribution

The surface current distribution at different orientation angles is depicted in Fig. 12. It has been elucidated from these figures that the current distribution is intensively concentrated near the center of the metasurface and edges of the patch at 0° orientation angle. At 30° orientation angle, the distribution is strong across the right-portion of metasurface and left/right edge of the patch. More current flows near the extreme right part of both metasurface and patch corresponding to 60° orientation angle. In the case of 90° orientation angle, the current distribution is intensively accumulated along the center of the metasurface and edges of the patch.

Gain

Gain is an important performance parameter that describes how efficiently information is to be sent or received by an antenna in a particular direction [39]. The simulated and measured gain obtained at orientation angles corresponding to 0, 30, 60, and 90° [20] is presented in Fig. 13.

Fig. 14. Designed antenna in an anechoic chamber.

Radiation pattern

Figure 14 shows the designed antenna placed in an anechoic chamber. The 2D simulated and measured radiation characteristics of an antenna analyzed at resonant frequencies corresponding to different orientation angles are shown in Fig. 15. These patterns are defined for both the principal planes ($\varphi = 0°$ and $\varphi = 90°$). At $\varphi = 0°$, the pattern exhibited by the antenna is bidirectional and $\varphi = 90°$, the radiation pattern obtained is omnidirectional in shape. The radiation pattern plots indicate that the co-polarization observed along the y-axis radiates highly as compared to the cross-polarization that is observed along the x-axis. The value of the front-to-back ratio examined is also more than 20 dB at all orientation angles. Thus, the metasurface only reconfigures the operating frequency of an antenna without much affecting the shape of the radiation pattern and polarization at different orientation angles.

Table 5 compares the performance parameters of the proposed work with other existing frequency reconfigurable antennas. It is apparent from Table 5 that the proposed antenna achieves 19, 88.2, 48.16, and 48.16% reduction in size as compared to [20], [21], [41] and [25], respectively. On considering the bandwidth, it is observed that 50.66 and 169% hike as compared to [20] and [40], respectively. The comparative tuning range of the proposed antenna with other research in Table 5 indicates a 6.3 1.3, 6.3% rise in tuning range as compared to recent research in

https://doi.org/10.1017/S1759078721001434 Published online by Cambridge University Press

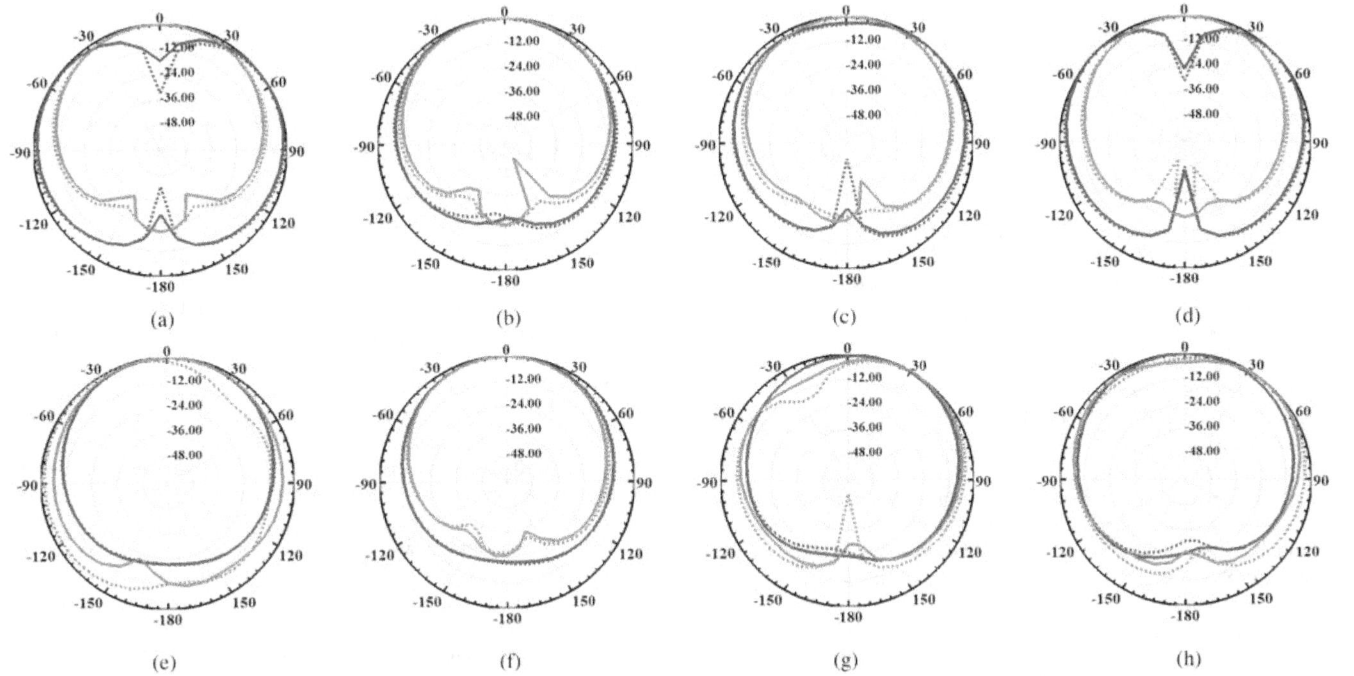

Fig. 15. Simulated (solid line) and measured (dotdot line) radiation pattern of FRPA-MSS at orientation angles (a) 0° (b) 30° (c) 60° (d) 90° in *x–z* plane and in *y–z* plane (e) 0° (f) 30° (g) 60° (h) 90°.

Table 5. Comparison of proposed work with other existing frequency reconfigurable antennas.

	[20]	[21]	[40]	[24]	Proposed work
Size	40 mm	105 mm × 105 mm	50 mm	50 mm	36 mm
Electrical size	0.67λ	0.735λ × 0.735λ	0.5λ	–	0.66λ
Operating frequency	5 GHz	–	3 GHz	–	5.55 GHz
Antenna	Patch	Slot	Slot	Slot	Patch
Metasurface	Rectangular loop unit cells	Meandered unit cells	Rectangular loop unit cells	Ellipse type and wire type unit cells	CDSRR unit cells
Tuning range	4.76–5.51 GHz	1.9–2.3 GHz	2.78–3.2 GHz	3.97–4.74 GHz and 3.84–4.55 GHz (ellipse) and 3.82–4.87 GHz (wire)	4.99–6.12 GHz
Bandwidth	750 MHz	–	420 MHz	–	1.13 GHz
Fractional tuning range	14%	19%	14%	21.1%, 18.9% (ellipse) and 24.2% (wire)	20.3%
Gain	5 dBi	5 dBi	4.8 dBi	–	> 6 dB
Technique used	–	–	–	Radially homogenous model	ANN

[20], [21], and [40], respectively. It can be examined from the comparison that the proposed antenna possesses smaller dimensions with acceptable gain, wide bandwidth, and tuning range at all orientation angles.

Conclusion

In this paper, the design of FRPA-MSS using the ANN has been proposed and investigated. The compounded double split ring-shaped resonator unit cells arranged periodically forming the metasurface are mounted atop the superstrate layer for accomplishing the desired tuning range. By mechanically tuning the metasurface with respect to the reference patch antenna, frequency reconfiguration is achieved within the 4.99–6.12 GHz tuning range. A good correlation is seen between the measured results and simulated predictions. Also, the proposed antenna owns wide bandwidth and acceptable gain at all orientation angles. The developed ANN model demonstrates its utility for the prediction of resonant frequencies at different orientation angles.

Acknowledgement. The authors would like to thank Rogers Corporation for providing support material for fabricating the antenna prototype and the

National Institute of Technical Teachers Training and Research (NITTTR), Chandigarh, and the Indian Institute of Technology (IIT), New Delhi for providing the facility to test the fabricated prototype.

References

1. **Chandra KV, Satyanarayana M and Battula KT** (2019) A novel miniature hexagonal shape switched pattern and frequency reconfigurable antenna. *International Journal of Communication Systems* **33**(5), 1–8.
2. **Dwivedy B, Behera SK and Singh V** (2018) A versatile triangular patch array for wideband frequency alteration with concurrent circular polarization and pattern reconfigurability. *IEEE Transactions on Antennas and Propagation* **67**(3), 1640–1649.
3. **Zhu HL, Cheung SW and Yuk TI** (2015) Mechanically pattern reconfigurable antenna using metasurface. *IET Microwaves, Antennas & Propagation* **9**(12), 1331–1336.
4. **Yashchyshyn Y** (2010) Reconfigurable antennas: the state of the Art. *INTL Journal of Electronics and Telecommunications* **56**(3), 319–326.
5. **Iqbal A, Smida A, Abdulrazak LF, Saraereh OA, Mallat NK, Elfergani I and Kim S** (2019) Low-profile frequency reconfigurable antenna for heterogeneous wireless systems. *Electronics* **8**(9), 1–11.
6. **Lim MC, Rahim SKA, Hamid MR, Eteng AA and Jamlos MF** (2017) Frequency reconfigurable antenna for WLAN application. *Microwave and Optical Technology Letters* **59**(1), 171–176.
7. **Kehn MNM, Quevedo-Reruel O and Rajo-Iglesias E** (2011) Reconfigurable loaded planar inverted-f antenna using varactor diodes. *IEEE Antennas and Propagation Letters* **10**, 466–468.
8. **Zhang C, Yang S, Pan HK, Fathy AE, Ghazaly SE and Nair VK** (2009) A reconfigurable multiband patch antenna for wireless applications using MEMS switches. *Microwave and Optical Technology Letters* **51**(8), 1892–1896.
9. **Liu Q, Wang N, Wu C, Wai G and Smolders AB** (2014) Frequency reconfigurable antenna controlled by multi-reed switches. *IEEE Antennas and Wireless Propagation Letters* **14**, 927–930.
10. **Pendharker S, Shevgaonkar RK and Chandorkar AN** (2014) Optically controlled frequency-reconfigurable microstrip antenna with low photoconductivity. *IEEE Antennas and Wireless Propagation Letters* **13**, 99–102.
11. **Ahmad A, Arshad F, Naqvi SI, Amin Y, Tenhunen H and Loo J** (2018) Flexible and compact spiral-shaped frequency reconfigurable antenna for wireless applications. *IETE Journal of Research* **66**(1), 22–29.
12. **Ouyang W, Vosoughi A and Gong X** (2019) A frequency-reconfigurable electronically-steerable parasitic array radiator using microstrip patch antennas. *Microwave and Optical Technology Letters* **62**(3), 1409–1422.
13. **Kim S, Kuester EF, Holloway CL, Scher AD and Jarvis JB** (2011) Boundary effects on the determination of metamaterial parameters from normal incidence reflection and transmission measurements. *IEEE Transactions on Antennas and Propagation* **59**(6), 2226–2240.
14. **Veselago VG** (1968) The electrodynamics of substances with simultaneously negative values of ϵ and μ. *Soviet Physics Uspekhi* **10**(4), 504–514.
15. **Ali T, Aw MS and Biradar RC** (2018) A fractal quad-band antenna loaded with L-shaped slot and metamaterial for wireless applications. *International Journal of Microwave and Wireless Technologies* **10**(7), 826–834.
16. **Ramachandran T, Faruque MRI and Islam MT** (2020) A dual band left-handed metamaterial enabled design for satellite applications. *Results in Physics* **16**, 1–8.
17. **Luo X** (2019) Metamaterials and metasurfaces. *Advanced Optical Materials* 7, 1900885.
18. **Haupt RL and Lanagan M** (2013) Reconfigurable antennas. *IEEE Antennas and Propagation Magazine* **55**(1), 49–61.
19. **Glybovski SB, Tretyakov SA, Belov PA, Kivshar YS and Simovski CR** (2016) Metasurfaces: from microwaves to visible. *Physics Reports* **634**, 1–72.
20. **Zhu HL, Liu XH, Cheung SW and Yuk TI** (2014) Frequency-reconfigurable antenna using metasurface. *IEEE Transactions on Antennas and Propagation* **62**(1), 80–85.
21. **Chatterjee J, Mohan A and Dixit V** (2018) A novel frequency reconfigurable slot antenna using metasurface. IEEE Indian Conference on Antennas and Propogation (InCAP) 16–19th Dec, 2018, Hyderabad, India.
22. **Majumder B, Krishnamoorthy K, Mukherjee J and Ray KP** (2016) Frequency reconfigurable slot antenna enabled by thin anisotropic double layer metasurface. *IEEE Transactions on Antennas and Propagation* **64**(4), 1218–1225.
23. **Ni C, Chen MS, Zhang ZX and Wu XL** (2018) Design of frequency-and-polarization-reconfigurable antenna based on the polarization conversion metasurface. *IEEE Antennas and Wireless Propagation Letters* **17**(1), 78–81.
24. **Li H, Man X and Qi J** (2019) Accurate and robust characterization of metasurface-enabled frequency reconfigurable antennas by radially homogeneous model. *IEEE Access* **7**, 122605–122612.
25. **Sivia JS, Pharwaha APS and Kamal TS** (2013) Analysis and design of circular fractal antenna using artificial neural networks. *Progress in Electromagnetics Research B* **56**, 251–267.
26. **Kaur N, Sivia and JS and Rajni** (2021) Metasurface incorporated frequency reconfigurable planar antenna for wireless applications. *Progress in Electromagnetics Research C* **113**, 265–275.
27. **Kaur N, Sivia and JS and Rajni** (2021) Artificial neural network based metasurface inspired planar frequency reconfigurable antenna for wireless applications. *International Journal of RF and Microwave Computer-Aided Journal* **31**(9), 1–13.
28. **Rajni and Marwaha A** (2015) Magnetic resonance in spiral resonators. *International Journal of Applied Engineering Research.* **10**(13), 33291–33295.
29. **Sharma N and Bhatia SS** (2019) Double split labyrinth resonator- based CPW-fed hybrid fractal antennas for PCS/UMTS/WLAN/Wi-MAX applications. *Journal of Electromagnetic Waves and Applications* **33**(18), 2476–2498.
30. **Rajni R and Marwaha A** (2013) Role of geometry of split ring resonators in magnetic resonance of metamaterials. *International Journal of Electronics and Communication Engineering & Technology* **4**(7), 279–285.
31. **Sethi A** and Rajni (2018) Determination of electromagnetic parameters of a new metasurface comprising of square loop. *Journal of Engineering Science and Technology* **13**(1), 048–057.
32. **Rajni and Marwaha A** (2015) Resonance characteristics and effective parameters of new left hand metamaterial. *Telkomnika Indonesian Journal of Electrical Engineering* **15**(3), 497–503.
33. **Varamini G, Keshtkar A, Daryasafar N and Moghadasi MN** (2018) Microstrip Sierpinski fractal carpet for slot antenna with metamaterial loads for dual-band wireless application. *International Journal of Electronics and Communications* **84**, 93–99.
34. **Bilotti F, Toscano A, Vegni L, Aydin K, Alici KB and Ozbay E** (2007) Equivalent-circuit models for the design of metamaterials based on artificial magnetic inclusions. *IEEE Transactions on Microwave Theory and Techniques* **55**(12), 2865–2873.
35. **Kaur M and Sivia JS** (2019) Giuseppe Peano and Cantor set fractals based miniaturized hybrid fractal antenna for biomedical applications using artificial neural network and firefly algorithm. *International Journal of RF and Microwave Computer-Aided Engineering* **30**(2), 1–11.
36. **Kaur M and Sivia JS** (2020) ANN and FA based design of hybrid fractal antenna for ISM band applications. *Progress in Electromagnetics Research C* **98**, 127–140.
37. **Kaur M and Sivia JS** (2019) ANN-based design of hybrid fractal antenna for biomedical applications. *International Journal of Electronics* **106**(8), 1184–1199.
38. **Kaur M and Sivia JS** (2019) Minkowski, Giuseppe Peano and Koch curves based design of compact hybrid fractal antenna for biomedical applications using ANN and PSO. *International Journal of Electronics and Communications* **99**, 14–24.
39. **Balanis CA** (2005) *Antenna Theory: Analysis and Design*. Hoboken, NJ: John Wiley & Sons.
40. **Zhu HL, Cheung SW, Liu XH, Cao YF and Yuk TI** (2005) Frequency reconfigurable slot antenna using metasurface. The 8th European Conference on Antennas and Propagation (EuCAP), April 2014, The Hague, Netherlands, pp. 2575–2577.

Ms. Navneet Kaur obtained his bachelor' (B.Tech.) in electronics and instrumentation engineering from Punjab Technical University, Jalandhar and master' (M.Tech.) in electronics and communication engineering from Punjabi University Patiala, Punjab, India in 2005 and 2007, respectively. She is currently working toward the Ph.D. degree in electronics and communication engineering (ECED) from Punjabi University Patiala, Punjab, India. She has published more than 10 research papers in several international journals, international and national conferences. Her current research interests include microstrip antennas, artificial neural networks, and reconfigurable antennas in wireless communication systems.

Dr. Jagtar Singh Sivia born in Bathinda, Punjab in 1976. He has obtained his B.Tech from Punjab Technical University, Jalandhar, Punjab in electrical and electronics communication engineering in 1999 and he had obtained his master's from Punjab Technical University, Jalandhar in 2005. He obtained his Ph.D. degree from Sant Longowal Institute of Engineeering and Technology, Longowal, Punjab. Currently, he is a professor in electronics and communication engineering at Yadavindra College of Engineering, Off-Campus of Punjabi University, Patiala, Punjab, India. He has published more than 60 papers in several international journals and international and national conferences. His main interests are in neural networks, electromagnetic waves, genetic algorithms, antenna system engineering. Mr. Sivia is a member of Institution of Engineers in India, Indian Society of Technical Education and International Association of Engineers.

Dr. Rajni is currently professor at Shaheed Bhagat Singh State University (formerly known as Shaheed Bhagat Singh State Technical Campus) Ferozepur, India. She has done her B.Tech. from National Institute of Technology (formerly known as Regional Engineering College) Kurukshetra and M.E. from National Institute of Technical Teacher Training and Research (NITTTR), Chandigarh. She did her Ph.D. in metamaterial antennas from Sant Longowal Institute of Engineering and Technology, Longowal (SLIET), Sangrur, Punjab. She has approximately 23 years of academic experience. She has authored more than 80 papers in international journals, national and international conferences. Her research interests include wireless communication, antenna design and signal processing.

Progress In Electromagnetics Research C, Vol. 113, 265–275, 2021

Metasurface Incorporated Frequency Reconfigurable Planar Antenna for Wireless Applications

Navneet Kaur[1, *], Jagtar S. Sivia[2], and Rajni[3]

Abstract—In this paper, the design of a Metasurface incorporated Frequency Reconfigurable Planar Antenna (MS-FRPA) for Wireless Applications is presented. The structure of the projected MS-FRPA consists of a patch with a metasurface placed one above the other with no gap between them. The MS is composed of an array of alternately placed dual split ring resonators arranged periodically in both horizontal and vertical directions. Frequency reconfiguration is achieved by rotating the MS relative to the designed patch antenna. The projected reconfigurable antenna is constructed on Rogers RO4350B material with thickness 1.524 mm. High Frequency Structure Simulator software is employed for analysis of the structure. The results clearly reveal that frequency tuning is achieved in 4.35 to 5.33 GHz with a fractional tuning range of 20.2%. The proposed structure provides appreciable realized gain with stable radiation patterns at all rotation angles. Further, the measured outcomes of the developed prototype show good correlation with the simulated outcomes.

1. INTRODUCTION

In the past few decades, a prodigious development has been observed in various systems such as radio-frequency and microwaves due to widespread multi-functionality of wireless communication devices [1–4]. The recent research mainly pays attention towards developing smart systems having potential to perform multiple operations in one device as compared to traditional single operational device [5–7] due to reduction of multipath fading, augmented channel properties, and being resistant to interrupting signals. All these characteristics prompt the development of reconfigurable antennas in present-day wireless communication systems. These antennas have the capacity to reconfigure the important characteristics like frequency, polarization, radiation pattern, and combination of two characteristics or all three [8]. Out of these, frequency reconfigurable antennas are widely preferred as they have the ability to resonate at multiple tuning frequencies [9]. A large number of frequency reconfigurable antennas have been designed and published so far by deploying the electrical methods using positive intrinsic negative (PIN) diodes, varactor diodes, and radiofrequency micromechanical systems (RF-MEMS) & mechanical tuning methods using actuator and large reflector antennas [10, 11]. However, they possess some drawbacks such as requirement of biasing lines and direct current (DC) electrical sources which in turn degrades their performance.

In recent years, to deal with the above discussed hitches, a few accomplishments are made in the exploration of reconfigurability using other means such as metamaterials. Metamaterials are synthetically designed material that displays some notable unnatural electromagnetic (EM) properties which have broadened its importance towards numerous significant applications in science, technology, and medicine. A two-dimensional equivalent of metamaterials is metasurface formed by periodically

Received 27 May 2021, Accepted 4 July 2021, Scheduled 9 July 2021

* Corresponding author: Navneet Kaur (navsandhu31696@gmail.com).

[1] Department of Electronics and Communication Engineering, Punjabi University, Patiala, Punjab, India. [2] YCoE, Punjabi University Guru Kashi Campus, Talwandi Sabo, Bathinda, Punjab, India. [3] Shaheed Bhagat Singh State Technical Campus, Ferozepur, Punjab, India.

arranging the array of electrically small scatterers or holes in the form of rings [12]. They occupy less Euclidean space and provide lossless structures in comparison to their 3-D counterparts. Several works have been reported in literature based on this. In [10], the performance of a metasurface based frequency reconfigurable antenna is analyzed by periodically arranging the rectangular loop unit cells atop the patch antenna. A similar idea is demonstrated in [13] to acknowledge a frequency tunable slot antenna with a bidirectional radiation pattern. A meandered unit cell structure based frequency tunable slot antenna is designed in [14]. Though wide tuning range is achieved, there exists a gap between the antenna and MS layer. A frequency reconfigurable antenna is demonstrated in [15] in which elliptical-shaped unit cells are utilized for designing. Frequency and polarization reconfigurability using double layer metasurface is demonstrated in [16]. Li et al. in [17] proposed an equivalent radially homogenous model for a metasurface enabled frequency slot reconfigurable antenna. Wire type unit cells were opted for designing the MS and to estimate the central frequencies with enhanced accuracy, simplicity, and robustness.

Keeping this in view, the aim of this paper is to design a metasurface incorporated frequency reconfigurable planar antenna for wireless applications. The manuscript is presented in five sections. Section 2 illustrates the topology of reconfigurable antenna along with its geometrical details. A metamaterial unit cell is analyzed for EM characteristics in Section 3. The performance results of projected MS-FRPA are elucidated in Section 4. The comparative performance of proposed antenna with other existing antennas is discussed in this section. The work is concluded in Section 5.

2. TOPOLOGY OF PROJECTED MS-FRPA

The layout of the projected MS-FRPA is demonstrated in Fig. 1. The structure of the projected MS-FRPA is designed using two substrate layers: one for patch antenna and the other for metasurface. On the top of lower substrate, a rectangle-shaped patch antenna is designed, and on its bottom, a circle-shaped ground plane is implemented using planar technology. The geometrical view of the patch antenna is demonstrated in Fig. 1(a). An array of unit cells of alternately placed dual split ring resonators (DSRRs) joined with thin wire represents the proposed MS. The whole arrangement is designed on the top of the upper substrate as illustrated in Fig. 1(b). In order to achieve frequency reconfigurability of an antenna, MS is rotated across its centre with reference to the designed patch antenna. The rotation angle θ_r is evaluated along the y-axis. The unit cells exhibit similarity in both horizontal and vertical directions. Therefore, it is noticed that $\theta_r = -\theta_r$, and its maximum value considered is 90°. During the manufacturing of the antenna structure, the radiating side of the lower substrate and non-radiating side of upper substrate are placed together. Between the two substrates there is no gap present thereby resulting in a compact structure. The side view of the two-layered MS-FRPA structure is shown in Fig. 1(c). For the implementation of designed structure, Rogers RO4350B material with dielectric constant (ε_r) of 3.48, loss tangent ($\tan\delta$) of 0.0037, and thickness (h) of 1.524 mm is selected for both the substrates. A SubMiniature version A (SMA) connector of 50 Ω impedance is chosen for proper impedance matching. The photographic view of fabricated prototype of the patch & metasurface and the pictorial view of MS-FRPA is illustrated in Fig. 1(d) and Fig. 1(e), respectively. Table 1 shows the optimized parameters of the projected reconfigurable antenna.

Table 1. Parametric description of MS-FRPA (units in mm).

D	L_p	W_p	P_e	s
39	16	12	2	2.4

3. ANALYSIS OF METAMATERIALISTIC BEHAVIOR

The simulation model of a 3 × 3 DSRR array is placed inside a waveguide medium with boundary conditions and excitations applied along respective faces. The boundary conditions: perfect electric

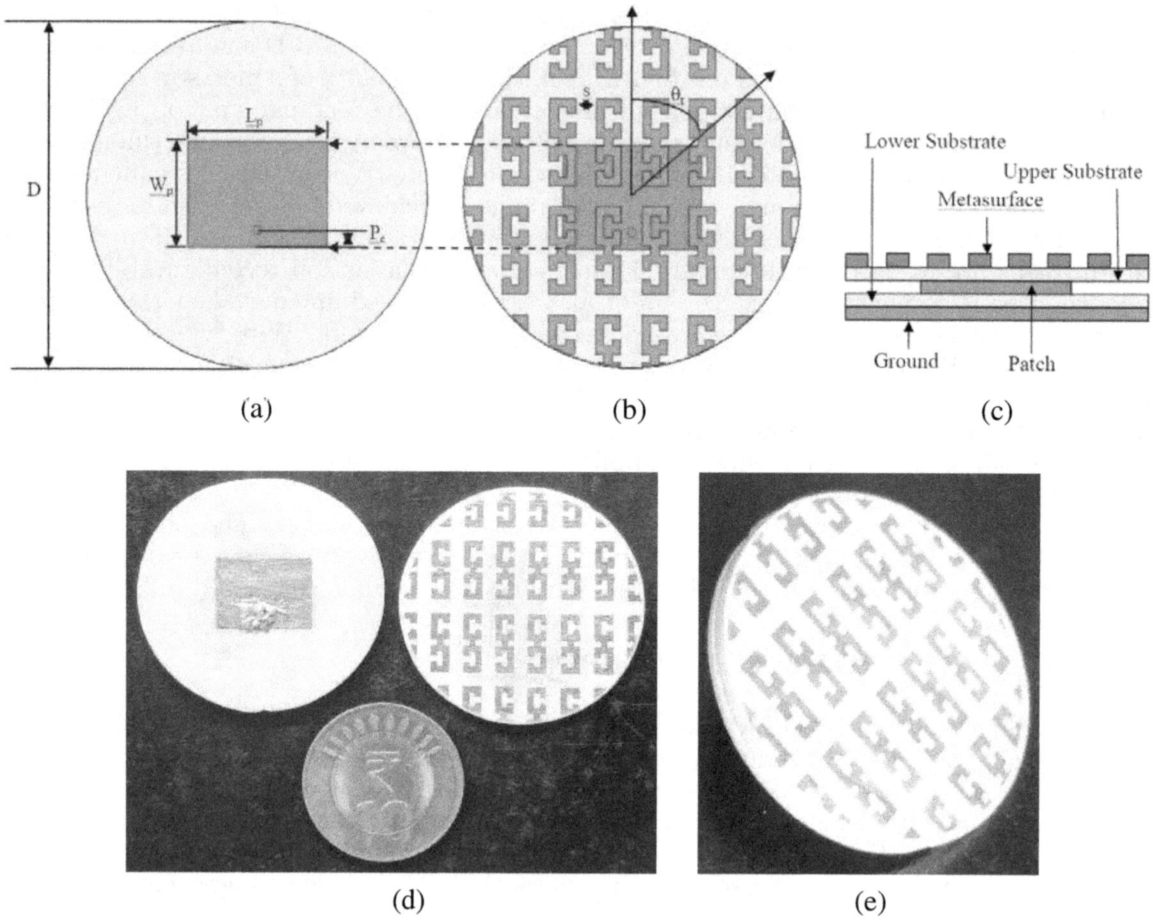

Figure 1. Geometrical structure of (a) patch antenna, (b) metasurface, (c) side view, (d) fabricated prototype of patch antenna and metasurface, (e) MS-FRPA.

conductor (PEC) and perfect magnetic conductor (PMC) boundary conditions are applied along the z- and y-faces of the unit cell. On the x-faces from $-x$ to $+x$ direction, the two wave ports 1 and 2 are allocated. Thus, a triad of E-H and k is created [18–20]. Ansys High Frequency Structure Simulator (HFSS) software is deployed for simulating the structure and to characterize the EM properties of the synthesized material. This behaviour is confirmed by examining the phase reversal characteristics of reflection coefficient (S_{11}) and transmission coefficient (S_{21}). The enlarged form of unit cell is shown in Fig. 2(a). The structure of SRR generally consists of two metallic rings with a gap in between. Whenever a current moves inside the coil, a magnetic dipole moment is generated. This dipole moment vector is perpendicular to the coil plane. Thus, the coil and capacitor generate an LC circuit with increased dipole moment at the resonance. Thus, the SRR works like an LC circuit with metallic ring and gap representing the inductor (L) and parallel plate capacitor (C), respectively [21, 22]. The LC equivalent circuit of the DSRR is depicted in Fig. 2(b). The geometrical description of DSRR unit cell is tabulated in Table 2.

Figure 3 specifies the transmission and reflection coefficients of the metamaterial structure with

Table 2. Parametric description of DSRR (units in mm).

U_a	U_b	a	b	c	d	e
12.4	5.4	10	3	4.5	1	1

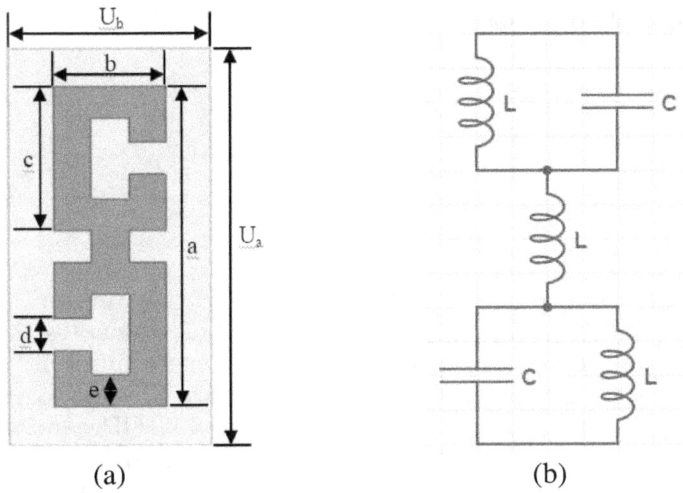

Figure 2. (a) Enlarged unit cell, (b) LC equivalent structure.

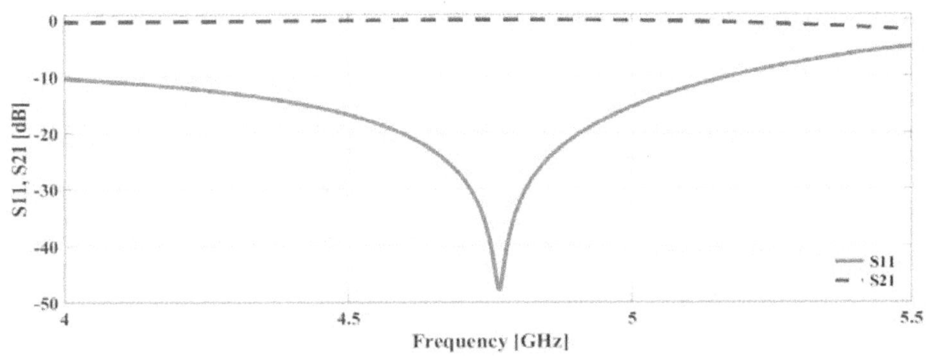

Figure 3. Reflection coefficient (S_{11}) and transmission coefficient (S_{21}) of the proposed structure.

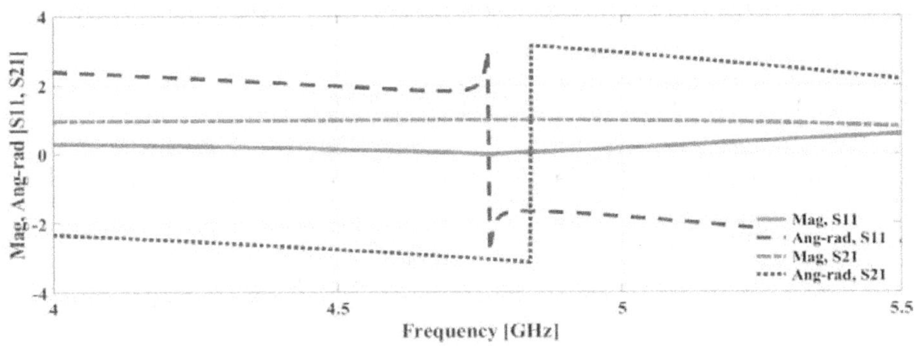

Figure 4. Magnitude and phase response of S_{11} and S_{21}.

respect to frequency. The structure reveals the maximum reflection at 47.67 dB below 0 dB. Figure 4 depicts the magnitude and phase angle plots of S_{11} and S_{21}. The magnitude curve and phase curve represent the group velocity and phase velocity, respectively. The phase reversal response at particular frequency indicates the metamaterial behaviour of the proposed structure [21]. The negative characteristics of permeability and permittivity are evaluated with the help of real and imaginary parts of S_{11} and S_{21}. Nicolson Ross Weir approach is implemented using Matrix Laboratory (MATLAB) for characterizing the values of effective parameters, i.e., permeability and permittivity with S_{11} and

S_{21} [18]. It is expressed mathematically with the help of following Eqs. (1) to (4)

$$V_1 = S_{21} + S_{11} \quad (1)$$

$$V_2 = S_{21} - S_{11} \quad (2)$$

$$\mu_r = \frac{2}{jk_o d}\frac{1 - V_2}{1 + V_2} \quad (3)$$

$$\varepsilon_r = \frac{2}{jk_o d}\frac{1 - V_1}{1 + V_1} \quad (4)$$

where V_1 and V_2 represent the composite terms that express the sum and difference of S_{11} and S_{21} of scattering parameters; k_o specifies the free space wave number; d denotes the thickness of substrate; μ_r and ε_r signify the effective permeability and permittivity of metamaterial.

The real and imaginary parts of effective parameters are illustrated in Fig. 5. The permeability and permittivity has negative frequency regions from 4.0 to 4.92 GHz and 4.0 to 4.81 GHz as shown in Fig. 5 and Table 3, respectively. The effective parameters are simultaneously negative between 4.0 and 4.81 GHz frequency range. The real value of refractive index is also negative in this frequency range. Thus, the proposed 3×3 array of DSRRs behaves as a left-handed medium where the real parts of both permittivity and permeability are negative.

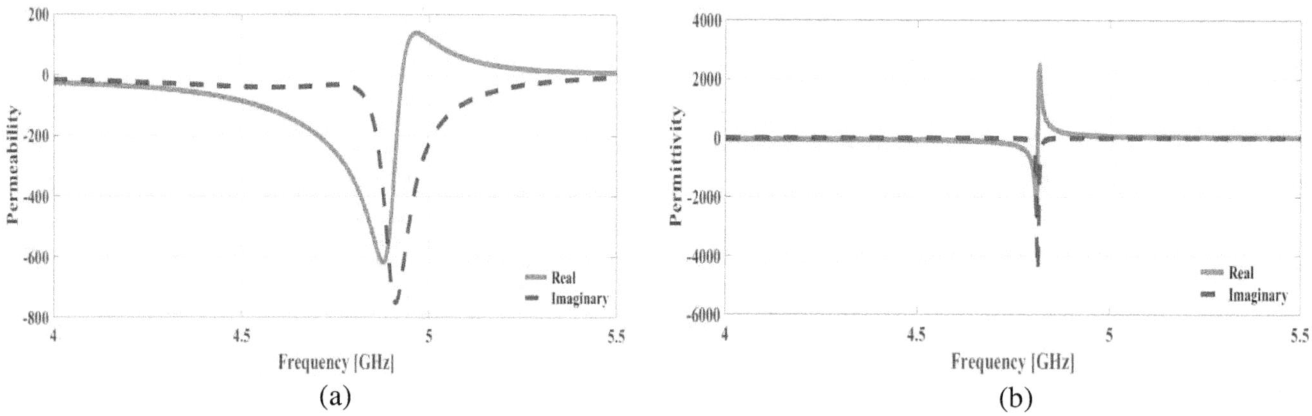

Figure 5. Real and imaginary parts of effective parameters (a) permeability, and (b) permittivity.

Table 3. Negative index frequency region of effective parameters.

Parameters	Negative index frequency region (in GHz)
Permeability (μ_r)	4.0–4.92
Permittivity (ε_r)	4.0–4.81

4. RESULTS AND DISCUSSION

The design and analysis of the projected antenna is done using full wave electromagnetic solver HFSS V15. The structure of fabricated prototype is tested using vector network analyzer (VNA) Anritsu MS46322A.

4.1. Projected DSRR Frequency Reconfiguration

The simulated and measured results of S_{11} presented in Fig. 6 reveal a noble trend over all frequencies. The resonant frequency increases continuously from 4.35 to 4.72, 5.09, and 5.33 GHz as the rotation

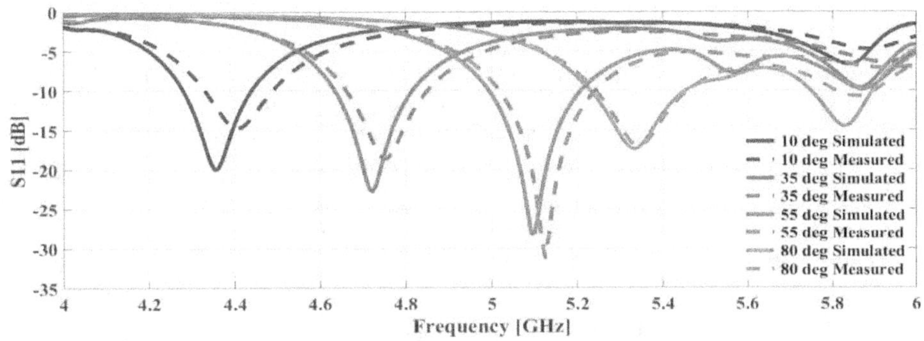

Figure 6. Simulated and measured S_{11} at different rotation angles.

angle changes its value from 10° to 35°, 55°, and 80°, respectively. The best matching condition occurs at 5.09 GHz that corresponds to 55° rotation angle. The resulting condition degrades as the rotation angle moves away from 55°. The simulated and measured results of reflection coefficient at various rotation angles are shown in Table 4. A reasonable agreement is seen between the simulated and experimentally observed values. Small discrepancies occur among these values and are mainly due to fabrication tolerances, cable effects, environmental conditions, and SMA connector losses.

Table 4. Simulated and measured results of reflection coefficient at different rotation angles.

Rotation angle	Simulated		Measured	
	Frequency (GHz)	Reflection coefficient	Frequency (GHz)	Reflection coefficient
10°	4.35	−19.9617	4.40	−14.7277
35°	4.72	−22.7394	4.75	−18.5627
55°	5.09	−28.1995	5.12	−31.1497
80°	5.33	−17.4077	5.34	−17.0907

The relation between rotation angle and resonant frequency can be analyzed from the graph when θ increases from 10° to 80°. The resonant frequency exhibits a linear relationship with the rotation angle. This relation can be approximated using linear regression analysis as shown in Fig. 7. The simulated and measured results display desirable agreements. Thus, as the rotation angle extends from 10° to 80°, the resonant frequency increases consistently from 4.35 to 5.33 GHz resulting in fractional tuning range of 20.2%.

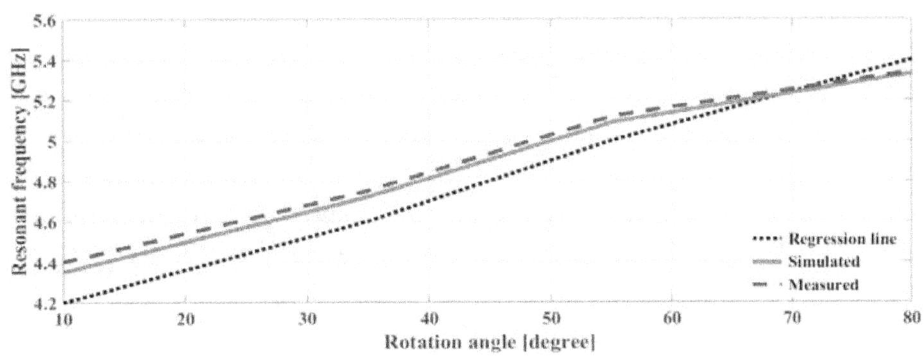

Figure 7. Resonant frequency versus rotation angle.

4.2. Parametric Analysis

The operational performance of an antenna is examined by varying optimized dimensions of unit cell for carrying out the parametric analysis of the proposed antenna. This study observes four different cases: varying parameters 'a', 'b', 'c', and 's' of unit cell. The effect of parameter 'a' on reflection coefficient is shown in Fig. 8(a). It is visualized from this plot that when the value of parameter 'a' is increased to 11 mm and 12 mm, the resonant frequency shifts to the higher side. By decreasing the value of parameter 'a' to 8 mm and 9 mm, the resonant frequency shifts to the lower side. The variation of reflection coefficient with respect to parameter 'b' is illustrated in Fig. 8(b). From this figure, it is noticed that when the value of parameter 'b' is increased to 4 mm and 5 mm, the resonant frequency shifts towards lower frequencies, whereas when the value of parameter 'b' is decreased to 1 mm and 2 mm, the resonant frequency shifts towards the higher frequencies. The variation of parameter 'c' on reflection coefficient is elucidated in Fig. 8(c). When the value of parameter 'c' is increased to 5.5 mm and 6.5 mm, the resonant shifts towards the lower level, whereas on decreasing it to 3.5 mm and 2.5 mm, the resonant frequency shifts towards upper levels. The influence of parameter 's' on reflection coefficient is elucidated in Fig. 8(d). From this figure, it is analyzed that when the value of 's' changes from 2.4 to 3.4 mm and 4.4 mm, the resonant frequency is shifted towards the higher frequencies, whereas when the value changes from 2.4 to 1.4 mm and 0.4 mm, the resonant frequency is shifted towards the lower frequencies.

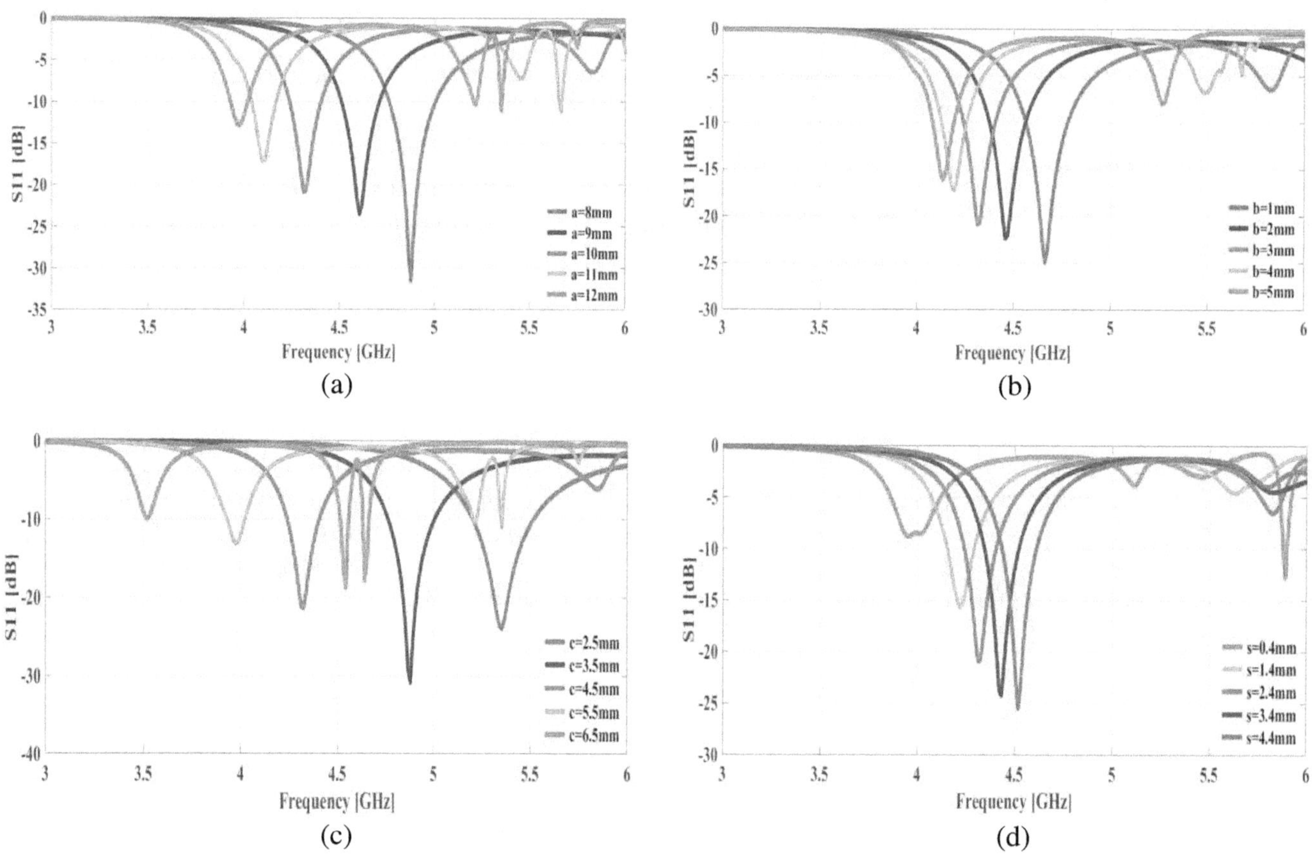

Figure 8. (a) Effect of parameter 'a' on reflection coefficient, (b) effect of parameter 'b' on reflection coefficient, (c) effect of parameter 'c' on reflection coefficient, (d) effect of parameter 's' on reflection coefficient.

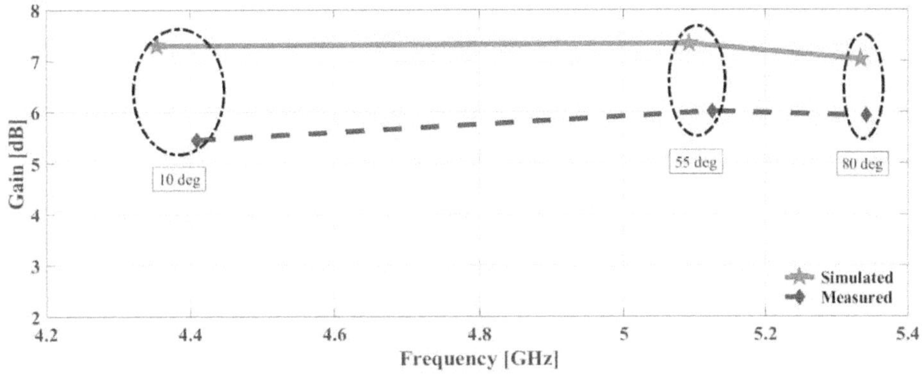

Figure 9. Gain versus frequency at different rotation angles.

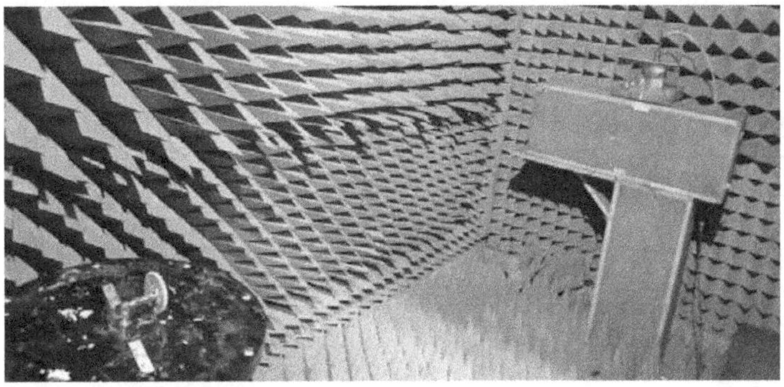

Figure 10. Projected antenna in an anechoic chamber.

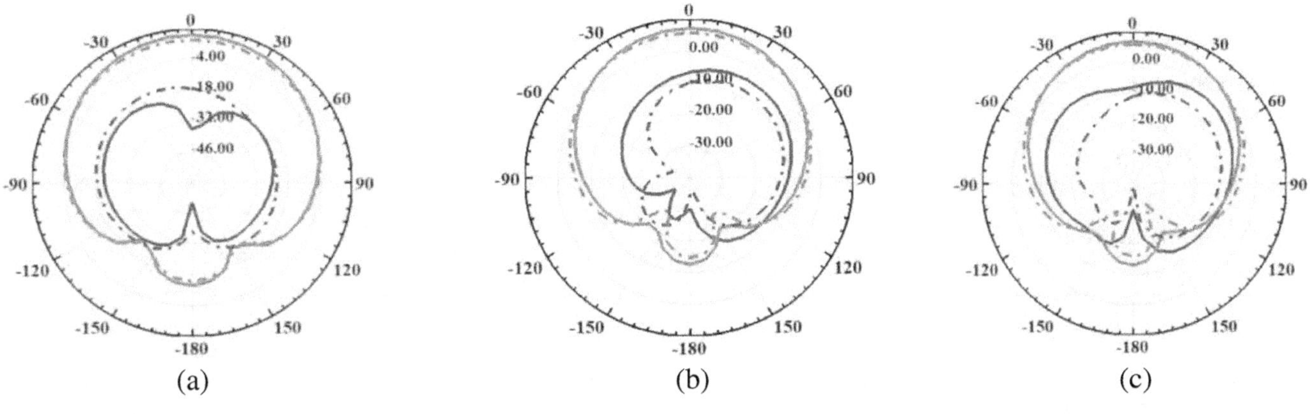

Figure 11. Simulated (bold line) and measured (dotdashed line) radiation patterns in zx plane at rotation angles (a) 10°, (b) 55°, (c) 80° (The red line indicates co-polarization and the blue line signifies cross-polarization).

4.3. Gain and Radiation Pattern of Projected MS-FRPA

The important antenna parameters such as gain and radiation pattern are described here at different resonating frequencies in correspondence to rotation angles 10°, 55°, and 80°. The simulated and measured graphs of gain versus frequency are shown in Fig. 9. From the results, it is observed that gains around 7.29, 7.33, and 7.02 dB have been achieved corresponding to resonant frequencies 4.35 GHz, 5.09 GHz, and 5.33 GHz, respectively. The projected antenna placed in an anechoic chamber is shown

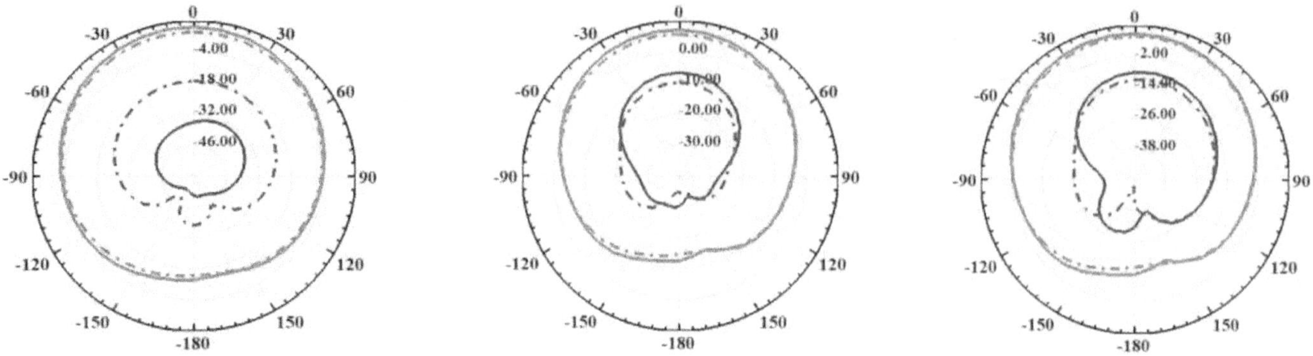

(a) (b) (c)

Figure 12. Simulated (bold line) and measured (dotdashed line) radiation patterns in yz plane at rotation angles (a) 10°, (b) 55°, (c) 80° (The red line denotes co-polarization and the blue line specifies cross-polarization).

Table 5. Performance comparison of the projected antenna with the other reported reconfigurable antennas.

Reference No.	[10]	[13]	[14]	[16]	[17]	**Projected antenna**
Overall size (mm)	40	50	105 × 105	-	50	39
Tuning Range (GHz)	4.76–5.51	2.78–3.2	1.9–2.3	4–4.35	3.97–4.74, 3.84–4.55 (ellipse) and 3.82–4.87 (wire)	4.35–5.33
Bandwidth (MHz)	750	420	-	350	-	980
Fractional Tuning Range (%)	14.6	14	19	8.4	21.1, 18.9 (ellipse) and 24.2 (wire)	20.2
Realized Gain	> 5 dBi	4.8 dBi	5 dBi	5 dBi		> 7 dB
Reconfigurability type	Frequency	Frequency	Frequency	Frequency and polarization	Frequency	Frequency

in Fig. 10. Figs. 11 and 12 show the simulated and measured results of radiation pattern at frequencies 4.35 GHz, 5.09 GHz, and 5.33 GHz in zx and yz planes respectively with different rotation angles. The radiation pattern plots indicate that the co-polarization (linear polarization observed along y-axis) radiates highly as compared to cross-polarization (linear polarization observed along x-axis). The cross polarization component shows maximum value when the dual split ring resonator gaps are placed orthogonal to each other. Thus, as the rotation angle θ varies from 10° towards 80°, gradual increase in cross polarization transmission amplitude is observed [23]. The value of front to back ratio examined is also more than 20 dB at all rotation angles. The simulated radiation efficiencies observed are also greater than 94% at all rotation angles. Thus, metasurface only shifts the frequency of operation without much affecting the shape of radiation pattern and polarization at different rotation angles.

A brief comparison of various performance parameters of projected MS-FRPA with the other reported antennas is shown in Table 5. It is observed that the designed antenna structure exhibits better performance in terms of size, tuning range, gain, and bandwidth.

5. CONCLUSION

The design of a metasurface incorporated planar frequency reconfigurable antenna printed on a Rogers RO4350B substrate is presented in this manuscript. Alternately placed dual split ring resonators joined by a thin wire representing the MS are used to reconfigure the frequency. A unit cell structure of DSRR is placed inside a waveguide medium to analyze the phase reversal behavior of metamaterial. By rotating the MS relative to the designed patch antenna, it is possible to reconfigure continuously the antenna's operating frequency from 4.35 GHz to 5.33 GHz range resulting in fractional tuning range of 20.2% and bandwidth of 980 MHz without much affecting the shape of the radiation pattern and polarization of the antenna. The proposed structure also provides acceptable gain results.

ACKNOWLEDGMENT

The authors would like to thank Rogers Corporation for providing support material for fabricating the antenna prototype, National Institute of Technical Teachers Training and Research (NITTTR), Chandigarh and Indian Institute of Technology (IIT), New Delhi for providing the facility to test the fabricated prototype.

REFERENCES

1. Sabapathy, T., M. F. Bin Jamlos, R. B. Ahmad, M. Jusoh, M. I. Jais, and M. R. Kamarudin, "Electronically reconfigurable beam steering antenna using embedded RF PIN based parasitic arrays (ERPPA)," *Progress In Electromagnetics Research*, Vol. 140, 241–261, 2013.
2. Bhangi, I. K. and J. S. Sivia, "Minkowski and Hilbert curves based hybrid fractal antenna for wireless applications," *International Journal of Electronics and Communications*, Vol. 85, 159–168, Feb. 2018.
3. Sivia, J. S., A. P. S. Pharwaha, and T. S. Kamal, "Analysis and design of circular fractal antenna using artificial neural networks," *Progress In Electromagnetics Research B*, Vol. 56, 251–267, 2013.
4. Singh, J., A. P. Singh, and T. S. Kamal, "Estimation of resonant frequency of a circular microstrip antenna using artificial neural network," *Journal of the Institution of Engineers (India): Series B*, Vol. 93, No. 1, 7–13, Mar.–May 2012.
5. Ge, L. and K. M. Luk, "Frequency-reconfigurable low-profile circular monopolar patch antenna," *IEEE Transactions on Antennas and Propagation*, Vol. 62, No. 7, 3443–3449, Jul. 2014.
6. Kaur, K. and J. S. Sivia, "A compact hybrid multiband antenna for wireless applications," *Wireless Personal Communications*, Vol. 97, No. 4, 5917–5927, Dec. 2017.
7. Bhatia, S. S. and J. S. Sivia, "On the design of fractal antenna array for multiband applications," *Journal of the Institution of Engineers (India): Series B*, Vol. 100, 471–476, May 2019.
8. Anantha, B., L. Meregu, and P. V. D. S. Rao, "A novel single feed frequency and polarization reconfigurable microstrip patch antenna," *International Journal of Electronics and Communications*, Vol. 72, 8–16, Feb. 2017.
9. Li, T., H. Zhai, and C. H. Liang, "Frequency reconfigurable bow-tie antenna array," *Electronics Letters*, Vol. 50, No. 18, 1264–1266, Aug. 2014.
10. Zhu, H. L., X. H. Liu, S. W. Cheung, and T. I. Yuk, "Frequency-reconfigurable antenna using metasurface," *IEEE Transactions on Antennas and Propagation*, Vol. 62, No. 1, 80–85, Jan. 2014.
11. Haupt, R. L. and M. Lanagan, "Reconfigurable antennas," *IEEE Antennas and Propagation Magazine*, Vol. 55, No. 1, 49–61, Feb. 2013.
12. Holloway, C. L., E. F. Kuester, J. A. Gordon, J. O. Hara, J. Booth, and D. R. Smith, "An overview of theory and applications of metasurfaces: The two dimensional equivalents of metamaterials," *IEEE Antennas and Propagation Magazine*, Vol. 54, No. 2, 10–35, Apr. 2012.
13. Zhu, H. L., S. W. Cheung, X. H. Liu, Y. F. Cao, and T. I. Yuk, "Frequency reconfigurable slot antenna using metasurface," *The 8th European Conference on Antennas and Propagation (EuCAP)*, 2575–2577, The Hague, Netherlands, Apr. 2014.

14. Chatterjee, J., A. Mohan, and V. Dixit, "A novel frequency reconfigurable slot antenna using metasurface," *IEEE Indian Conference on Antennas and Propogation (InCAP)*, Hyderabad, India, Dec. 16–19, 2018.
15. Zhu, M. and L. Sun, "Design of frequency reconfigurable antenna based on metasurface," *IEEE 2nd Advanced Information Technology, Electronic, and Automation Control Conference (IAEAC)*, Chongqing, China, Mar. 2017.
16. Chen, X. and Y. Zhao, "Dual-band polarization and frequency reconfigurable antenna using double layer metasurface," *International Journal of Electronics and Communications*, Vol. 95, 82–87, Oct. 2018.
17. Li, H., X. Man, and J. Qi, "Accurate and robust characterization of metasurface-enabled frequency reconfigurable antennas by radially homogeneous model," *IEEE Access*, Vol. 7, 122605–122612, Sept. 2019.
18. Sethi, A. and Rajni, "Determination of electromagnetic parameters of a new metasurface comprising of square loop," *Journal of Engineering Science and Technology*, Vol. 13, No. 1, 48–57, 2018.
19. Rajni, R. and A. Marwaha, "Electrically small microstrip patch antenna loaded with spiral resonator for wireless applications," *Wireless Personal Communications*, Vol. 96, No. 2, 2621–2632, Sept. 2017.
20. Sharma, N. and S. S. Bhatia, "Double split labyrinth resonator-based CPW-fed hybrid fractal antennas for PCS/UMTS/WLAN/Wi-Max applications," *Journal of Electromagnetic Waves and Applications*, Vol. 33, No. 18, 2476–2498, Dec. 2019.
21. Rajni, and A. Marwaha, "Resonance characteristics and effective parameters of new left hand metamaterial," *Telkomnika Indonesian Journal of Electrical Engineering*, Vol. 15, No. 3, 497–503, Sept. 2015.
22. Rajni, R. and A. Marwaha, "An accurate approach of mathematical modeling of SRR and SR for metamaterials," *Journal of Engineering Science and Technology Review*, Vol. 9, No. 6, 82–86, Dec. 2016.
23. Rao, S. J. M., R. Sarkar, G. Kumar, and D. B. Chowdhury, "Gradual cross polarization conversion of transmitted waves in near field coupled planar terahertz metamaterials," *OSA Continuum*, Vol. 2, No. 3, 603–614, Mar. 2019.

Different Reconfiguration Mechanisms and Applications in Planar Antennas: A Review

Navneet Kaur[a], Jagtar Singh Sivia[b], Rajni[c]

[a]Research Scholar, Department of Electronics and Communication Engineering, Punjabi University, Patiala (147002), India
[b]Professor, YCoE, Punjabi University Guru Kashi Campus, Talwandi Sabo (151302), India
[c]Professor, Shaheed Bhagat Singh State Technical Campus, Ferozepur (152004), India

Email: navsandhu31696@gmail.com

Abstract: There has been an increasing demand to design reconfigurable antennas during the last few decades. Based on its ability to radiate frequency, radiation pattern and polarization, a reconfigurable antenna is able to perform multiple functions. This paper briefly discusses the challenges faced in the design of these antennas. In the first part of the paper, various types of reconfigurable antennas are described that are characterized on the basis of reconfiguration mechanisms used and the parameter to be reconfigured. The design aspects of reconfigurable antennas along with the components involved in designing are illustrated with advantages and shortcomings in the next part. Some of the applications of these antennas are also explained in the latter part.

Keywords: Reconfigurable Antenna, Wireless System, PIN diodes, Gain, Resonant Frequency, Polarization

1. Introduction

A reconfigurable antenna had been a topic of interest of researchers for the past few years due to their suitability for various wireless applications. The reconfiguration capability of antennas can maximize the performance in a changing scenario by altering some of the antenna parameters in an adjustable manner. The different standards in handheld gadgets require compact multi-band antennas/smart antennas with reconfigurable features. Hence, there is a necessity to develop reconfigurable antennas so that it can cover the requirements of the latest communication devices and reduce the system's complexity (Borakhde & Pokle, 2015). Several techniques have been developed to achieve the reconfigurability of these antennas. They can either be one antenna or a combination of many antennas (Haupt & Lanagan 2013). Due to the several features such as small size, better signal quality, low cost, immune to signal interferences, less fading effects, more system capacity, etc (Anantha, Meregu, & Rao, 2017) (Panahi, Bao, Yang, Conchubhair, & Ammann, 2015) the investigation of the "Reconfigurable Antennas" is an alternative leap to enhance the general framework execution as they can contribute variety of features (Bernhard, 2007).

The design of any reconfigurable antenna type includes numerous performance parameters – gain, bandwidth, polarization, input impedance, frequency of operation, radiation patterns and variability over the entire range of operation, and mechanical/electrical structural flexibility. These performance parameters can be changed by changing the distribution of current through the use of movable parts, attenuators, diodes or the use of dynamic materials (Haupt & Lanagan 2013).

The reconfigurable antennas were first proposed in 1926 by A. N. Goldsmith so as to make use of the same antenna for a number of different purposes at different frequencies. Initial demonstrated was focused on only frequency reconfigurability. Bruce and Beck in 1935 redesign the structure of the rhombic antenna by expanding its wires through the use of rotating parts. Several ideas were explored later for other reconfigurability options. Schaubert in 1983 got the first patent on designing frequency and polarization reconfigurable antenna using switching diodes by suitably choosing the position of shorting posts (Schaubert, 1983). After that, a multi-university program was launched in 1999 by Defence Advanced Research Projects Agency (DARPA) under the name Reconfigurable Aperture Program (RECAP) in the United States between various companies, research institutes and universities (Smith, 1999). Further this led to more investigation in the developments of reconfigurable antennas.

The organization of this paper is as follows. Section 2 demonstrates the various challenges faced by the researchers while designing reconfigurable antennas. Section 3 describes the types of reconfigurable antennas on the basis of the reconfiguration mechanism and reconfigured parameter. Applications of these antennas in various fields are presented in Section 4. Finally, the paper is concluded in Section 5.

Abbreviations

DARPA – Defence Advanced Research Projects Agency
RECAP – Reconfigurable Aperture Program
dB – Decibel
dBi – Decibel per inch
LP – Linear Polarization
CP – Circular Polarization
LHCP – Left Hand Circular Polarization
RHCP – Right Hand Circular Polarization

2. Challenges posed in the design of Reconfigurable Antennas

Configuring a reconfigurable antenna is a demanding factor as it leads to the development of versatile antenna systems. There are a lot of factors that influence the design of reconfigurable antennas but the main challenges which the engineers have taken into account are:

- Which radiation characteristic – frequency, polarization, radiation pattern or compound is to be varied in order to get better performance?
- How the distinct structural flexibility is reconfigured to attain the required characteristic?
- Which method of reconfiguration counteracts against the false effects better?

3. Types of Reconfigurable Antennas

The reconfigurable antennas can be categorized depending on

- Reconfiguration Mechanism
- Reconfigured Parameter

3.1. Reconfiguration Mechanisms

It is imperative to select the apt mechanism in order to achieve the desired function. Various methods have been designed to configure the characteristics of an antenna and to redistribute their current.

3.1.1. Electrically Reconfigurable Antennas

Electrically reconfigurable antennas are generally designed using band switching and continuous tuning techniques. The band switching is attained by means of PIN diodes (Han, Wang, & Zhang, 2016) and RF-MEMS switch (Escuderos, Bataller, Escudero, & Herranz, 2011) whereas varactor diode (Kehn, Teruel, & Iglesias, 2011) is used for achieving continuous tuning. In both the types, direct current biasing is used for the operation. However, there are few limitations of electrically reconfigurable antennas; for example, negative biasing effects to control switching conditions, nonlinearity effects due to switching, power consumption, and reliability of used components and slow tuning may cause unfavorable effects on antenna performances (Zhu, Liu, Cheung, & Yuk, 2014).

3.1.2. Mechanically Reconfigurable Antennas

In mechanically reconfigurable antennas, the entire structure is composed of various movable parts like a pulley, weights, and motor. The main limitation of such antennas is that the variation in size in accordance with the tuned frequency. Moreover, the actuators employed to generate mechanical movements were too complex, bulky and costly (Haupt & Lanagan, 2013).

3.1.3. Optically Reconfigurable Antennas

In optically reconfigurable antennas, photoconductive elements are used where electrons move from valence band to conduction band. Thus switching takes place from OFF to ON state. This is accomplished from a laser diode by enlightening the switch with the light of a suitable wavelength (Keiser, 2000). These antennas are preferred due to fast switching and activation, possession of linear behavior and intermodulation. Besides this, no bias lines are required for their operation (DaCosta & Spadoti, 2017) (Pendharker, Shevgaonkar, & Chandorkar, 2014).

3.1.4. Physically Reconfigurable Antennas

Physical reconfiguration is generally obtained by changing the structure of an antenna. These antennas do not require switching, biasing and optical integration. But they do suffer from the device's physical reconfiguration effect.

3.1.5. Material Change based Reconfigurable Antennas

The antennas which are designed using smart materials such as ferrites (Pozar & Sanchez, 1988), liquid crystal (Hu, Ismail, Cahill, Encinar, Fusco, Gamble, Linton, Dickie, Grant & Rea, 2007) and metasurfaces (Zhu, Cheung &Yuk, 2015) are called material change based reconfigurable antennas. The material properties are altered by altering the relative permittivity and permeability. Liquid crystal is a type of matter having flow the same as that of liquid but ordered like molecules. In case of ferrites e.m. field is applied that in turn changes its permittivity and permeability whereas metasurface is a two dimensional equivalent of metamaterials that change its permittivity and permeability. It not only minimizes the cost and size but provides high gain and efficiency also (Zhu, Liu, Cheung, & Yuk, 2014).

3.2. Reconfigured Parameter

Different types of reconfigurable antennas based on the parameter to be reconfigured to attain the desired characteristics are categorized as follows:

3.2.1. Frequency Reconfigurable Antennas

Frequency reconfigurable antennas are those that can dynamically change the frequency of an antenna while keeping the pattern and polarization unchanged. They are widely popular due to their ability to select the resonant frequency and the proper use of spectrum (Han, Wang, Chen & Zhang, 2016). It can easily adapt to changing environmental conditions (Li, Zhai, Wang & Liang, 2015). Thus, frequency reconfigurable antennas have the ability to support several applications of wireless systems (Majid, Rahim, Hamid & Ismail 2014). Example: cognitive radio (Mansoul,

Ghanem, Hamid & Trabelsi 2014). Figure 1 describes the structures of various frequency reconfigurable antennas having different designs and shapes. The design of compact and efficient reconfigurable slot antennas is presented in Figure 1 (a). Dual-frequency microstrip antenna using varactor diodes is described in Figure 1 (b). Planar inverted F-antenna is analyzed in Figure 1 (c) using pin and varactor diodes.

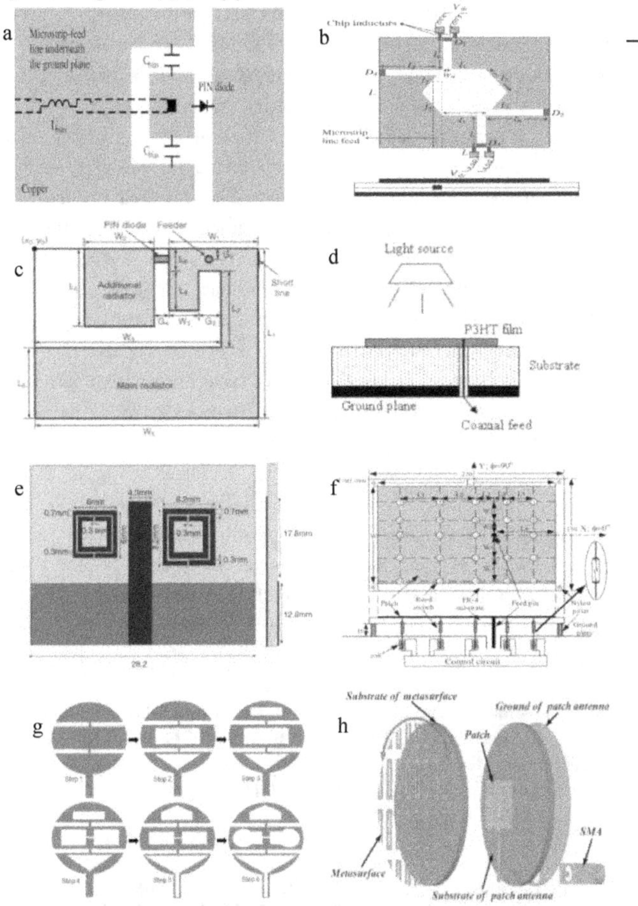

Fig. 1- Frequency Reconfigurable Antennas
(a) Switching bias network (Peroulis, Sarabandi & Linda, 2005) (b) Dual frequency micro-strip antenna (Shynu, Augustin, Aanandan, Mohanan & Vasudevan, 2006) (c) Planar inverted F-antenna (Lim, Back, Ko, Song & Yun, 2010) (d) P3HT antenna (Sathi, Ehteshami & Nourinia, 2012) (e) Coplanar fed straight-line monopole with two DSRRs (Cheribi, Ghunam & Kimouche, 2013) (f) FRA with multi-reed switches (Liu, Wang, Wu, Wei & Smolders, 2015) (g) Patch antenna with bias tee (Chattha, Aftab, Akram, Sheriff, Huang & Abbasi, 2018) (h) Frequency Reconfigurable Metasurface antenna (Zhu, Liu, Cheung & Yuk, 2014)

The structure of optically tuned frequency-reconfigurable square and the square-ring shaped antenna is described in Figure 1 (d) whose operating frequency is changed by continuously varying the optical intensity of the light source. Metamaterial-based frequency reconfigurable antenna using coplanar-fed straight away monopole and two dual split-ring resonators are presented in Figure 1 (e). Frequency reconfigurability using multi-reed switches is depicted in Figure 1 (f). A micro-strip frequency reconfigurable patch antenna that covers various bands of wireless applications is expressed in Figure 1 (g).

Table 1: Summary of Frequency Reconfigurable Antennas

Reconfiguration Mechanism (Ref.)	Frequency Bands	Gain	Features
PIN diodes (Peroulis, Sarabandi & Linda, 2005)	540-890 MHz Bandwidth-1.7:1	--	No matching network
Varactor diodes (Shynu, Augustin, Aanandan, Mohanan & Vasudevan, 2006)	(1.037-1.394 GHz) (1.359-1.485 GHz)	2.1 dB 1.2 dB	No matching network
Capacitor (Yang, Kishk & Lee, 2008)	2.6-3.35 GHz	--	Reduces crosstalk
PIN & Varactor diodes (Lim, Back, Ko, Song & Yun, 2010)	(1.85-1.99 GHz) (1.92-2.18 GHz) (5.15-5.825 GHz) (3.4-3.6 GHz)	2.84 dBi 2.81 dBi 1.49 dBi 1.25 dBi	Good impedance matching
Organic semiconductor polymer (Sathi, Ehteshami & Nourinia, 2012)	950 MHz 1.5 GHz	3.6 dB 3.1 dB	--
Metamaterial (Cheribi, Ghunam & Kimouche, 2013)	Monopole at 5 GHz DSRR at 2.6 and 4.2 GHz	--	--
MEMS, PIN diodes and reed switches (Liu, Wang, Wu, Wei & Smolders, 2015)	0.3-3 GHz	2.8-5.7 dBi	free from bias effect
PIN diodes (Borhani, Rezaei & Valizade, 2016)	2.3-2.51 GHz 3.35-3.75 GHz 4.95-5.53 GHz	--	--
PIN diodes (Chattha, Aftab, Akram, Sheriff, Huang & Abbasi, 2018)	2.4 GHz, 3.6 GHz, 4.9 GHz, 5.1 GHz, and 5.9 GHz	1.6 dBi 2.12 dBi 3.13 dBi 4.12 dBi	Biasing required >75 %
PIN diodes (Shah, Hayat, Basir, Zada, Shah & Ullah, 2019)	3.5-4.8 GHz 2.10-5.2 GHz	1.85-3.46 dBi	Compact, low cost and simple in integration
Metasurface (Majumder, Krishnamoorthy, Mukherjee & Ray, 2016)	2.55-3.45 GHz	Peak gain 8.3 dB	> 90% efficiency

Metasurface (Zhu, Liu, Cheung & Yuk, 2014)	4.76-5.51 GHz	5 dB	>80 % efficiency

Metasurface based planar frequency reconfigurable antenna is designed in Figure 1 (h). As illustrated in Table 1, a list of various frequency reconfigurable antennas is specified including the reconfiguration mechanisms, frequency bands, their respective gain, and efficiency.

3.2.2. Pattern Reconfigurable Antennas

Antenna pattern is described in the form of directional coordinates such as unidirectional, bidirectional, multidirectional or omnidirectional (Balanis, 2005).

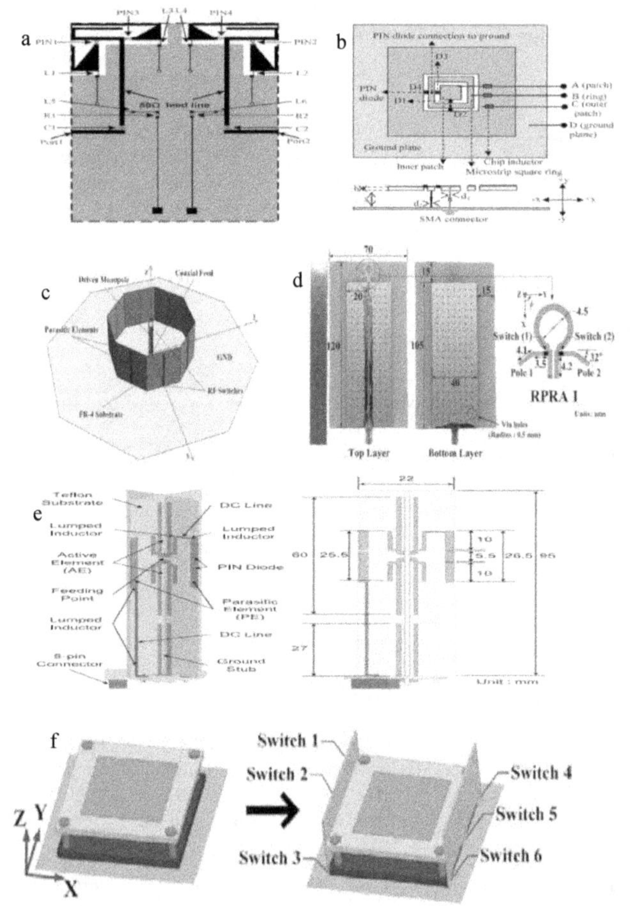

Fig. 2- Pattern Reconfigurable Antennas (a) Antenna array using two monopoles (Cai & Du, 2009) (b) Antenna with integrated p-i-n diode switches (Nair & Ammann, 2010) (c) Antenna with switches printed elements (Shi, Zheng, Ding & Guo, 2012) (d) Pattern MIMO element (Rhee, Kim, Park, Kwoun, Mun, Lee & Jung, 2014)] (e) Dual pattern reconfigurable antenna (Ji, 2016) (f) Multi-direction beam antenna (Yang, Li, Wei, Zhou & Xu, 2019)

They can easily change the pattern from one form to another (Ji, 2016). Example: mobile antenna systems (Li, Ma, Chountalas & Lau, 2015). In 1959, a radiation pattern reconfigurable antenna was proposed by W. Rotman. In this, the beam scanning was performed through the use of mechanically tuned leaky mode. In 1979, Matthews described a multiple beam shaped reconfigurable satellite antenna. For the analysis of coverage zone six antennas were developed. In 1990 radiation pattern was controlled by changing the reflecting surface of parabolic reflector antenna by A. D. Monk (Haupt & Lanagan, 2013).

Figure 2 describes the structures of various pattern reconfigurable antennas. Pattern reconfigurable antenna array using two equally placed complementary monopoles is presented in Figure 2 (a) using PIN diodes to vary the radiation structure and circulation of the current. Figure 2 (b) illustrated the design of a single-feed reconfigurable micro-strip antenna using integrated pin diodes for pattern switching of 65^0 and 45^0 in elevation and azimuth planes. Pattern reconfigurable antenna using switched printed elements and corner reflector antenna are illustrated in Figure 2 (c). In Figure 2 (d) pattern reconfigurable antenna using loop-dipole is designed using two switches covering the range in three distinct directions for multi-input multi-output applications. Dual-band pattern reconfigurable antenna is presented in Figure 2 (e) for wireless multi-input multi-output applications. Miniaturized pattern reconfigurable aperture feed microstrip antenna for wireless communication systems using two metal walls and six-pin diodes is demonstrated in Figure 2 (f). A brief summary of various features, frequency bands, and gain of pattern reconfigurable antennas are described in Table 2.

Table 2 - Summary of various Pattern Reconfigurable Antennas

Reconfiguration Mechanism (Ref.)	Frequency Bands and beam	Gain	Features
PIN diodes (Cai & Du, 2009)	2.05 to 2.18 GHz	3 dBi, 5.65 dBi, 3.3 dBi	Isolation > 13 dB
PIN diodes (Nair & Ammann, 2010)	Beam switching of 65^0 and 45^0 in the E and H planes	4.58 dBi, 2.71 dBi, 1.11 dBi, 3.2 dBi	Less lumped components
Switches (Tao, Wang, Ma& Leng, 2012)	5.15–5.35 GHz Six azimuth patterns having HPBW 60^0	5.46 dB	FBR >9 dB, Good impedance matching
RF switch (Shi, Zheng, Ding & Guo, 2012)	2.4-2.8 GHz, 17 beams	8 dB	--
Switches (Rhee, Kim, Park, Kwoun, Mun, Lee & Jung, 2014)	5.15-5.35 GHz, Orthogonal directional radiation pattern	5.4 dBi, 5.38 dBi	High isolation >21dB, low correlation

PIN diodes (Shi, & Ding, 2015)	3.44-3.6 GHz, 90^0 in azimuth and 30^0 deflection in elevation	> 8 dBi	Compact structure
PIN diodes (Ji, 2016)	nine patterns at 5.8 GHz & omni-directional pattern at 2.4 GHz	5.6-10.4 dBi	--
PIN diodes (Yang, Li, Wei, Zhou & Xu, 2019)	3.5-3.9 GHz, 6 beams	--	Low cross-polarization
Metasurface (Zhu, Cheung & Yuk, 2015)	5.4-5.6 GHz, Main beam has an angle of 32^0 from boresight direction	7.2 dB	Fractional operating BW 4 %
PIN diodes (Yang, Lu, Li, Liu & Yin, 2019)	5.0-5.27 GHz Horizontal, azimuth pattern with 15 beams	5.09-8.52 dBi	Efficiency 78 %

3.2.3. Polarization Reconfigurable Antennas

It is one of the important parameters of reconfigurable antennas and an essential characteristic of the wireless communication system due to the small size and less cost. The antenna which has the capability to interchange between different polarization modes while keeping the frequency unchanged is called polarization reconfigurable antenna (Zhu, Cheung, Liu & Yuk, 2014). They are also called as polarization agile antennas. Example: Multi Input Multi Output channels (Piazza, Kirsch, Forenza, Heath & Dandekar, 2008). Various types of polarization reconfigurable antennas are presented in Figure 3. In Figure 3 (a), the design of the polarization reconfigurable slot antenna is presented using PIN diodes. A reconfigurable microstrip antenna is presented in Figure 3 (b) that allows switching between left-hand and right-hand circular polarization states using 3 dB hybrid coupler and square patch.

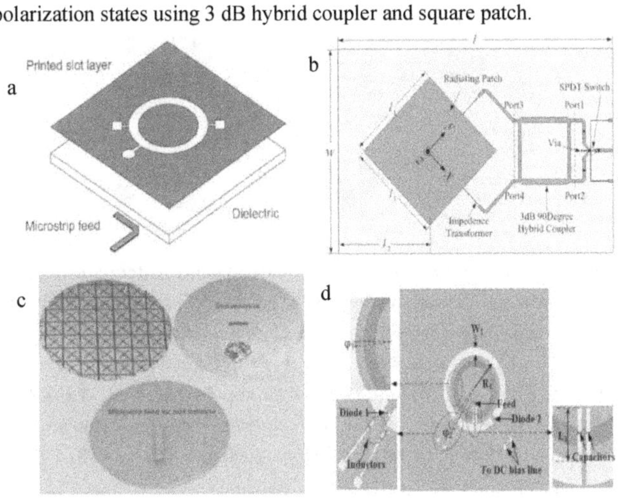

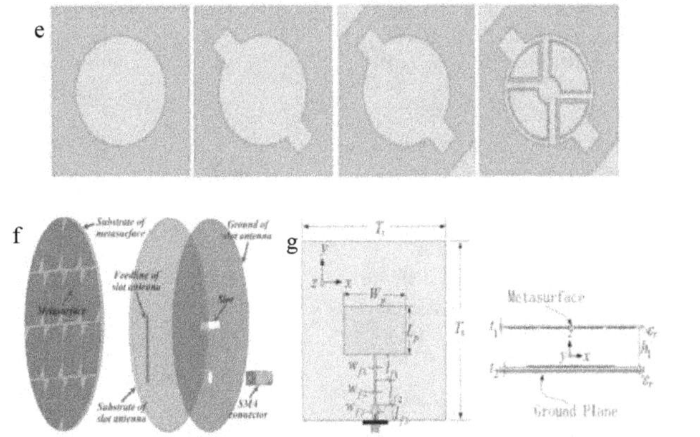

Fig. 3- Structures of Polarization Reconfigurable Antennas (a) Microstrip-fed circularly polarized slot ring (Fries, Grani &Vahldieck, 2003) (b) Square micro-strip patch antenna (Wei, Liu, Yin & Zhou, 2007) (c) Polarization reconfigurable antenna using Metasurface (Krishnamoorthy, Majimder, Mukherjee & Ray, 2015) (d) Wideband loop antenna (Zhang, Gao, Luo, Young & Li, 2016) (e) Wideband SRR inspired slot antenna (Rahimi, Maleki, Soltani, Arezomand & Zarrabi, 2016) (f) Polarization reconfigurable antenna using Metasurface (Zhu, Cheung, Liu & Yuk, 2014) (g) LP to CP using Metasurface (Zhu, Cheung, Chung & Yuk, 2013)

Polarization reconfigurable antenna with reduced radar cross-section is presented in Figure 3 (c) using slot antenna and cross slot based metasurface. A wideband loop antenna with circular polarization is presented in Figure 3 (d) using loop antenna and a PIN diode. SRR based wideband slot antenna is presented in Figure 3 (e) for wireless application. A metasurface based polarization reconfigurable antenna has been reported in Figure 3 (f). Furthermore, metasurface based linear to circular polarization conversion is designed in Figure 3 (g) using slot antenna. In Table 3, features of various polarization reconfigurable antennas are described along with their gain, axial ratio, switching states, and bandwidth ranges.

Table 3: Summary of various Polarization Reconfigurable Antennas

Reconfiguration Mechanism (Ref.)	Frequency Bands & Gain	Polarization	Features
PIN diodes (Fries, Grani &Vahldieck, 2003)	2.4 GHz	Circular, linear & between two circular polarizations	Realized on low-cost dielectric materials
FET switch (Wei, Liu, Yin & Zhou, 2007)	1.5175GHz, 5.12dB and 5.26dB	LHCP and RHCP	Axial ratio 1.59 dB
PIN diodes and capacitor (Qin, Weily, Guo & Liang, 2010)	5.6-6.3 GHz 5.72-6.08 GHz	LP and CP	Axial ratio of 5.7–5.86 GHz

RF switches (Khidre, Lee, Yang & Elsherbeni, 2013)	2.4 – 2.57 GHz, 8.7 dBi	RHCP to LHCP & vice versa	AR 2.4-2.6 GHz (8 %), No matching networks
Metasurface (Krishnamoorthy, Majimder, Mukherjee & Ray, 2015)	4.4 GHz	LP, LHCP, RHCP	AR 120 MHz
PIN diode (Zhang, Gao, Luo, Young & Li, 2016)	8 dBic for LHCP & 7 dBic for RHCP	RHCP to LHCP	AR 12.7 % and 14.9 %
Metamaterial (Rahimi, Maleki, Soltani, Arezomand & Zarrabi, 2016)	2-3.8 GHz, 2-3.5 dB	LP and CP	Efficiency > 90 %
Substrate integrated waveguide & PIN diodes (Hu, Hao & Miao, 2017)	7.98 to 8.75 GHz, 8.18 to 8.45 GHz, 10.47, 9.9, and 10.75 dBi	LP, LHCP, RHCP	AR 8.01–8.24 GHz
Truncated corner patch (McMichael, 2018)	1.0 – 1.8 GHz	LHCP & RHCP	AR 0.4 dB
PIN diodes (Yang, Yang, Zhu, Yoshitomi & Kanaya, 2019)	5.78-5.96 GHz, 6.84 dBi	LHCP & RHCP	AR 5.64-5.91 GHz (4.7 %)
Metasurface (Zhu, Cheung, Liu & Yuk, 2014)	3.3–3.7 GHz, 5 dBi	LP and CP	high-polarization isolation > 15 dB, ARBW 400 MHz
Metasurface (Zhu, Cheung, Chung & Yuk, 2013)	2.47-2.52GHz, 5.8dB	LP to CP	FBR 26 dB, HPBW 54^0

3.2.4. Compound Reconfigurable Antennas

Compound reconfiguration is the synchronous reconfiguration of multiple parameters, thereby enhancing the spectral efficiency of wireless links (Rodrigo, Cetiner & Jofre, 2014). In the first approach, two parameters are to be combined: frequency-polarization (Anantha, Meregu & Rao, 2017), polarization-pattern (Narbudowicz, Bao & Ammann, 2014) and pattern-frequency (Li, Shao, Wang & Cheng, 2015). In the second approach frequency, pattern and polarization all three parameters are simultaneously combined together (Rodrigo, Cetiner & Jofre, 2014).

The design of reconfigurable antennas using pin diodes, lumped capacitors, L-shaped slot and bias networks for portable devices are reported in Figure 4 (a). Pattern reconfiguration is obtained by switching the positions of diode and capacitor thereby inducing current across the slot. A reconfigurable micro-strip antenna using switches and power dividers for pattern selectivity and polarization diversity is presented in Figure 4 (b). Frequency and pattern reconfigurable antenna is introduced by employing loaded stubs with varactors and dc bias networks are depicted in Figure 9 (c) for smart communication systems. In Figure 9 (d), a low profile, cost-effective frequency, and pattern reconfigurable antenna are designed using five-pin diodes, planar monopole and micro-strip patch for multi-standard wireless communication applications. Dual-Band frequency and polarization reconfigurable antenna using double-layer metasurface on patch antenna are presented in Figure 9 (e). This antenna has the tendency to operate at 4 GHz for frequency reconfiguration and 5 GHz for linear to left-hand and right-hand circular polarization reconfiguration.

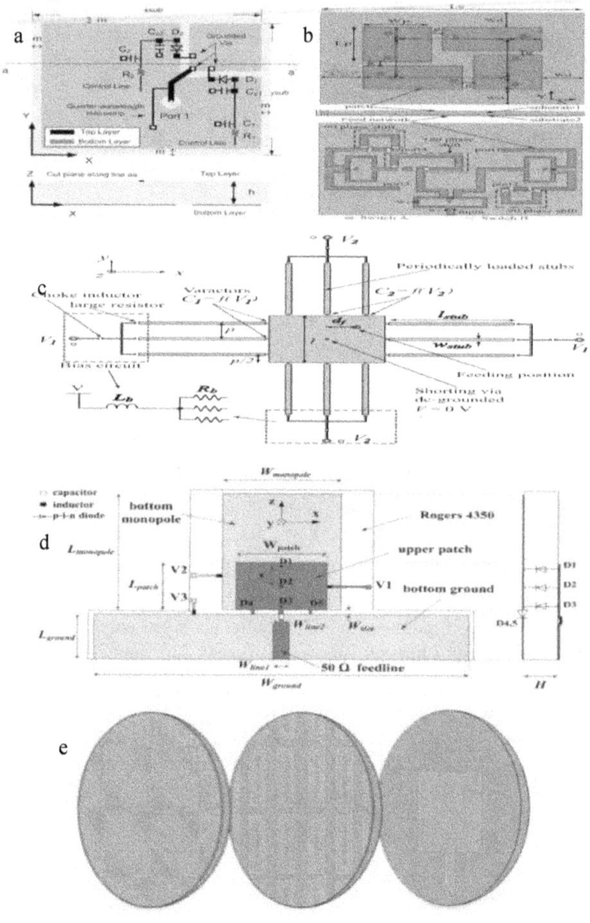

Fig. 4- Compound Reconfigurable Antennas (a) Antenna using L-shaped slot and PIN diodes (Lai, Wu, Hsieh, Wang & Jeng, 2009) (b) Antenna with pattern selectivity and polarization diversity (Cao, Zhang, Liu, Yu, Guo & Pan, 2012) (c) Stub loaded antenna (Trong, Hall & Fumeaux, 2015) (d) Planar monopole (Li, Shao, Wang & Cheng, 2015) (e) Polarization and Frequency reconfigurable antenna using double-layer metasurface (Chen & Zhao, 2018)

Table 4 describes a brief overview of various compound reconfigurable antennas along with their reconfiguration mechanisms and other features.

Table 4: Summary of various Compound Reconfigurable Antennas

Reconfiguration Mechanism (Ref.)	Frequency Bands & Gain	Polarization	Features
Varactor diode, PIN diodes, and capacitor (Lai, Wu, Hsieh, Wang & Jeng, 2009)	2 and 2.7 GHz, 0.72 dBi gain	--	--
Switches (Cao, Zhang, Liu, Yu, Guo & Pan, 2012)	1.55-2.37 GHz, 2.1 dBi for conical mode, 7.9 dBi for broadside mode	LP & CP	AR BW 14 %
PIN diodes (Rodrigo, Cetiner & Jofre, 2014)	Tuning range 12-25 %, 4 dB gain	LP, LHCP, RHCP	45 to 55 % efficiency, beam switching over $\pm30^0$ in E and H plane
Phase-shifting technique (Narbudowicz, Bao & Ammann, 2014)	360^0 in either elevation or azimuth plane	Full coverage polarization	No switching elements
Varactors and dc bias networks (Trong, Hall & Fumeaux, 2015)	2.4-3.6 GHz	LP, CP, LHCP, RHCP	Efficiency 90%
PIN diodes (Li, Shao, Wang & Cheng, 2015)	2.21-2.79 GHz 5.27-5.56 GHz 1.9 dBi, 2.1 dBi, 4.8 dBi, 5 dBi	--	71 %, 80 %, 51 %, 47 %, Omni-directional and directional patterns
PIN diodes (Pengfei, Shizhong, Rongrong & Xinglin, 2016)	2.38 and 2.46 GHz, Gain 5 dBi	LHCP, RHCP	Efficiency > 75%
PIN diodes (Anantha, Meregu & Rao, 2017)	5.2 and 5.8 GHz	LP, LHCP, RHCP	--
Metasurface (Chen & Zhao, 2018)	4 GHz (LP) and 5 GHz (CP), 4GHz-4.35GHz (8.4%) for CP, Gain 5 dBi	LP,CP LHCP, RHCP	ARBW 5.0-5.2 GHz (4%)

4. Applications

Reconfigurable antennas play an integral role in a wide variety of fields for the designing of compact and low profile antennas. They have applications in cognitive radio, multi-input multi-output channels, space, and wireless systems. The various types of antennas based on these applications are discussed below:

4.1. Reconfigurable Antennas for Cognitive Radio Applications

Cognitive radio is a versatile, adroit radio and system innovation that can naturally recognize accessible occupies in a remote range and change transmission parameters empowering more correspondences to run simultaneously and furthermore improve radio working behavior. Generally, the system has two antennas. One is for sensing and the other for communication purposes (Mansoul, Ghanem, Hamid & Trabelsi 2014).

4.2. Reconfigurable Antennas for Wireless Applications

Wireless networks and its applications are increasing day by day everywhere. They are one of the important communication devices as they provide multi-standard features and multifunctional capabilities (McMichael, 2018) (Yang, Yang, Zhu, Yoshitomi & Kanaya, 2019). Polarization conversion metasurface based antenna is described in Figure 5 to modify frequency and polarization characteristics. The metasurface design is composed of an array of 64 patches placed on the top of the substrate. A double slot-shaped structure is used for the slot antenna to increase the bandwidth. Reconfiguration is achieved by changing the positions of metasurface and the planar slot antenna. Linear, left-hand and right-hand circular polarizations are reconfigured. A maximum gain of 16.5 dB and bandwidth around 8 to 11.2 GHz has been achieved.

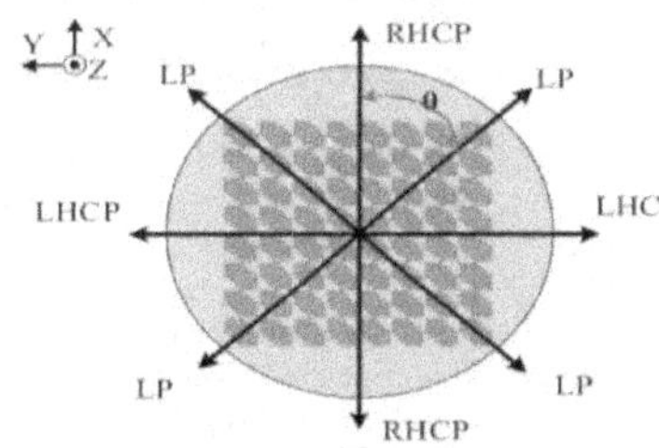

Fig. 5- Polarization of an antenna using Metasurface (Ni, Chen, Zhang & Wi, 2018)

5. Conclusion

In this paper, various approaches employed for designing the reconfigurable antennas have been investigated and illustrated. Challenges and problems concerned with the designing process have also been discussed. After reviewing the literature, it is noticed that several traditional methods are based on switching techniques that makes the design complex and cumbersome. Further, progress towards metasurface based designs is presented as they don't require switching, biasing, optical integration and other physical effects of the device. Despite the fact, that the basic work has been started in designing material change based reconfigurable antennas, but much more has to be done which in turn will provide low cost and small size antennas along with high gain and efficiency.

REFERENCES

Borakhde, D. K., & Pokle, S. B. (2015) Pentagon slot resonator frequency reconfigurable antenna for wideband reconfiguration. *International Journal of Electronics and Communications, 69 (10),* 1562-1568.

Haupt. R. L, & Lanagan, M. (2013) Reconfigurable Antennas. *IEEE Antennas and Propagation Magazine, 55 (1),* 49-61.

Anantha, B, Meregu, L, Rao, P. V. D. S. (2017) A novel single feed frequency and polarization reconfigurable microstrip patch antenna. *International Journal of Electronics and Communications, 72,* 8-16.

Panahi, A, Bao, X. L, Yang, K, Conchubhair, O. O, Ammann, M. J. (2015) A Simple Polarization Reconfigurable Printed Monopole Antenna. *IEEE Transactions on Antennas and Propagation, 63 (11)*, 5129-5134.

Bernhard, J. T. (2007) Reconfigurable Antenna. *Morgan & Claypool.*

Schaubert, D. (1983) Frequency-agile polarization diversity microstrip antennas and frequency scanned arrays. *US Patent, 4*, 367-474.

Smith, J. K. (1999) Reconfigurable aperture antenna (RECAP), *DARPA*. [Online]. Available: www.darpa.mil

Han, L, Wang, C, Zhang, W. (2016) Compact Frequency Reconfigurable Slot Antenna for Wireless Applications. *IEEE Antennas and Wireless Propagation Letters, 15*, 1795-1798.

Escuderos, D. S, Bataller, M. F, Escudero, M. B, Herranz, J. I. (2011) Reconfigurable slot array antenna with RF-MEMS. *IEEE Antennas and Wireless Propagation Letters, 10*, 721-725.

Kehn, M. N. M, Teruel, O. Q, Iglesias, E. R. (2011) Reconfigurable Loaded Planar Inverted F-antenna Using Varactor Diodes. *IEEE Antennas and Wireless Propagation Letters, 10*, 466-468.

Zhu, H. L, Liu, X. H, Cheung, S. W, Yuk, T. I. (2014) Frequency-reconfigurable antenna using metasurface *IEEE Transactions on Antennas and Propagation, 62 (1)*, 80-85.

Keiser, G. (2000) *Optical Fiber Communications (3rd Edition),* McGraw Hill. Singapore.

Da Costa, I. F, & Spadoti, D. H. (2017) Optically controlled reconfigurable antenna for 5G future broadband cellular communication networks. *Journal of Microwaves, Optoelectronics and Electromagnetic Applications, 16(1)*, 208-217.

Pendharker, S, Shevgaonkar, R. K, Chandorkar, A. N. (2014) Optically Controlled Frequency Reconfigurable Microstrip Antenna with low Photoconductivity. *IEEE Antennas and Propagation Letters, 13*, 99-102.

Pozar, D. M, & Sanchez, V. (1988) Magnetic tuning of a microstrip antenna on a ferrite substrate. *Electronic Letters, 24 (12)*, 729-731.

Hu, W, Ismail, M. Y, Cahill, R, Encinar, J. A, Fusco, V, Gamble, H. S, Linton, D, Dickie, R, Grant, N, Rea, S. P. (2007) Liquid-crystal-based reflectarray antenna with electronically switchable monopulse patterns. *Electronic Letters,* 43 (14).

Zhu, H. L, Cheung, S. W, Yuk, T. I. (2015) Mechanically pattern reconfigurable antenna using metasurface. *IET Microwaves, Antennas & Propagation, 9 (12),* 1331-1336.

Li, T, Zhai, H, Wang, X, Li, L, Liang, C. (2015) Frequency-Reconfigurable Bow-Tie Antenna for Bluetooth, WiMAX and WLAN Applications. *IEEE Antennas and Wireless Propagation Letters, 14*, 171-174.

Majid HA, Rahim MKA, Hamid MR, Ismail MF. (2014) Frequency Reconfigurable Microstrip Patch-slot Antenna with Directional Radiation Pattern. *Progress In Electromagnetics Research PIER 144*, 319-328.

Mansoul A, Ghanem F, Hamid MR, Trabelsi M. (2014) A selective frequency-reconfigurable antenna for cognitive radio applications. *IEEE Antennas and Wireless Propagation Letters, 13*, 515-518.

Peroulis, D, Sarabandi, K, Linda, P. B. K. (2005) Design of reconfigurable slot antennas. *IEEE Transactions on Antennas and Propagation,* 53 (2), 645-654.

Shynu, S. V, Augustin, G, Aanandan, C. K, Mohanan, P, Vasudevan, K. (2006) Design of compact reconfigurable dual frequency microstrip antennas using varactor diodes. *Progress In Electromagnetics Research PIER 60*, 197-205.

Yang, S. S, Kishk, A. A, Lee, K. F. (2008) Frequency reconfigurable U-slot microstrip patch antenna. *IEEE Antennas and Wireless Propagation Letters, 7*, 127-129.

Lim, J. H, Back, G. T, Ko, Y, Song, C. W, Yun, T. Y. (2010) A reconfigurable PIFA using a switchable PIN-diode and a fine-tuning varactor for USPCS/WCDMA/m-WiMAX/WLAN. *IEEE Transactions on Antennas and Propagation, 58 (7)*, 2404-2411.

Sathi, V, Ehteshami, N, Nourinia, J. (2012) Optically tuned frequency-reconfigurable microstrip antenna. *IEEE Antennas and Wireless Propagation Letters, 11*, 1018-1020.

Cheribi, H, Ghunam, F, Kimouche, H. (2013) Metamaterial-based frequency reconfigurable antenna. *Electronics Letters,* 49 (5).

Liu, Q, Wang, N, Wu, C, Wei, G, Smolders, A. B. (2015) Frequency reconfigurable antenna controlled by multi-reed switches. *IEEE Antennas and Wireless Propagation Letters, 14*, 927-930.

Borhani, M, Rezaei, P, Valizade, A. (2016) Design of a reconfigurable miniaturized microstrip antenna for switchable multiband systems. *IEEE Antennas and Wireless Propagation Letters, 15*, 822-825.

Chattha, H. T, Aftab, N, Akram, M, Sheriff, N, Huang, Y, Abbasi, Q. H. (2018) Frequency reconfigurable patch antenna with bias tee for wireless LAN applications. *IET Microwaves, Antennas and Propagation, 12 (14)*, 2248-2254.

Shah, I. A, Hayat, S, Basir, A, Zada, M, Shah, S. A. A, Ullah, S. (2019) Design and analysis of a hexa-band frequency reconfigurable antenna for wireless communication. *International Journal of Electronics and Communication, 98*, 80-88.

Majumder, B, Krishnamoorthy, K, Mukherjee, J, Ray, K. P. (2016) Frequency reconfigurable slot antenna enabled by thin anisotropic double layer metasurface. *IEEE Transactions on Antennas and Propagation, 64 (4)*, 1218-1225.

Balanis, C. A. (2005) Antenna theory: analysis and design. Hoboken, NJ: John Wiley & Sons.

Ji, J. K. (2016) Dual band pattern reconfigurable antenna for wireless MIMO applications. *The Korean Institute of Communications and Information Sciences, 2 (4)*, 199-203.

Li, H, Ma, R, Chountalas, J, Lau, B. K. (2015) Characteristic Mode Based Pattern Reconfigurable Antenna for Mobile Handset. *European Conference on Antennas and Propagation (EUCAP).*

Cai, Y, & Du, Z. (2009) A novel pattern reconfigurable antenna array for diversity systems. *IEEE Antennas and Wireless Propagation Letters, 8*, 1227-1230.

Nair, S. V. S, & Ammann, M. J. (2010) Reconfigurable antenna with elevation and azimuth beam switching. *IEEE Antennas and Wireless Propagation Letters, 9*, 367-370.

Tao, C. X, Wang, A, Ma, N, Leng, W. (2012) Novel radiation pattern reconfigurable antenna with six beam choices. *The Journal of China Universities of Posts and Telecommunications, 19 (2)*, 123-128.

Shi, Z, Zheng, R, Ding, J, Guo, C. (2012) A novel pattern reconfigurable antenna using switched printed elements. *IEEE Antennas and Wireless Propagation Letters, 11*, 1100-1103.

Rhee, C, Kim, Y, Park, T, Kwoun, S, Mun, B, Lee, B, Jung, C. (2014) Pattern-reconfigurable MIMO antenna for high isolation and low correlation. *IEEE Antennas and Wireless Propagation Letters, 13*, 1373-1376.

Shi, S. J, & Ding, W. P. (2015) Radiation pattern reconfigurable microstrip antenna for WiMAX application. *Electronic Letters,* 51 (9), 662-664.

Yang, G, Li,, J, Wei, D, Zhou, S, Xu, R. (2019) Pattern reconfigurable microstrip antenna with multi-directional beam for wireless communications. *IEEE Transactions on Antennas and Propagation, 67 (3).*

Yang, L, Lu, C, Li, X, Liu, L, Yin, X. (2019) A Horizontal Azimuth Pattern Reconfigurable Antenna Using Omnidirectional Microstrip Arrays for WLAN Application. *Hindawi International Journal of Antennas and Propagation*, 1-10.

Zhu, H. L, Cheung, S. W, Liu, X. H, Yuk, T. I. (2014) Design of polarization reconfigurable antenna using metasurface. *IEEE Transactions on Antennas and Propagation, 62 (6)*, 2891-2898.

Piazza, D, Kirsch, N. J, Forenza, A, Heath, R. W, Dandekar, K. P. (2008) Design and Evaluation of a Reconfigurable Antenna Array for MIMO Systems. *IEEE Transactions on Antennas and Propagation,* 56 (3), 869-881.

Fries, M. K, Grani, M, Vahldieck, R. (2003) A reconfigurable slot antenna with switchable polarization. *IEEE Microwaves and Wireless Component Letters,* 13 (11), 490-492.

Wei, W. B, Liu, Q. Z, Yin, Y. Z, Zhou, H. J. (2007) Reconfigurable Microstrip Patch Antenna with Switchable Polarization. *Progress In Electromagnetics Research PIER 75*, 63-68.

Qin, P. Y, Weily, A. R, Guo, Y. J, Liang, C. H. (2010) Polarization reconfigurable u-slot patch antenna. *IEEE Transactions on Antennas and Propagation, 58 (10)*, 3383-3388.

Khidre, A, Lee, K. F, Yang, F, Elsherbeni, A. Z. (2013) Circular polarization reconfigurable wideband E-shaped patch antenna for wireless applications. *IEEE Transactions on Antennas and Propagation, 61 (2)*, 960-964.

Krishnamoorthy, K, Majimder, B, Mukherjee, J, Ray, K. P. (2015) Low RCS and polarization reconfigurable antenna using cross slot based metasurface. *IEEE Antennas and Wireless Propagation Letters, 14.*

Zhang, L, Gao, S, Luo, Q, Young, P, Li, Q. (2016) Wideband loop antenna with electronically switchable circular polarization. *IEEE Antennas and Wireless Components Letters, 16*, 242-245.

Rahimi, M, Maleki, M, Soltani, M, Arezomand, A. S, Zarrabi, F. B. (2016) Wideband SRR-inspired slot antenna with circular polarization for wireless application. *International Journal of Electronics and Communications,* 70 (9), 1199-1204.

Hu, J, Hao, Z. C, Miao, Z. W. (2017) Design and Implementation of a Planar Polarization Reconfigurable Antenna. *IEEE Antennas and Wireless Propagation Letters, 16*, 1557-1560.

McMichael, I. T. (2018) A mechanically reconfigurable patch antenna with polarization diversity. *IEEE Antennas and Wireless Component Letters, 17 (7)*, 1186-1189.

Yang, L. S, Yang, L, Zhu, Y. A, Yoshitomi, K, Kanaya, H. (2019) Polarization reconfigurable slot antenna for 5.8 GHz wireless applications. *International Journal of Electronics and Communications, 101*, 27-32.

Zhu, H. L, Cheung, S. W, Chung, K. L, Yuk, T. I. (2013) Linear-to-circular polarization conversion using metasurface. *IEEE Transactions on Antennas and Propagation, 61 (9)*, 4615-4623.

Rodrigo, D, Cetiner, B. A, Jofre, L. (2014) Frequency, radiation pattern and polarization reconfigurable antenna using a parasitic pixel layer. *IEEE Transactions on Antennas and Propagation, 62 (6)*, 3422-3427.

Narbudowicz, A, Bao, X, Ammann, M. J. (2014) Omnidirectional microstrip patch antenna with reconfigurable pattern and polarization. *IET Microwaves, Antennas and Propagation, 8 (11)*, 872-877.

Li, P. K, Shao, Z. H, Wang, Q, Cheng, Y. J. (2015) Frequency and pattern reconfigurable antenna for multistandard wireless applications. *IEEE Antennas and Wireless Propagation Letters, 14*, 333-336.

Lai, M. I, Wu, T. Y, Hsieh, J. C, Wang, C. H, Jeng, S. K. (2009) Design of reconfigurable antennas based on an L-shaped slot and PIN diodes for compact wireless devices. *IET Microwaves, Antennas and Propagation, 3 (1)*, 47-54.

Cao, W, Zhang, B, Liu, A, Yu, T, Guo, D, Pan, K. (2012) A reconfigurable microstrip antenna with radiation pattern selectivity and polarization diversity. *IEEE Antennas and Wireless Component Letters, 11*, 453-456.

Trong, N. N, Hall, L, Fumeaux, C. (2015) A frequency and Polarization reconfigurable stub-loaded microstrip patch antenna. *IEEE Transactions on Antennas and Propagation, 63 (11)*, 5235-5240.

Pengfei, Z, Shizhong, L, Rongrong, C, Xinglin, H. (2016) A reconfigurable microstrip patch antenna with frequency and circular polarization diversities. *Chinese Journal of Electronics, 25 (2)*, 379-383.

Chen, X, & Zhao, Y. (2018) Dual-band polarization and frequency reconfigurable antenna using double layer metasurface. *International Journal of Electronics and Communications, 95*, 82-87.

Ni, C, Chen, M. S, Zhang, Z. X, Wi, X. L. (2018) Design of frequency and polarization reconfigurable antenna based on the polarization conversion metasurface. *IEEE Antennas and Wireless Propagation Letters, 17 (1)*, 78-81.

Analysis of Metasurface based Frequency Reconfigurable Planar Antenna using Artificial Neural Network

Navneet Kaur
Electronics and Communication Engineering
Punjabi University
Patiala, India
navsandhu31696@gmail.com

Jagtar Singh Sivia
Electronics and Communication Engineering
YDoE, Punjabi University Guru Kashi Campus, Talwandi Sabo
Bathinda, India
jagtarsivian@gmail.com

Rajni
Electronics and Communication Engineering
Shaheed Bhagat Singh State University
Ferozepur, India
rajni.c123@gmail.com

***Abstract*- Artificial Neural Network (ANN), an information processing paradigm provide a lot of promising applications in micro-engineering fields. In this paper, a feed forward backpropagation ANN (FFBP-ANN) model is developed for estimating the dimensions of a unit cell of the projected Metasurface based Frequency Reconfigurable Planar Antenna (MS-FRPA). During the analysis, 41 samples are generated that forms the entire data set. In each sample, length and width of the unit cell associated with projected antenna is varied. The performance of the neural network is then verified by comparing it with the simulated results obtained from the selected software. Results reveal that the average estimation error obtained is quite less leading to the effectiveness of the designed approach.**

Keywords—Artificial neural network, Frequency reconfigurable antenna, Metasurface, Mean squared error, Unit cell

I. Introduction

An antenna is a vital component of any communication system. A single antenna device can resonate at distinct frequency bands by applying the approach of frequency reconfiguration. Multiple approaches and processes are recommended in the previous literature illustrating the concept of change in antenna's resonant frequency. Mechanical and electrical mechanisms are common among them. There are two types of frequency reconfigurable antennas that use an electrical mechanism: continuous and switched tuning. Varactor diodes can be used for continuous tuning, whereas PIN diodes, RF-MEMS switches can be used for switched tuning [1]. The antenna is made up of movable elements in the mechanical configuration. The frequency is changed by varying the total size of the antenna with the use of actuators. The use of bulky and expensive actuators is a major disadvantage of this mechanism. Thus, metasurfaces can be utilized instead of cumbersome actuators to achieve good antenna characteristics, compact size, and low cost. Metamaterials represented in two-dimensional form constitute the metasurface [2].

In the previous decade, different types of soft computing techniques are employed widely for the designing and optimization of the antennas. ANN is the most recognized and intelligent technique that solves various engineering problems, thereby eliminating complex and time-consuming mathematical procedures. The learning and simplification features of neural processing offer a new approach to storing and manipulating information. It is a system that is designed to mimic the human brain [3]. It consists of different types of nonlinear functional blocks that are termed as neurons. These neurons are presented effectively in the form of layers. All these neurons are mutually interconnected with parallel synaptic weights that in turn are strengthened or weakened throughout the process of learning. Thus, information is stored in the neural network [4]. Several papers have been published in the available literature that indicates how ANN can be efficiently applied to analyze and synthesize antennas. The ANN-based approach is applied for the design and analysis of circular fractal antenna is presented [5]. This approach can efficiently bypass the complex mathematical process, thereby reducing the computational time. The implementation of ANN-based metasurface incorporated frequency reconfigurable antenna is presented in [6]. Here the ANN model is developed to estimate the output parameters which in turn provide the minimum absolute error during analysis. ANN and particle swarm optimization (PSO) based hybrid fractal antenna is designed using four distinct fractal curves to compute the feed position [7]. The design of a virtual instrument for fault detection in a fractal antenna array is developed. The ANN model efficiently develops the fitted points which in turn minimize the mean square error [8].

In view of the above discussion, an ANN model has been developed to analyze the performance of the metasurface incorporated unique type of frequency reconfigurable antenna. This model can predict the frequency and return loss parameters. The whole paper is organized effectively. It incorporates five sections. The detailed procedure of the projected frequency reconfigurable antenna is illustrated in Section II. Section III presents the ANN framework. All the results are discussed in Section IV. The whole paper is briefly compiled in Section V.

II. Design Configuration

Figure 1 depicts the proposed MS-FRPA layout. The proposed MS-structure FRPA's is made up of two substrate layers. The first substrate layer is for the patch antenna and the other substrate layer is for the metasurface. For achieving the desired reconfiguration, both the substrates possess the same shape and size. A rectangular-shaped patch antenna is developed on top of the lower substrate, and a ground plane of circular shape is implemented at the bottom. Figure 1 shows the geometrical view of a patch antenna (a). Dual split ring resonators (DSRRs) are alternately placed and connected with thin wire in a periodic pattern, generating an array of unit cells that represents the MS. As seen in Figure 1, the whole set is presented at the top side of the upper substrate (b). MS is mechanically rotated across its center about the patch antenna to achieve frequency reconfigurability.Along the y-axis, the rotation angle θ is calculated. In both the directions i.e. horizontal and vertical directions, the unit cells are similar. As a result, θ = -θ is seen, and the greatest value examined is 90^0. The conducting side belonging to the lower substrate and the non- conducting side belonging to the top substrate are put together during antenna structure construction. There is no space between these two substrates, which is responsible for compact structure. The optimized parameters of the projected MS-FRPA are depicted in Table I. Table II illustrates the parametric description of DSRR [9].

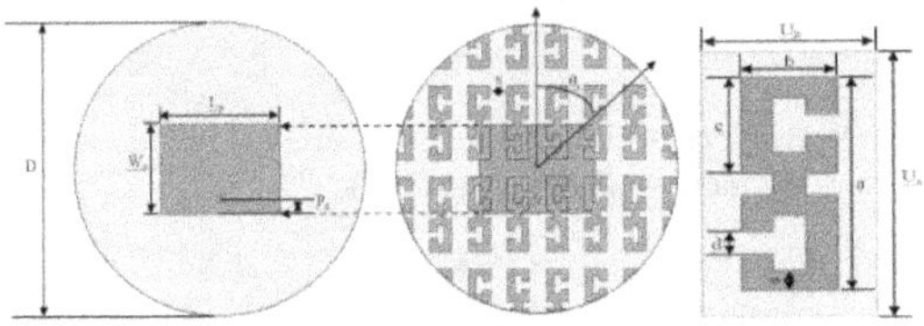

Figure 1: Geometrical structure of projected MS-FRPA (a) patch antenna (b) metasurface (c) enlarged unit cell

TABLE I. PARAMETRIC DESCRIPTION OF MS-FRPA (UNITS IN MM)

D	L_p	W_p	P_e	s
39	16	12	2	2.4

TABLE II. PARAMETRIC DESCRIPTION OF DSRR (UNITS IN MM)

U_a	U_b	a	b	c	D	e
12.4	5.4	10	3	4.5	1	1

III. ANN FRAMEWORK

Artificial Neural Network (ANN) is basically a sub-field of artificial intelligence that is biologically inspired and is modelled according to the human brain. The first ANN was created by famous psychologist Frank Rosenblatt in 1958. ANN is usually an effective computational network in which all the neurons are mutually interconnected and are presented at different layers. These networks can capture data and give responses in the form of predictions or classifications. They use learning algorithms that can make the adjustments independently. In the architecture, the three primarily layers are: input, hidden and output. The input layer takes all the inputs in various formats provided by the programmers [10]. Hidden layer is presented in-between the input and output layers. This layer is responsible for all the calculations to examine the hidden characteristics such as hidden features and patterns. The output layer conveys the output. ANN accepts the inputs and provides the weighted sum including bias. Bias is a constant that allows the fitting of the model in best possible way. They are classified as the best tools for non-linear statistical data modelling. These tools provide the most cost-effective and best methods for achieving best solutions [3].

The FFBP-ANN model for analyzing the proposed frequency reconfigurable antenna is effectively delineated in Figure 3. This model is developed with 2 input, 10 hidden, and 2 output layer neurons. For this, the unit cell dimensions 'a' and 'b' are taken as inputs and 'f' and 'r' are taken as outputs. During the analysis, 41 samples are generated that forms the entire data set. Out of this, training set contains 29 samples and validation and testing set contains 6 samples.

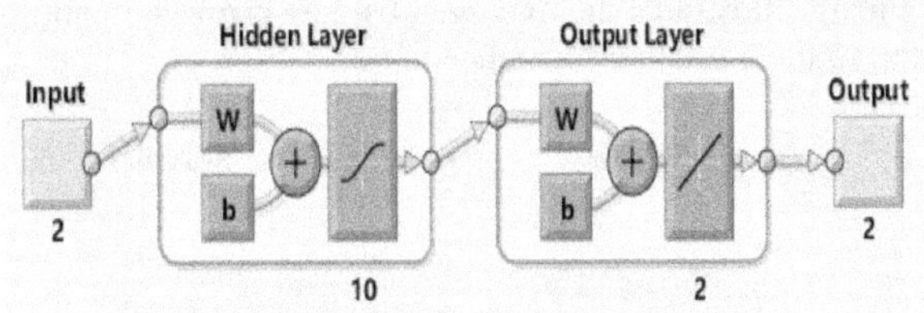

Figure 3: The FFBP-ANN model

IV. RESULTS AND DISCUSSION

For the purpose of training, 41 distinct samples are generated. For each sample, dimensions of each unit cell belonging to the antenna are varied.Here 'a' and 'b' are considered as input and 'f' and 'r' output parameters, respectively.The value of parameter 'a' is varied from 9 mm to 11mm and parameter 'b' is varied from 2 mm to 4mm. The Levenberg-Marquardt (LM) algorithm is selected because it helps in providing desired accuracy and best estimation of output parameters. The transfer function used at hidden layer is Tansig whereas at the output layer, it is purelin. The three statistical parameters: mean squared error (MSE), number of epochs taken, and the maximum absolute error is determined to evaluate the model's performance. During the analysis phase, the evaluated performance characteristics of the projected MS-FRPA are shown in Table III. Out of the total 41 samples, 29 samples are present in the training set, 6 in validation set and 6 in testing set. Mean squared error (MSE) is calculated from ANN and HFSS outputs and then take difference between them. Smaller value of MSE is responsible for better results. During the training phase, the mean square error and regression observed is 2.66172e-2 and 9.99906e-1, respectively. During validation phase, the observed values are 6.659775e-2 and 9.99767e-1, respectively. during testing phase the values examined are 5.45709e-2 and 9.99813e-1, respectively. Figure 4 shows the performance plot of the LM-based ANN model. The best validation performance is found at 0.065978 at epoch 3 according to the graph.

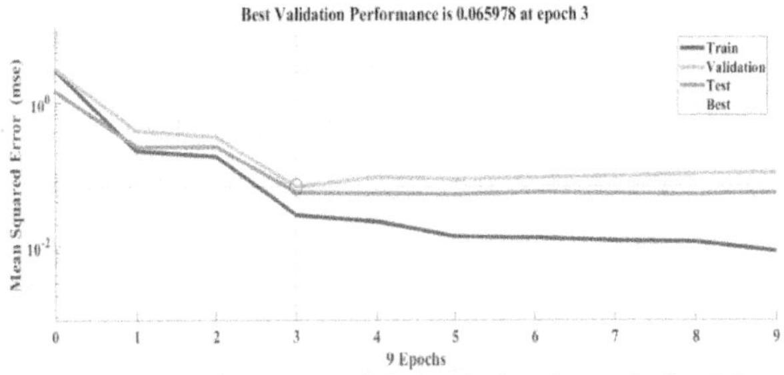

Figure 4: Performance validation during the analysis of the proposed antenna

Figure 5 effectively represents the regression (R) plot during the analysis phase for all cases including training, validation, testing, and overall output. The total value of R obtained during this process is 0.99986. The results showing estimation of absolute error are illustrated in Table IV. 10 samples are presented in the table. Based on these values, outputs are taken and an average of the absolute error is estimated. The estimated average error value corresponding to output parameters such as resonant frequency and return loss value is 0.00233 and 0.0082, respectively. Figure 6 graphically illustrates the average absolute error estimations related to the output performance parameters.

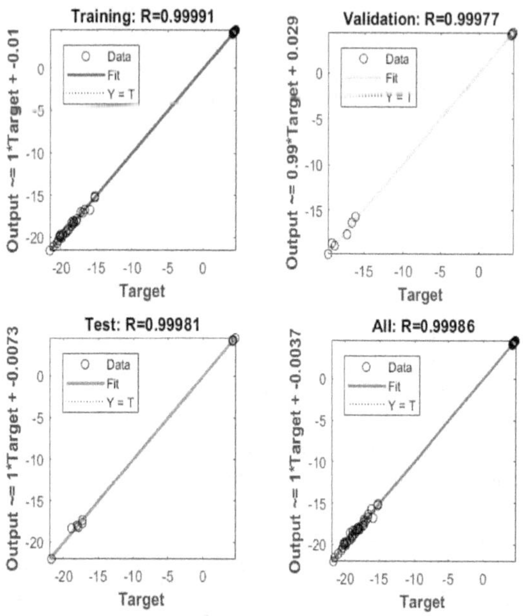

Figure 5: Scatter plot showing the target value and ANN output for training, validation, testing and total output during the analysis phase

TABLE III. PERFORMANCE EVALUATION DURING ANALYSIS

	Samples	*MSE*	*Regression*
Training	29	2.66172e-2	9.99906e-1
Validation	6	6. 659775e-2	9.99767e-1
Testing	6	5.45709e-2	9.99813e-1

TABLE IV. ESTIMATION OF ABSOLUTE ERROR

Inputs		*HFSS outputs*		*ANN outputs*		*Absolute error*	
a	**B**	**f**	**r**	**f**	**r**	**f**	**r**
10	3.1	4.32	-18.5	4.33	-18.2	-.013	-.217
10	3.7	4.26	-17.2	4.31	-17.3	-.050	.0948
10	2.9	4.34	-19.2	4.31	-18.6	.026	-.637
10	2.4	4.40	-19.7	4.42	-19.8	-.010	.0528
10	2	4.48	-20.0	4.48	-19.7	-.005	-.324
10.1	3	4.30	-18.8	4.30	-18.3	-.002	-.523
11	3	4.13	-15.2	4.11	-15.2	.0169	.0196
9.7	3	4.43	-19.2	4.43	-19.4	.0027	.1370
9.3	3	4.54	-20.5	4.53	-20.7	.0066	.1795
9	3	4.61	-21.7	4.58	-22.0	.0370	.2993
Average absolute error						.0023	.0082

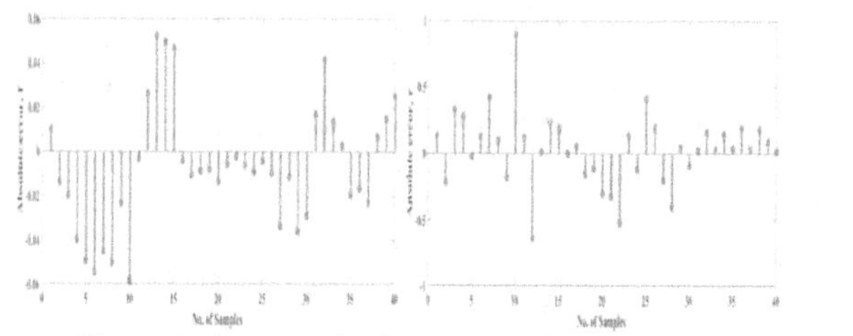

Figure 6: Average absolute error estimations (a) resonant frequency 'f' (b) return loss 'r'

V. CONCLUSION

The development and analysis of FFBP-ANN based frequency reconfigurable antenna using metasurfaceis presented in this paper. 41 samples are created by varying the length and width of the unit cell belonging to an antenna. The estimated value of average absolute error for the frequency and return loss are 0.00233 and 0.0082, respectively. Thus, it is observed that the suggested model is very effective and supportive in estimating the antenna dimensions, thereby eliminating the lengthy and time-consuming cycles with a short production time.

REFERENCES

[1] H. L. Zhu, S. W. Cheung, and T. I. Yuk, "Frequency Reconfigurable Slot Antenna with Wide Tuning Range using Metasurface," Microw. Opt. Tech. Lett., vol. 57, no. 6, pp. 1475-1481, June 2015.

[2] H. L. Zhu, X. H. Zhu, S. W. Cheung, and T. I. Yuk, "Frequency Reconfigurable Antenna using Metasurface," IEEE Trans. Antennas Propag., vol. 62, no. 1, pp. 80-85, Jan. 2014.

[3] M. Kaur, J. S. Sivia, "ANN and FA based Design of Hybrid Fractal Antenna for ISM band applications," Progress in Electromagnetic Research C, vol. 98, pp. 127-140, 2020.

[4] S. Haykin, Neural Networks: A Comprehensive Foundation, Englewood Cliffs, New Jersey, Macmillan Publishing Company, 1994.

[5] J. S. Sivia, A. P. S. Pharwaha, T. S. Kamal, "Analysis and design of circular fractal antenna using artificial neural networks," Progress in Electromagnetics Research B, vol. 56, pp. 251-267, 2013.

[6] N. Kaur, J. S. Sivia, and Rajni, "Artificial neural network based metasurface inspired planar frequency reconfigurable antenna for wireless applications," Int. J. of RF and Microw. Computer-Aided Engineering, vol. 31, issue 9, pp. 1-13, July 2021.

[7] M. Kaur, and J. S. Sivia, "Minkowski, Giuseppe Peano and Koch curves based design of compact hybrid fractal antenna for biomedical applications using ANN and PSO," Int. J. of Electron. Commun., Vol. 99, 14–24, Feb. 2019.

[8] S. Rani, and J. S. Sivia, "Design and development of virtual instrument for fault diagnosis in fractal antenna array," Int. J. of RF Microw. Computer-Aided Engineering, Oct. 2019.

[9] N. Kaur, J. S. Sivia, and Rajni, "Metasurface Incorporated Frequency Reconfigurable Planar Antenna for Wireless Applications," Progress In Electromgnetics Research C, vol. 113, pp. 265-275, 2021.

LIST OF PUBLICATIONS

International Journals

1. Navneet Kaur, Jagtar Singh Sivia, and Rajni, "Artificial neural network based metasurface inspired planar frequency reconfigurable antenna for wireless applications" , ***International Journal of RF and Microwave Computer-Aided Engineering***, Vol. 31, Issue 9, pp. 1-13, July 2021.

(SCIE Indexed, Impact Factor: 1.739)

2. Navneet Kaur, Jagtar Singh Sivia, and Rajni, "Design of Frequency Reconfigurable Planar Antenna using Artificial Neural Network" , ***International Journal of Microwave and Wireless Technologies***, Vol. 14, Issue 9, pp. 1107-1118, November 2022.

(SCI Indexed, Impact Factor: 1.064)

3. Navneet Kaur, Jagtar Singh Sivia, and Rajni, "Metasurface Incorporated Frequency Reconfigurable Planar Antenna for Wireless Applications" , ***Progress In Electromgnetics Research C***, Vol. 113, pp. 265-275, July 2021.

(Scopus Indexed, Impact Factor: 1.48)

4. Navneet Kaur, Jagtar Singh Sivia, and Rajni, "Determination of Resonanace Characteristics and Electromagnetic Properties of H-I Shaped Resonator based Metasurface" , ***Journal of The Institution of Engineers (India): Series B (IEIB)***, May 2020. **(Communicated)**

(Scopus Indexed)

International Conferences

5. Navneet Kaur, Jagtar Singh Sivia, and Rajni, "Different Reconfiguration Mechanisms and Applications in Planar Antennas: A Review" , in ***Elsevier SSRN, International Conference on Intelligent Communication and Computational Research (ICICCR-2020)***, Punjab Institute of Technology, Rajpura, 25th Jan 2020.

6. Navneet Kaur, Jagtar Singh Sivia, and Rajni, "Analysis of Metasurface based Frequency Reconfigurable Planar Antenna Using Artificial Neural Network" , in ***International Virtual Conference on Artificial Intelligence, 5G Communications and Network Technologies (ICA5NT 2022)***, Velammal Institute of Technology, Chennai, 28th - 29th April 2022.

Received: 8 February 2021 | Revised: 28 April 2021 | Accepted: 14 June 2021

DOI: 10.1002/mmce.22793

RESEARCH ARTICLE

INTERNATIONAL JOURNAL OF RF AND MICROWAVE COMPUTER-AIDED ENGINEERING WILEY

Artificial neural network based metasurface inspired planar frequency reconfigurable antenna for wireless applications

Navneet Kaur[1] | **Jagtar Singh Sivia**[2] | **Rajni**[3]

[1]Department of Electronics and Communication Engineering, Punjabi University, Patiala, Punjab, India

[2]YCoE, Punjabi University Guru Kashi Campus Talwandi Sabo, Bathinda, Punjab, India

[3]Department of Electronics and Communication Engineering, Shaheed Bhagat Singh State Technical Campus, Ferozepur, Punjab, India

Correspondence
Navneet Kaur, Research Scholar, Department of Electronics and Communication Engineering, Punjabi University, Patiala, Punjab, India.
Email: navsandhu31696@gmail.com

Abstract

The growing interest in attaining various appealing features of wireless communication systems has motivated researchers to design innovative antennas. This paper analyzes the behavior of a low profile artificial neural network-based metasurface (MS) inspired two-layered frequency reconfigurable antenna (ANN-MSFRA) using planar technology. The designed two-layered structure is a combination of two substrates mounted one above the other, having no air gap between them. The prototype of the proposed antenna is fabricated on Rogers RO4350B material having permittivity (ε_r) = 3.48, and thickness (h) = 1.524 mm. The MS is represented as an artificially generated periodical array of H and I-shaped metallic inclusions. Numerically analyzed results validate the double negative properties of metamaterial. To verify the effectiveness of the projected two-layered approach, the performance of the reconfigurable antenna is analyzed through both simulations and measurements. The antenna successfully reconfigures the operating frequency from 4.86 to 5.89 GHz, covering the operating bandwidth of 1.03 GHz with a fractional tuning range of 19.1%. The presented simulated and measured outcome provides a positive correlation.The developed ANN model suggested for the estimation of specific output parameters shows minimum error during analysis and synthesis.

KEYWORDS

artificial neural network, frequency reconfigurable antenna, metamaterial, metasurface, reflection coefficient

1 | INTRODUCTION

The technology sector is developing very rapidly according to the growing demands of the users.[1] The technological advancements in wireless systems have stimulated the market demand for developing novel antennas with unique functionalities.[2,3] These antennas can modify dynamically the important characteristics in a controlled and reversible way.[4] The fundamental requirements such as multifunctionality, strong reliability, small volume, high data rate are accomplished by embedding the wireless devices with reconfigurable antennas. Therefore, reconfigurable antennas with their diverse attributes are deployed to cater all these functionalities.[5] These antennas have gained huge interest in the last decade as they have the strong ability to reduce the problems associated with single-band and multiband antennas.[6] Moreover, they have the potential to switch between different

International Journal of Microwave and Wireless Technologies

cambridge.org/mrf

Design of frequency reconfigurable planar antenna using artificial neural network

Navneet Kaur[1], Jagtar Singh Sivia[2] and Rajni[3]

[1]Department of Electronics and Communication Engineering, Punjabi University, Patiala, Punjab, India; [2]YCoE, Punjabi University Guru Kashi Campus, Talwandi Sabo, Bathinda, Punjab, India and [3]Shaheed Bhagat Singh State Technical Campus, Ferozepur, Punjab, India

Research Paper

Cite this article: Kaur N, Sivia JS, Rajni (2022). Design of frequency reconfigurable planar antenna using artificial neural network. *International Journal of Microwave and Wireless Technologies* **14**, 1107–1118. https://doi.org/10.1017/S1759078721001434

Received: 15 May 2021
Revised: 11 September 2021
Accepted: 18 September 2021
First published online: 14 October 2021

Keywords:
Artificial electromagnetic materials; artificial neural network; metamaterial; metasurface superstrate; reconfigurable antenna; *S*-parameters; wireless communications

Author for correspondence:
Navneet Kaur,
E-mail: navsandhu31696@gmail.com

Abstract

In this paper, the design of frequency reconfigurable planar antenna by incorporation of metasurface superstrate (FRPA-MSS) is presented using an artificial neural network. The dual-layer radiating structure is created on a 1.524 mm thick Rogers RO4350B substrate board ($\epsilon_r = 3.48$, $\tan \delta = 0.0037$). The candidate antenna is designed and analyzed using a high-frequency structure simulator (HFSS) tool. The transfer matrix method is employed for the successful retrieval of electromagnetic properties of the metamaterial. Frequency reconfiguration is achieved by placing the metasurface superstrate onto the rectangular patch antenna. A simplified ANN approach has been employed for the design of metasurface incorporated proposed antenna. Presented prototypes are characterized through experimental measurements. It is found from the practical observations that the proposed antenna effectively reconfigures the tuning range from 5.03 to 6.13 GHz. Moreover, the presented antenna operates efficiently with agreeable gain, good impedance matching, and stable pattern characteristics across the entire operational bandwidth. The experimental results obtained validate the simulated performance.

Introduction

In the present scenario, reconfigurable antennas have grabbed huge attention from the research community due to their ability to integrate multiple standards into a single platform [1]. Therefore, the wireless systems are empowered with reconfigurable antennas to enhance the overall performance and providing cost-effective solutions [2]. The important characteristics that are to be considered while designing these antennas are operating frequency, polarization, and radiation pattern [3]. Modern-day wireless communication systems such as mobile phones, laptops, watches, tablets, etc. support several wireless standards. To fulfill such requirements, multiband, wideband and frequency reconfigurable antennas are the probable choices. Frequency reconfigurable or tunable antennas act as the best alternative by opening up new horizons, thereby providing additional functionality levels [4]. These antennas can change their operating frequency while maintaining stable polarization and radiation pattern modes over the entire frequency range [5]. This feature is accomplished by redistributing the surface current within the radiating element by employing positive intrinsic negative (PIN) diode [6], varactor diode [7], radio frequency micro-electro-mechanical system (RF-MEMS) switches [8], multi-reed switches [9], and optical element [10]. Numerous reconfigurable antennas have been demonstrated based on different switching techniques. In [11], the spiral-shaped flexible and compact frequency reconfigurable antenna is implemented for wireless applications. Ouyang *et al.* [12] proposed a microstrip patch antenna with an electronically steerable parasitic array radiator. With the employment of switches and biasing networks, the non-linear effects and insertion loss increase, that in turn, degrades the performance of an antenna.

Over the previous decades, artificial materials have garnered prodigious attention in designing smart antenna structures with improved performance parameters [13]. The origination of metamaterial reveals an outstanding achievement in comparison to conventional materials. This idea first came into existence in 1967 [14]. After that, the concept of metamaterial has been explored widely to provide a wide tuning range, thus offering a promising solution to various research-oriented problems. The remarkable electromagnetic properties of metamaterial such as negative refractive index, permittivity, and permeability values, anti-parallel phase and group velocities, etc. are responsible for designing fascinating antenna structures with superior characteristics [15]. Ramachandran *et al.* [16] proposed a left-handed metamaterial design for satellite applications constructed using a combination of circular and square ring structures. Though the three-dimensional metamaterial is a young field and has achieved blooming technological advancements in several research areas such as microwaves and infrared regions yet they lack paucity in realizing lossless optical metamaterials. Thus to provide easy fabrication, two-dimensional metasurfaces have emerged out as a multifaceted branch

Progress In Electromagnetics Research C, Vol. 113, 265–275, 2021

Metasurface Incorporated Frequency Reconfigurable Planar Antenna for Wireless Applications

Navneet Kaur[1, *], Jagtar S. Sivia[2], and Rajni[3]

Abstract—In this paper, the design of a Metasurface incorporated Frequency Reconfigurable Planar Antenna (MS-FRPA) for Wireless Applications is presented. The structure of the projected MS-FRPA consists of a patch with a metasurface placed one above the other with no gap between them. The MS is composed of an array of alternately placed dual split ring resonators arranged periodically in both horizontal and vertical directions. Frequency reconfiguration is achieved by rotating the MS relative to the designed patch antenna. The projected reconfigurable antenna is constructed on Rogers RO4350B material with thickness 1.524 mm. High Frequency Structure Simulator software is employed for analysis of the structure. The results clearly reveal that frequency tuning is achieved in 4.35 to 5.33 GHz with a fractional tuning range of 20.2%. The proposed structure provides appreciable realized gain with stable radiation patterns at all rotation angles. Further, the measured outcomes of the developed prototype show good correlation with the simulated outcomes.

1. INTRODUCTION

In the past few decades, a prodigious development has been observed in various systems such as radio-frequency and microwaves due to widespread multi-functionality of wireless communication devices [1–4]. The recent research mainly pays attention towards developing smart systems having potential to perform multiple operations in one device as compared to traditional single operational device [5–7] due to reduction of multipath fading, augmented channel properties, and being resistant to interrupting signals. All these characteristics prompt the development of reconfigurable antennas in present-day wireless communication systems. These antennas have the capacity to reconfigure the important characteristics like frequency, polarization, radiation pattern, and combination of two characteristics or all three [8]. Out of these, frequency reconfigurable antennas are widely preferred as they have the ability to resonate at multiple tuning frequencies [9]. A large number of frequency reconfigurable antennas have been designed and published so far by deploying the electrical methods using positive intrinsic negative (PIN) diodes, varactor diodes, and radiofrequency micromechanical systems (RF-MEMS) & mechanical tuning methods using actuator and large reflector antennas [10, 11]. However, they possess some drawbacks such as requirement of biasing lines and direct current (DC) electrical sources which in turn degrades their performance.

In recent years, to deal with the above discussed hitches, a few accomplishments are made in the exploration of reconfigurability using other means such as metamaterials. Metamaterials are synthetically designed material that displays some notable unnatural electromagnetic (EM) properties which have broadened its importance towards numerous significant applications in science, technology, and medicine. A two-dimensional equivalent of metamaterials is metasurface formed by periodically

Received 27 May 2021, Accepted 4 July 2021, Scheduled 9 July 2021

* Corresponding author: Navneet Kaur (navsandhu31696@gmail.com).
[1] Department of Electronics and Communication Engineering, Punjabi University, Patiala, Punjab, India. [2] YCoE, Punjabi University Guru Kashi Campus, Talwandi Sabo, Bathinda, Punjab, India. [3] Shaheed Bhagat Singh State Technical Campus, Ferozepur, Punjab, India.

Different Reconfiguration Mechanisms and Applications in Planar Antennas: A Review

Navneet Kaur[a], Jagtar Singh Sivia[b], Rajni[c]

[a]Research Scholar, Department of Electronics and Communication Engineering, Punjabi University, Patiala (147002), India
[b]Professor, YCoE, Punjabi University Guru Kashi Campus, Talwandi Sabo (151302), India
[c]Professor, Shaheed Bhagat Singh State Technical Campus, Ferozepur (152004), India

Email: navsandhu31696@gmail.com

Abstract: There has been an increasing demand to design reconfigurable antennas during the last few decades. Based on its ability to radiate frequency, radiation pattern and polarization, a reconfigurable antenna is able to perform multiple functions. This paper briefly discusses the challenges faced in the design of these antennas. In the first part of the paper, various types of reconfigurable antennas are described that are characterized on the basis of reconfiguration mechanisms used and the parameter to be reconfigured. The design aspects of reconfigurable antennas along with the components involved in designing are illustrated with advantages and shortcomings in the next part. Some of the applications of these antennas are also explained in the latter part.

Keywords: Reconfigurable Antenna, Wireless System, PIN diodes, Gain, Resonant Frequency, Polarization

1. Introduction

A reconfigurable antenna had been a topic of interest of researchers for the past few years due to their suitability for various wireless applications. The reconfiguration capability of antennas can maximize the performance in a changing scenario by altering some of the antenna parameters in an adjustable manner. The different standards in handheld gadgets require compact multi-band antennas/smart antennas with reconfigurable features. Hence, there is a necessity to develop reconfigurable antennas so that it can cover the requirements of the latest communication devices and reduce the system's complexity (Borakhde & Pokle, 2015). Several techniques have been developed to achieve the reconfigurability of these antennas. They can either be one antenna or a combination of many antennas (Haupt & Lanagan 2013). Due to the several features such as small size, better signal quality, low cost, immune to signal interferences, less fading effects, more system capacity, etc (Anantha, Meregu, & Rao, 2017) (Panahi, Bao, Yang, Conchubhair, & Ammann, 2015) the investigation of the "Reconfigurable Antennas" is an alternative leap to enhance the general framework execution as they can contribute variety of features (Bernhard, 2007).

The design of any reconfigurable antenna type includes numerous performance parameters – gain, bandwidth, polarization, input impedance, frequency of operation, radiation patterns and variability over the entire range of operation, and mechanical/electrical structural flexibility. These performance parameters can be changed by changing the distribution of current through the use of movable parts, attenuators, diodes or the use of dynamic materials (Haupt & Lanagan 2013).

The reconfigurable antennas were first proposed in 1926 by A. N. Goldsmith so as to make use of the same antenna for a number of different purposes at different frequencies. Initial demonstrated was focused on only frequency reconfigurability. Bruce and Beck in 1935 redesign the structure of the rhombic antenna by expanding its wires through the use of rotating parts. Several ideas were explored later for other reconfigurability options. Schaubert in 1983 got the first patent on designing frequency and polarization reconfigurable antenna using switching diodes by suitably choosing the position of shorting posts (Schaubert, 1983). After that, a multi-university program was launched in 1999 by Defence Advanced Research Projects Agency (DARPA) under the name Reconfigurable Aperture Program (RECAP) in the United States between various companies, research institutes and universities (Smith, 1999). Further this led to more investigation in the developments of reconfigurable antennas.

The organization of this paper is as follows. Section 2 demonstrates the various challenges faced by the researchers while designing reconfigurable antennas. Section 3 describes the types of reconfigurable antennas on the basis of the reconfiguration mechanism and reconfigured parameter. Applications of these antennas in various fields are presented in Section 4. Finally, the paper is concluded in Section 5.

Abbreviations

DARPA – Defence Advanced Research Projects Agency
RECAP – Reconfigurable Aperture Program
dB – Decibel
dBi – Decibel per inch
LP – Linear Polarization
CP – Circular Polarization
LHCP – Left Hand Circular Polarization
RHCP – Right Hand Circular Polarization

Analysis of Metasurface based Frequency Reconfigurable Planar Antenna using Artificial Neural Network

Navneet Kaur
Electronics and Communication Engineering
Punjabi University
Patiala, India
navsandhu31696@gmail.com

Jagtar Singh Sivia
Electronics and Communication Engineering
YDoE, Punjabi University Guru Kashi Campus, Talwandi Sabo
Bathinda, India
jagtarsivian@gmail.com

Rajni
Electronics and Communication Engineering
Shaheed Bhagat Singh State University
Ferozepur, India
rajni.c123@gmail.com

***Abstract*- Artificial Neural Network (ANN), an information processing paradigm provide a lot of promising applications in micro-engineering fields. In this paper, a feed forward backpropagation ANN (FFBP-ANN) model is developed for estimating the dimensions of a unit cell of the projected Metasurface based Frequency Reconfigurable Planar Antenna (MS-FRPA). During the analysis, 41 samples are generated that forms the entire data set. In each sample, length and width of the unit cell associated with projected antenna is varied. The performance of the neural network is then verified by comparing it with the simulated results obtained from the selected software. Results reveal that the average estimation error obtained is quite less leading to the effectiveness of the designed approach.**

Keywords—Artificial neural network, Frequency reconfigurable antenna, Metasurface, Mean squared error, Unit cell

I. INTRODUCTION

An antenna is a vital component of any communication system. A single antenna device can resonate at distinct frequency bands by applying the approach of frequency reconfiguration. Multiple approaches and processes are recommended in the previous literature illustrating the concept of change in antenna's resonant frequency. Mechanical and electrical mechanisms are common among them. There are two types of frequency reconfigurable antennas that use an electrical mechanism: continuous and switched tuning. Varactor diodes can be used for continuous tuning, whereas PIN diodes, RF-MEMS switches can be used for switched tuning [1]. The antenna is made up of movable elements in the mechanical configuration. The frequency is changed by varying the total size of the antenna with the use of actuators. The use of bulky and expensive actuators is a major disadvantage of this mechanism. Thus, metasurfaces can be utilized instead of cumbersome actuators to achieve good antenna characteristics, compact size, and low cost. Metamaterials represented in two-dimensional form constitute the metasurface [2].

In the previous decade, different types of soft computing techniques are employed widely for the designing and optimization of the antennas. ANN is the most recognized and intelligent technique that solves various engineering problems, thereby eliminating complex and time-consuming mathematical procedures. The learning and simplification features of neural processing offer a new approach to storing and manipulating information. It is a system that is designed to mimic the human brain [3]. It consists of different types of nonlinear functional blocks that are termed as neurons. These neurons are presented effectively in the form of layers. All these neurons are mutually interconnected with parallel synaptic weights that in turn are strengthened or weakened throughout the process of learning. Thus, information is stored in the neural network [4]. Several papers have been published in the available literature that indicates how ANN can be efficiently applied to analyze and synthesize antennas. The ANN-based approach is applied for the design and analysis of circular fractal antenna is presented [5]. This approach can efficiently bypass the complex mathematical process, thereby reducing the computational time. The implementation of ANN-based metasurface incorporated frequency reconfigurable antenna is presented in [6]. Here the ANN model is developed to estimate the output parameters which in turn provide the minimum absolute error during analysis. ANN and particle swarm optimization (PSO) based hybrid fractal antenna is designed using four distinct fractal curves to compute the feed position [7]. The design of a virtual instrument for fault detection in a fractal antenna array is developed. The ANN model efficiently develops the fitted points which in turn minimize the mean square error [8].

In view of the above discussion, an ANN model has been developed to analyze the performance of the metasurface incorporated unique type of frequency reconfigurable antenna. This model can predict the frequency and return loss parameters. The whole paper is organized effectively. It incorporates five sections. The detailed procedure of the projected frequency reconfigurable antenna is illustrated in Section II. Section III presents the ANN framework. All the results are discussed in Section IV. The whole paper is briefly compiled in Section V.

II. DESIGN CONFIGURATION

Figure 1 depicts the proposed MS-FRPA layout. The proposed MS-structure FRPA's is made up of two substrate layers. The first substrate layer is for the patch antenna and the other substrate layer is for the metasurface. For achieving the desired reconfiguration, both the substrates possess the same shape and size. A rectangular-shaped patch antenna is developed on top of the lower substrate, and a ground plane of circular shape is implemented at the bottom. Figure 1

Document Information

Analyzed document	Navneet_Plagiarism_Report.docx (D156431091)
Submitted	1/20/2023 2:19:00 PM
Submitted by	
Submitter email	navsandhu31696@gmail.com
Similarity	3%
Analysis address	jagtarsivian.pununi@analysis.urkund.com

Sources included in the report

W	URL: https://www.researchgate.net/publication/308826009_Design_and_analysis_of_a_frequency_reconfig... Fetched: 7/25/2020 7:09:16 PM	1
SA	**Punjabi University, Patiala / Navneet Synopsis.doc** Document Navneet Synopsis.doc (D41059860) Submitted by: er_navneetsandhu01@yahoo.co.in Receiver: jagtarsivian.pununi@analysis.urkund.com	20
W	URL: https://www.hrpub.org/download/20190930/UJEEE6-14913674.pdf Fetched: 2/9/2021 4:29:24 AM	2
W	URL: http://ceur-ws.org/Vol-3058/Paper-019.pdf Fetched: 10/25/2022 11:49:28 AM	4
W	URL: https://www.hindawi.com/journals/ijap/2018/3678018/ Fetched: 10/22/2019 8:29:21 AM	1
SA	**Punjabi University, Patiala / full thesis new desktop.docx** Document full thesis new desktop.docx (D133542193) Submitted by: navjot905@gmail.com Receiver: jagtarsivian.pununi@analysis.urkund.com	1

Entire Document

www.ingramcontent.com/pod-product-compliance
Lightning Source LLC
LaVergne TN
LVHW082337200926
848481LV00012B/3372
* 9 7 9 8 2 3 2 0 1 1 6 2 8 *